Music
in Boston

National Endowment for the Humanities
Learning Library Program
Boston Public Library
Publication Number 3

Music
in Boston
Readings from the
First Three Centuries

Compiled and Edited by
John C. Swan

Boston, Trustees of the Public Library
of the City of Boston, 1977

Library of Congress Cataloging in Publication Data

Music in Boston.

   (Publication—National Endowment for the Humanities Learn-
ing Library Program, Boston Public Library; no. 3)
   1. Music—Massachusetts—Boston. I. Swan, John C., 1945-
II. Series: Boston. Public Library. National Endowment for the
Humanities Learning Library Program. Publication—National
Endowment for the Humanities Learning Library Program,
Boston Public Library; no. 3.
ML200.8.B7M9   781.7'744'61   78-6167
ISBN 0-89073-052-0

Contents

Preface

From the time of the first English settlements, the New England corner of the New World—and Boston in particular—has played a large role in the shaping of this country's multifarious musical identity. This is as true of writings about music as it is of music itself. Indeed, many of the sermons, tracts and journalistic essays about music which came from the pens of New Englanders had a greater impact on American culture than did the music composed or performed here. Included in this anthology are several selections which exercised a vital influence upon our musical development, but it is not by any means devoted exclusively to such historically important documents. There are several which primarily reflect or report the progress of music in Boston and environs; the purpose of the collection is not so much to present the major works as to provide a diverse record of the development of music in a changing society.

Inevitably, the earliest pieces here deal for the most part with issues of immediate practical and religious significance. However, although they offer little extended description of actual musical activity, there is much to be discovered between the lines. This is especially true of the work of Thomas Symmes, who qualifies as this country's first real commentator upon the musical scene. In the course of his vigorous prosecution of the cause of musical literacy, he included many observations of (and wry comments about) the opinions and practices of the adherents to the oral tradition of learning and singing that had grown up in the first century of American psalmody.

The nineteenth century is far more heavily represented in this collection than its predecessors. That was the time of greatest change in the social dimensions of music, and it was also the time when music began to receive intensive and widespread coverage from journalists, crusaders, and journalist-crusaders. Chief among the last is John Sullivan Dwight, to whom a great deal of space is given here because of his personal significance, because of his informativeness, and because he most clearly exemplifies the most important feature of Boston's contribution to the growth of American musical culture. With few important exceptions (the grandest of them is William Billings), the best early Boston writers functioned as inheritors and disseminators of the great music and musical standards and practices of Europe. This is ironically true of Mather and Symmes and their fellow Regular Singers, who desired only that their congregations acquire the technical skills necessary for the accurate performance of psalm- and hymn-tunes, but who ultimately created, in many of their students, the desire to put their skills to more sophisticated use. Men such as Hubbard, John Parker, Mason and Dwight were consciously devoted to shaping our musical culture according to European models. This very (but by no means exclusively) Bostonian cause resulted, on the one hand, in the suppression of our first great native art, the music of the American psalmodists; on the other hand, it resulted, particularly through the efforts of Mason and Dwight, in the spread of musical education and cultural awareness. For all its idiosyncrasies, Dwight's essay, "The History of Music in Boston," is the most sensitive and complete account of the positive achievements of these musical pioneers in the nineteenth century.

The nineteenth century is rich in musical reportage, and examples are included here from the work of John Rowe Parker, creator of the nation's first musical magazine, from *Dwight's Journal of Music,* and from the newspaper work of Philip Hale and Henry Taylor Parker. Also included are extracts from the autobiographies of Thomas Ryan and George Root, both musicians with important Boston connections.

Most of the material collected here is drawn from the original sources. The earliest essays were transcribed from facsimiles or microtext sources. I have as far as possible retained the original spelling, punctuation and capitalization, although I have corrected a few obvious misprints. Much that is important has perforce been omitted from this anthology and will, no doubt, be missed. I hope, however, that the readings which have been included offer a vivid representation of a city rich in musical history.

ACKNOWLEDGEMENTS

This anthology grew out of a collection of readings in primary sources assembled for use in a course, "From the Psalm Book to the Symphony: Music in the Culture of Boston," which I taught for the National Endowment for the Humanities Learning Library Program at the Boston Public Library during the Fall and Winter of 1976-77. I am grateful to Philip J. McNiff, Director of the Boston Public Library, for inviting me to augment that collection and make it available to a wider audience in the form of this book.

Many other members of the staff of the Boston Public Library have been very helpful to me during this project, but I owe a particularly large debt of gratitude to Paul Wright, director of the National Endowment for the Humanities Learning Library Program. Without his encouragement and assistance this anthology would never have been assembled.

J.S.

I

The Whole Booke of Psalmes Faithfully Translated into English Metre (Cambridge, Massachusetts, 1640)

[The "Bay Psalm Book," as it is generally called, is (aside from a lost Almanac) the first book-length publication to issue from English North America. The following is a facsimile of the Preface, written by John Cotton (1584-1652), "Teacher of the Church at Boston," New England patriarch, and one of the leaders of the committee of thirty Puritan clergymen who accomplished this new metrical translation of the Psalms of David. The motive for the project was characteristically Puritan: the ministers had become dissatisfied with the versions of the Psalms then in use for congregational singing because they did not adhere closely enough to the literal meaning of the original Hebrew. In the words of Cotton's Preface,

> [I]t is not unknowne to the godly learned that they have rather presented a paraphrase then the words of David . . . and that their addition to the words, detractions from the words are not seldome and rare, but very frequent and many times needles, (which we suppose would not be approved of if the psalmes were so translated into prose) and that their variations of the sense, and alterations of the sacred text too frequently, may iustly minister matter of offence to them that are able to compare the translation with the text; of which failings, some iudicious have oft complained, others have been grieved, whereupon it hath bin generally desired, that as wee doe inioye other, soe (if it were the Lords will) wee might inioye this ordinance also in its native purity: wee have therefore done our indeavor to make a plaine and familiar translation of the psalmes and words of David into english metre. . . .

The divines were particularly put out with the standard Anglican psalter, the Sternhold and Hopkins version, on the grounds of the liberties taken in the translations. They expressed a different kind of concern, however, when they found fault with "the difficulty of *Ainsworth's* tunes." The psalter of Henry Ainsworth had been brought to Plymouth from Leyden by the original Pilgrims, who in many cases were "very expert in music." Ainsworth, an important scholar and leader among the Dissenters, designed his translations to be sung to a wide variety of tunes that were often quite demanding musically. The congregation at Plymouth clung to the Ainsworth psalter until 1692, long after the Bay Psalm Book had conquered most of the rest of New England. The Bay Psalm Book, then, did more than satisfy scrupulous Puritan textual standards; it served the needs of a people who, pressed by the hardships of carving a new society out of the wilderness, were becoming less and less musically sophisticated. The Psalms were crammed into a few simple metrical schemes in order to accommodate a shrinking musical repertory, and they were also crudely adapted to the purposes of singing—"Gods Altar needs not our pollishings," it says in the final paragraph of the Preface. The third edition, of 1651, was, however, thoroughly revised and improved by Dunster and Lyon: the people did want some polish to their simple meters.

The Preface stands as a cogent statement of the Puritan view of music. The strictly ordered argument, bristling with Biblical references, concentrates upon both the doctrinal and practical aspects of the place of singing in worship—the singing of Psalms, that is: for the early Puritans, nothing else was acceptable. The intensity with which these men addressed the question of music, and the very fact that they chose the Psalms for the first book from their little Cambridge printing press, should demonstrate the depth of their commitment to music, "to sing praise unto the Lord, with the words of David."

There was no music included with the early

editions of the Bay Psalm Book. The people relied for the most part upon (fading) memories and oral tradition to pass the music from generation to generation. The earliest extant edition to contain musical notation is the ninth, of 1698, which helped to arrest the inevitable shrinkage of the repertory.

An actual facsimile of the Preface is included here in order to evoke something of the cultural ambience of this important document. It should not be too difficult to decipher, as long as one remembers that the lower-case "s" closely resembles the "f"

when it appears in the beginning or middle of a word, and that a line over a vowel is the equivalent of that vowel plus an "n" in modern print. Thus, "filéce" is "silence."

An excellent discussion of the Bay Psalm Book is to be found in Irving Lowens' *Music and Musicians in Early America* (Norton, 1964). A more extensive treatment is *The Enigma of the Bay Psalm Book,* by Zoltan Haraszti (University of California Press, 1956).]

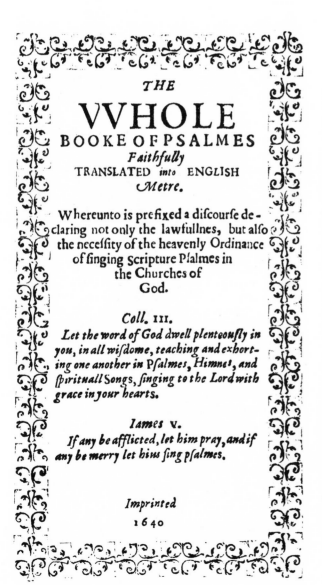

THE

VVHOLE

BOOKE OF PSALMES
Faithfully
TRANSLATED *into* ENGLISH
Metre.

Whereunto is prefixed a difcourfe declaring not only the lawfullnes, but alfo the neceffity of the heavenly Ordinance of finging Scripture Pfalmes in the Churches of God.

Coll. III.

Let the word of God dwell plenteoufly in you, in all wifdome, teaching and exhorting one another in Pfalmes, Himnes, and fpirituall Songs, finging to the Lord with grace in your hearts.

Iames v.

If any be afflicted, let him pray, and if any be merry let him fing pfalmes.

Imprinted
1 6 4 0

The Preface.

THe finging of Pfalmes, though it breath forth nothing but holy harmony, and melody : yet fuch is the fubtilty of the enemie, and the enmity of our nature againft the Lord, & his wayes, that our hearts can finde matter of difcord in this harmony, and crotchets of divifion in this holy melody .-for- There have been three queftiõs efpecially ftirrĩg cõcerning finging. Firft. what pfalmes are to be fung in churches? whether Davids and other fcripture pfalmes, or the pfalmes invented by the gifts of godly men in every age of the church. Secondly, if fcripture pfalmes, whether in their owne words, or in fuch meter as englifh poetry is wont to run in? Thirdly· by whom are they to be fung? whether by the whole churches together with their voices? or by one man finging alõe and the reft joynĩg in filéce, & in the clofe fayĩg amen.

Touching the firft, certainly the finging of Davids pfalmes was an acceptable worfhip of God, not only in his owne, but in fucceeding times. as in Solomons time 2 *Chron.* 5. 13. in Iehofaphats time 2 *chron.* 20. 21. in Ezra his time *Ezra* 3. 10, 11. and the text is evident in Hezekiahs time   they are commanded to fing praife in the words of David and Afaph, 2 *chron.* 29, 30. which one place may ferve to refolve two of the queftions (the firft and the laft) at once. for this commandement was it cerimoniall

* 2

2 .

moniall or morall? some things in it indeed were cerimoniall, as their musicall inſtruments &c but what cerimony was there in ſinging prayſe with the words of David and Aſaph? what if David was a type of Chriſt, was Aſaph alſo? was every thing of David typicall? are his words (which are of morall, univerſall, and perpetuall authority in all nations and ages) are they typicall? what type can be imagined in making uſe of his ſongs to prayſe the Lord? If they were typicall becauſe the cerimony of muſicall inſtruments was joyned with them, then their prayers were alſo typicall, becauſe they had that ceremony of incenſe admixt with them: but wee know that prayer then was a morall duty, notwithſtanding the incenſe; and ſoe ſinging thoſe pſalmes notwithſtanding their muſicall inſtruments. Beſide, that which was typicall (as that they were ſung with muſicall inſtruments, by the twenty-foure orders of Prieſts and Levites. 1 *chron* 2 5. 9.) muſt have the morall and ſpirituall accompliſhment in the new Teſtament, in all the Churches of the Saints principally, who are made kings & prieſts *Reu*. 1. 6. and are the firſt fruits unto God. *Reu*. 14 4. as the Levites were *Num*. 3. 45. with hearts & lippes, in ſtead of muſicall inſtruments, to prayſe the Lord; who are ſet forth (as ſome iudiciouſly thinke) *Reu*. 4. 4. by twēty foure Elders, in the ripe age of the Church, *Gal*. 4. 1, 2, 3. anſwering to the twenty foure orders of Prieſts and Levites 1 *chron*. 25. 9. Therefore not ſome ſelect members

members, but the whole Church is commaunded to teach one another in all the ſeverall ſorts of Davids pſalmes, ſome being called by himſelfe מִזְמוֹרִים: pſalms, ſome תְּהִלִּים: Hymns ſome שִׁירִים: ſpirituall ſongs. ſoe that if the ſinging Davids pſalmes be a morall duty & therfore perpetuall; then wee under the new Teſtamēt are bound to ſing them as well as they under the old: and if wee are expreſly commanded to ſing Pſalmes, Hymnes, and ſpirituall ſongs, then either wee muſt ſing Davids pſalmes, or elſe may affirm they are not ſpirituall ſongs: which being penned by an extraordīary gift of the Spirit, for the ſake eſpecially of Gods ſpirituall Iſraell; not to be read and preached only (as other parts of holy writ) but to be ſung alſo, they are therefore moſt ſpirituall, and ſtill to be ſung of all the Iſraell of God: and verily as their ſin is exceeding great, who will allow Davids pſalmes (as other ſcriptures) to be read in churches (which is one end) but not to be preached alſo, (which is another end ſoe their ſin is crying before God, who will allow them to be read and preached, but ſeeke to deprive the Lord of the glory of the third end of them, which is to ſing them in chriſtian churches. obj. 1 If it be ſayd that the Saints in the primitive Church did compile ſpirituall ſongs of their owne inditing, and ſing them before the Church. 1Cor. 14, 15, 16.

Anſ. We anſwer firſt, that thoſe Saints compiled theſe ſpirituall ſongs by the extraordinary gifts of

* 3   the

the spirit (common in those dayes) whereby they were inabled to praise the Lord in strange tongues, wherin learned *Pareus* proves those psalmes were uttered, in his Commēt on that place *uers* 14 which extraordinary gifts, if they were still in the Churches, wee should allow them the like liberty now. Secondly, suppose those psalmes were sung by an ordinary gift (which wee suppose cannot be evicted) doth it therefore follow that they did not, & that we ought not to sing Davids psalmes? must the ordinary gifts of a private man quench the spirit still speaking to us by the extraordinary gifts of his servant David? there is not the least foot-step of example, or precept, or colour reason for such a bold practise.

obj. 2. Ministers are allowed to pray conceived prayers, and why not to sing conceived psalmes? must wee not sing in the spirit as well as pray in the spirit?

Ans. First because every good minister hath not a gift of spirituall poetry to compose extemporary psalmes as he hath of prayer. Secondly. Suppose he had, yet seeing psalmes are to be sung by a joynt consent and harmony of all the Church in heart and voyce (as wee shall prove) this cannot be done except he that composeth a psalme, bringeth into the Church set formes of psalmes of his owne invētion; for which wee finde no warrant or president in any ordinary officers of the Church throughout the sciptures. Thirdly. Because the booke of psalmes is so compleat a System of psalmes

psalmes, which the Holy-Ghost himselfe in infinite wisdome hath made to suit all the conditions, necessityes, temptations, affections, &c. of men in all ages; (as most of all our interpreters on the psalmes have fully and perticularly cleared)there fore by this the Lord seemeth to stoppe all mens mouths and mindes ordinarily to compile or sing any other psalmes (under colour that the ocasions and conditions of the Church are new) &c. for the publick use of the Church, seing, let our condition be what it will, the Lord himselfe hath supplyed us with farre better; and therefore in Hezekiahs time, though doubtlesse there were among them those which had extraoridnary gifts to compile new songs on those new ocasions, as Isaiah and Micah &c. yet wee read that they are commanded to sing in the words of David and Asaph, which were ordinarily to be used in the publick worship of God: and wee doubt not but those that are wise will easily see; that those set formes of psalmes of Gods owne appoyntment not of mans conceived gift or humane imposition were sung in the Spirit by those holy Levites, as well as their prayers were in the spirit which themselves conceived, the Lord not then binding them therin to any set formes; and shall set formes of psalmes appoynted of God not be sung in the spirit now, which others did then?

Queston. But why may not one cōpose a psalme & sing it alone with a loud voice & the rest joyne with

with him in silence and in the end say **Amen?**
Ans. If such a practise was found in the Church
of Corinth, when any had a psalme suggested by
an extraordinary gift; yet in singing ordinary
psalmes the whole Church is to ioyne together
in heart and voyce to prayse the Lord. -for-
First. Davids psalmes as hath beene shewed,
were sung in heart and voyce together by the
twenty foure orders of the musicians of the Tem
ple, who typed out the twenty foure Elders all
the members especially of christian Churches *Rev*
5. 8. who are made Kings and Priests to God
to prayse him as they did: for if there were
any other order of singing Choristers beside
the body of the people to succeed those, the
Lord would doubtlesse have given direction
in the gospell for their quallification, election,
maintainance &c. as he did for the musicians of
the Temple, and as his faithfullnes hath done for
all other church officers in the new Testament.
Secondly. Others beside the Levites (the chiefe
Singers) in the Iewish Church did also sing the
Lords songs; else why are they commanded frequently to sing: as in pf. 100, 1,2,3. pf. 95, 1,2,3.
pf. 102. title. with vers 18. & *Ex.* 15. 1. not only
Moses but all Israell sang that song, they spake
saying (as it is in the *orig.*) all as well as Moses,
the women also as well as the men. v. 20 21. and
deut. 32. (whereto some thinke, Iohn had reference as well as to *Ex.* 15. 1. when he brings in the
protestant Churches getting the victory over the
Beast

Beast with harps in their hands and singing the
song of Moses. *Rev.* 15. 3.) this song Moses is
commanded not only to put it into their hearts
but into their mouths also: *deut.* 31. 19. which
argues, they were with their mouths to sing it together as well as with their hearts.
Thirdly. Isaiah foretells in the dayes of the new-
Testament that Gods watchmen and desolate
lost soules, (signified by wast places) should with
their voices sing together, Isa. 52. 8, 9. and *Rev.*
7. 9, 10. the song of the Lamb was by many together, and the Apostle expresly commands the
singing of Psalmes, Himnes, &c. not to any select christians, but to the whole Church Eph. 5. 19
coll. 3. 16. Paule & Silas sang together in private
Acts. 16. 25. and must the publick heare oly one
man sing? to all these wee may adde the practise
of the primitive Churches; the testimony of ancient and holy *Basil* is in stead of many *Epist.* 63
When one of us (saith he) hath begun a psalme,
the rest of us set in to sing with him, all of us with
one heart and one voyce; and this saith he is the
common practise of the Churches in Egypt,
Lybia, Thebes, Palestina, Syria and those that
dwell on Euphrates, and generally every where,
where singing of psalmes is of any account. To
the same purpose also *Eusebius* gives witnes,
Ecclef. Hist. lib. 2. *cap.* 17. The objections made
against this doe most of them plead against joyning to sing in heart as well as in voyce, as that by
this meanes others out of the Church will sing

**   as

as also that wee are not alway in a sutable estate to the matter sung, & likewise that all cannot sing with understanding; shall not therefore all that have understanding ioyne in heart and voyce to-gether? are not all the creatures in heaven, earth, seas: men, beasts, fishes, foules &c. commanded to praise the Lord, and yet none of these but men, and godly men too, can doe it with spirituall understanding?

As for the scruple that some take at the translatiō of the book of psalmes into meeter, because Davids psalmes were sung in his owne words without meeter: wee answer- First. There are many verses together in several psalmes of David which run in rithmes (as those that know the hebrew and as Buxtorf shews *Thesau.* pa. 629.) which shews at least the lawfulnes of singing psalmes in english rithmes.

Secondly. The psalmes are penned in such verses as are sutable to the poetry of the hebrew language, and not in the common style of such other bookes of the old Testament as are not poeticall; now no protestant doubteth but that all the bookes of the scripture should by Gods ordinance be extant in the mother tongue of each nation, that they may be understood of all, hence the psalmes are to be translated into our english tongue; and if in our english tongue wee are to sing them, then as all our english songs (according to the course of our english poetry) do run in metre, soe ought Davids psalmes to be translated into

into meeter, that soe wee may sing the Lords songs, as in our english tongue soe in such verses as are familar to an english eare which are commonly metricall: and as it can be no just offence to any good conscience to sing Davids hebrew songs in english words, soe neither to sing his poeticall verses in english poeticall metre: men might as well stumble at singing the hebrew psalmes in our english tunes (and not in the hebrew tunes) as at singing them in english meeter, (which are our verses) and not in such verses as are generally used by David according to the poetry of the hebrew language: but the truth is, as the Lord hath hid from us the hebrew tunes, left wee should think our selves bound to imitate them; soe also the course and frame (for the most part) of their hebrew poetry, that wee might not think our selves bound to imitate that, but that every nation without scruple might follow as the graver sort of tunes of their owne country songs, soe the graver sort of verses of their owne country poetry.

Neither let any think, that for the meetre sake wee have taken liberty or poeticall licence to depart from the true and proper sence of Davids words in the hebrew verses, noe; but it hath beene one part of our religious care and faithfull indeavour, to keepe close to the originall text.

As for other obiections taken from the difficulty of *Ainsworths* tunes, and the corruptions in

** 2 our

our common pſalme books, wee hope they are answered in this new edition of pſalmes which wee here preſent to God and his Churches. For although wee have cauſe to bleſſe God in many reſpects for the religious indeavours of the tranſlaters of the pſalmes into meetre uſually annexed to our Bibles, yet it is not unknowne to the godly learned that they have rather preſented a paraphraſe then the words of David tranſlated according to the rule 2 *chron*. 29. 30. and that their addition to the words, detractions from the words are not ſeldome and rare, but very frequent and many times needles, (which we ſuppoſe would not be approved of if the pſalmes were ſo tranſlated into proſe) and that their variations of the ſenſe, and alterations of the ſacred text too frequently, may iuſtly miniſter matter of offence to them that are able to compare the tranſlation with the text; of which failings, ſome iudicious have oft complained, others have been grieved, wherupon it hath bin generally deſired, that as wee doe inioye other, ſoe (if it were the Lords will) wee might inioye this ordinance alſo in its native purity: wee have therefore done our indeavour to make a plaine and familiar tranſlation of the pſalmes and words of David into engliſh metre, and have not ſoe much as preſumed to paraphraſe to give the ſenſe of his meaning in other words; we have therefore attended heerin as our chief guide the originall, ſhūning all additions, except ſuch as even the beſt tranſlators

tranſlators of them in proſe ſupply, avoiding all materiall detractions from words or ſence. The word י which wee tranſlate *and* as it is redundant ſometime in the Hebrew, ſoe ſomtime (though not very often) it hath been left out, and yet not then, if the ſence were not faire without it.

As for our tranſlations, wee have with our engliſh Bibles (to which next to the Originall wee have had reſpect) uſed the Idioms of our owne tongue in ſtead of Hebraiſmes, leſt they might ſeeme engliſh barbariſmes.
Synonimaes wee uſe indifferently: as *folk* for *people*, and *Lord* for *Iehovah*, and ſomtime (though ſeldome) *God* for *Iehovah*; for which (as for ſome other interpretations of places cited in the new Teſtament) we have the ſcriptures authority pſ. 14. with 53. Heb. 1. 6. with pſalme 97. 7. Where a phraſe is doubtfull wee have followed that which (in our owne apprehenſiō) is moſt genuine & edifying:

Somtime wee have contracted, ſomtime dilated the ſame hebrew word, both for the ſence and the verſe ſake: which dilatation wee conceive to be no paraphraſticall addition no more then the contraction of a true and full tranſlation to be any unfaithfull detraction or diminution: as when wee dilate *who healeth* and ſay *he it is who healeth*; ſoe when wee contract, *thoſe that ſtand in awe of God* and ſay *Gods fearers*.

Laſtly. Becauſe ſome hebrew words have a
** 3   more

more full and emphaticall fignification then any one englifh word can or doth fomtime expreffe, hence wee have done that fomtime which faithfull tranflators may doe, *viz.* not only to tranflate the word but the emphafis of it; as אל *mighty God*, for God. ברך *humbly bleffe* for *bleffe*; *rife to ftand*, pfalm 1. for *ftand*; *truth and faithfulnes* for *truth*. Howbeit, for the verfe fake wee doe not alway thus, yet wee render the word truly though not fully; as when wee fomtime fay *reioyce* for *fhout for ioye*.

As for all other changes of numbers, tenfes, and characters of fpeech, they are fuch as either the hebrew will unforcedly beare, or our englifh forceably calls for, or they no way change the fence; and fuch are printed ufually in an other character.

If therefore the verfes are not alwayes fo fmooth and elegant as fome may defire or expect; let them confider that Gods Altar needs not our pollifhings: Ex. 20. for wee have refpected rather a plaine tranflation, then to fmooth our verfes with the fweetnes of any paraphrafe, and foe have attended Confcience rather then Elegance, fidelity rather then poetry, in tranflating the hebrew words into englifh language, and Davids poetry into englifh meetre; that

that foe wee may fing in Sion the Lords fongs of prayfe according to his owne will; untill hee take us from hence, and wipe away all our teares, & bid us enter into our mafters ioye to fing eternall Halleluiahs.

Biblical References in the Preface to the Bay Psalm Book
(Given here in the King James Version)

2 Chron. 5.13—"It came even to pass, as the trumpeters and singers *were* as one, to make one sound to be heard in praising and thanking the Lord, and when they lifted up *their* voice with the trumpets and cymbals and instruments of music . . . then the house was filled with a cloud. . . ."

2 Chron. 20.21—"And when he had consulted with the people, he appointed singers unto the Lord. . . ."

Ezra 3.10, 11—"And when the builders laid the foundation of the temple of the Lord, they set the priests in their apparel with trumpets . . . to praise the Lord, after the ordinance of David King of Israel. And they sang together by course in praising the giving thanks unto the Lord. . . ."

2 Chron. 29.30—"Moreover, Hezekiah the king and the princes commanded the Levites to sing praise unto the Lord with the words of David. . . ."

II

Cotton Mather
A "Question" from *Magnalia Christi Americana,*
Book V (London, 1702) and excerpts from
The Accomplished Singer (Boston, 1721)

[Cotton Mather (1663-1728), last and most prodigiously active of the great Mather dynasty of Puritan leaders, managed to publish at least 444 books during a life devoted utterly, zealously to a magnificent rearguard action: the upholding and the chronicling of the intellectual and religious standards of conservative Puritanism. While much of his writing now appears pedantic, dull, reactionary, or worse (his closely reasoned attack on witches), sometimes his native brilliance and sensitivity yielded positive results. His works are enormously valuable historical sources, and some of them also have considerable literary merit. Mather's best-known literary accomplishment, the seven-book New England ecclesiastical history, *Magnalia Christi Americana,* contains a vast amount of information about matters of history and dogma. The selection included here is a statement of the conservative Puritan objections to the use of instrumental music in worship. This view prevailed in the form of a widespread rejection of church organs until well into the eighteenth century. Thus when Thomas Brattle died in 1713 and left his home organ, the earliest known to have been imported into New England, to the Brattle Square Church, it was indignantly rejected, and the instrument wound up in the Anglican King's Chapel.

The title page of *The Accomplished Singer* offers this description of the contents of the tract: "First, How the Piety of *Singing* with a True DEVOTION, may be obtained and expressed; the glorious GOD after an uncommon manner Glorified in it, and His People Edified. And then, How the MELODY of REGULAR SINGING, and the SKILL of doing it, according to the RULES of it, may be easily arrived unto." Mather was a leading combatant for the cause of "Regular Singing" (see the Symmes selection below) because as a strict Puritan he regarded the ability to sing the Psalms correctly as an important adjunct to correct worship. However, as the following passages reveal, he was motivated by much more than a desire for accuracy. These pages are illuminated with a sensitivity to the spiritual power of music; they express the profound Puritan belief in the positive effect of psalmody on the emotions of the worshipper. "Signifying our *Delight* in Divine *Truths* by Singing of them" is described as the method by which man can "come into a Holy *Symphony* with the Saints who had their *Hearts* burning within them, when they sang these things unto the Lord." Thus music had a place in the emotional core of the Puritan faith.]

Magnalia Christi Americana

QUESTION.
Whether Instrumental Musick may lawfully be
introduced into the Worship of God,
in the Churches of the New Testament?

Considered and answered in the following Conclusions.

I. The Instrumental Musick used in the old Church of *Israel,* was an Institution of God: It was (2 Chron. 29. 25.) the Commandment of the Lord *by the Prophets.* And the Instruments are called *God's Instruments,* (1 Chron. 16. 42) and *Instruments of the Lord,* (2 Chron. 7. 6.) Now there is not one word of Institution in the *New Testament,* for *Instrumental Musick* in the Worship of God. And because the Holy God rejects all he does not command in his Worship, he now therefore in effect says unto us, *I will not hear the Melody of thy Organs.* But, on the other side, the Rule given doth abundantly Intimate, that *no Voice* is now to be heard in the Church, but what is significant and edifying, by signification; which the Voice of *Instruments* is not.

II. Tho' Instrumental Musick were admitted and appointed in the Worship of God under the *Old*

9

Testament, yet we do not find it practised in the *Synagogue* of the Jews, but only in the *Temple.* It thence appears to have been a part of the *Ceremonial Pedagogy,* which is now abolished; nor can any say it was a part of *Moral Worship.* And, whereas the common Usage now hath confined *Instrumental Musick* to *Cathedrals,* it seems therein too much to *Judaize;* which to do is a part of the *Anti-Christian Apostacy,* as well as to *Paganize.*

III. In our asserting, a Matter of the *Old Testament,* to have been *Typical,* 'tis not needful, that we be always able to particularize any *future Mysteries* of the *New Testament* therein referred unto; *Truths* which were then of a *present* Consideration, were sometimes represented in the *Types* then used among the People of God, which helps to understand the Case of *Instrumental Musick.*

IV. *Instrumental Musick* in the Worship of God, is but a very late Invention and Corruption in the Church of the *New Testament.* The Writings that go under the name of *Justin Martyr* deny it and decry it. *Chrysostom* speaks meanly of it. Even *Aquinas* himself, about 400 years ago, determines against it, as *Jewish* and *Carnal. Bellarmine* himself confesses, that it was but late received in the Church.

V. If we admit *Instrumental Musick* in the Worship of God, how can we resist the Imposition of all the *Instruments* used among the ancient Jews? Yea, *Dancing* as well as *Playing,* and several other *Judaic Actions?* Or, how can we decline a whole *Rabble* of Church Officers, necessary to be introduced for *Instrumental Musick,* whereof our Lord Jesus Christ hath left us, no manner of Direction?

The Accomplished Singer

1. It is the Concern of everyone that would enjoy *Tranquillity* in this World, or obtain *Felicity* in the World to come, to follow that Holy Direction of Heaven, *Exercise thyself in PIETY.* And there is no *Exercise* of PIETY more unexceptionable than that of making *a joyful* Noise of SINGING in the Praises of our GOD; That of signifying our *Delight* in Divine *Truths* by SINGING of them; That of *Uttering* the Sentiments of Devotion, with the *Voice,* and such a *Modulation of the Voice,* as will naturally express the *Satisfaction* and *Elevation* of the *Mind,* which a Grave SONG shall be expressive of. 'Tis indeed a very *Ancient Way* of Glorifying the Blessed GOD; As *Ancient* as the Day *when the Foundations of the Earth were fastened,* and *the Corner-Stone thereof was laid. The Morning-Stars* then *Sang together.* And it is as *Extensive* an one; For it is Remarkable, That *All Nations* make SINGING to be one part of the *Worship* which they pay unto their

GOD. Those Few *Untuned Souls,* who affect upon Principle to distinguish themselves from the rest of Mankind, by the Character of *Non-Singers,* do seem too much to divest themselves of an *Humanity,* whereof it may be said unto them, *Doth not Nature itself teach it you?* Be sure, they sufficiently differ from the *Primitive Christians;* For, though the *Eastern* Churches were at first Superiour to the *Western,* for the *Zeal of the House of GOD* in this matter, yet both betimes Concurr'd in it. Not only *Justin* the *Martyr,* and *Clemens* of *Alexandria,* as well as *Tertullian,* and several others of the *Primitive Writers,* but also Governour *Pliny* himself will tell us, what *Singers* to their *GOD,* the Faithful were then known to be; and how much they *Worshipped* Him in these *Beauties of Holiness.*

2. BUT this piece of *Natural Worship* is further Confirmed by a *positive Institution* of GOD our SAVIOUR for it. The *Sacred Scriptures* with which the Holy SPIRIT of GOD has Enriched us, have directed us unto this *Way* of Worshipping. In our *Old Testament* we there find it as a Command of GOD; but Calculated particularly for Times under the *New-Testament:* Psal. LXVIII. 32. *Sing Praises unto GOD, ye Kingdoms of the Earth, O Sing Praises unto the Lord.* And Psal. C. 1, 2. *Make a Joyful Noise unto the Lord, All ye Lands, Come into his Presence with Singing. . . .* In our *New-Testament* itself 'tis a Thing so positively enjoined, that it must be a wonder, if any Christian can make any Question of it. How plainly is it commanded? Jam. V. 13. *Is any cheerful among you, Let him sing Psalms.* Yes, in the *Pauline* Epistles, we have it; how frequently, how earnestly inculcated! . . .

3. THE *Sacred Scriptures,* which have *Directed* us to *Sing unto the Lord, and Bless His Name;* have also *supplied* us with an admirable and sufficient *Matter* for our *Songs.*

WE have a PSALTER [the Bay Psalm Book], whereof the biggest part is of PSALMS, that were Composed by *David,* who being the *Last* of the Limitations which the Glorious GOD made of the *Line,* wherein the *First Promise* was to be accomplished, GOD for the sake of that REDEEMER, distinguished him, with doing of amazing Things for him, and by him; whereof *This* was one, that he was made the greatest *Instrument* for assisting the Devotions of the Church, that ever was in the World. The rest were Composed by other *Holy Men of GOD, who wrote as they were moved by the Holy SPIRIT. . . .*

6. . . . But let this be one of the First Things prescribed. Study and Labour for such Impressions of PIETY on our Minds, as we may easily discover to have been upon the Minds of the *Inspired Writers,*

at the Time when they wrote the *spiritual songs,* which we are now *singing unto the Lord.* An Exultation of PIETY in *singing unto GOD,* has an Infinite Recommendation of it, from This; That the *Prophetic* SPIRIT, falling according to the Good Pleasure of GOD, upon the Children of Men, and His *Good Angels possessing* of them, one of the *Gifts* with which they were endowed, and one of the *Acts* to which they were excited, was that of *singing unto GOD.* They could not but break forth into songs, wherein the *Great Things of GOD* were celebrated. . . . The Writers of our *spiritual songs* were *Holy Men of GOD;* and had a Principle of PIETY Sanctifying of them. There can be no doubt of it, but that when the Holy SPIRIT . . . disposed them to write what we have in our Hands, He produced in their *Heart,* those *Motions of Piety,* which were agreeable and answerable to the *Matter* then flowing from their *Pens.* In what they have written, there is very Legible, and a very ordinary Capacity may *see,* A *Confession* of Holy Truths, with an Heart *Believing* of them, Consenting to them; A *Desire* of Promised Blessings, with a *Value* for them; a *Love* to GOD, (and Man;) and a *Zeal* for His Kingdom; and His *Word* and *Ordinances;* a *Faith* in GOD, and our SAVIOUR, and His Promises; with a Joy in Him; and a Rapturous *Admiration* of Him; An *horror* of sin, and a *sorrow* for it; and a *Fear* of the *Judgments* threatned unto it; a *Resolution* for the Service of GOD; and a Retreat unto Him: with a Despair to find Relief in Creatures; with other *motions of Piety,* which belong to the *Life of GOD* in the Soul. In Singing our *spiritual songs,* let us be Inquisitive after those *Motions of piety,* which are discernible in the Verse now before us; and let us with a Soul flying away to GOD, for them, try whether we cannot fly *with* them; and strive to come at *the like;* and give not over the struggle, till we feel our selves come into an Holy *Symphony* with the Saints who had their *Hearts burning* within them, when they *sang* these things unto the Lord. *Christian,* Behold a lovely Method of getting into those Heavenly *Frames & Strains* which will assure thee of thy arriving one Day, to the same state of Blessedness, and those *Everlasting Habitations,* which these *Favourites* and *Amanuenses* of Heaven, thro' whom our *spiritual songs* were convey'd unto us, have been renew'd into. Yea, Thou art already *Caught* up to Paradise in them. Nor is there a Nobler Method, among all our *Hermeneutic Instruments,* to come at the *True sense* of our spiritual songs, than . . . an *Experimental Taste,* of the PIETY which was working in the Hearts of the Writers at the Time of their Inspiration.

III

Thomas Symmes
Utile Dulci. Or, A Joco-Serious Dialogue, Concerning Regular Singing
(Boston, 1723)

[Thomas Symmes (1678-1725), graduate of the Harvard class of '98, minister at Bradford, Massachusetts, and a man whose attachment to music led him to sign himself "Philomusicus," published a sermon in 1720 in Boston entitled *The Reasonableness of, Regular Singing, or, Singing by Note.* This was the first published declaration of the great New England Singing War. The only violence in this conflict was verbal, but there was a great deal of that, and it was to have an enormous impact upon early American musical culture. The combatants were, on the one hand, the Regular Singers, a group of reformers determined to reintroduce musical literacy to the congregations of New England; on the other hand were the Usual Singers, the traditionalists who defended the practices of "lining out" the Psalms and passing down the tunes by purely oral methods. The Usual Singers were at first the majority, albeit a relatively obscure lot, because it was naturally the literate opposition that did most of the writing. The dependence on oral methods was originally a matter of necessity, particularly in the first, hard century of settlement. For instance, in John Cotton's 1647 *Singing of Psalmes a Gospel Ordinance,* "lining out" is defined in purely practical terms: "It will be a necessary helpe, that the words of the *Psalme* be openly read before hand, line after line, or two lines together, that so they who want either books or skill to read, may know what is to be sung, and joyne with the rest in the dutie of singing." The practical, however, was not long in becoming ritual. In *The Reasonableness of, Regular Singing, or Singing by Note,* Symmes gives an account of the process by which a music-reading society became a society whose music was based upon oral traditions:

> The Declining from, and getting beside the Rule was gradual and insensible. Singing-Schools and Singing-Books being laid aside, there was no Way to learn; but only by hearing of Tunes Sung, or by taking the Run of the Tune (as it is phrased). The Rules of Singing not being taught or learnt, every one sang as best pleased himself, and every Leading-Singer would take the Liberty of raising any Note of the Tune, or lowering of it, as best pleas'd his Ear, and add such Turns and Flourishes as were grateful to him; and this was done so gradually, as that but few if any took Notice of it. One Clerk or Chorister would alter the Tunes a little in his Day, the next, a little in his and so on one after another, till in Fifty or Sixty Years it caus'd a Considerable Alteration.

This is a Regular Singer's version of history, of course, but it is quite plausible. In general, however, the reformers neglected the positive aspects of the Usual Way, and modern scholars have demonstrated that it very probably had developed into a rich folk art, at least in some areas. Still, the Usual Way was doomed by the vigorous efforts of the reformers, particularly when such men as John Tufts and Thomas Walter published practical instructional works and Psalms with musical notation, thus giving their fellow Regular Singers the wherewithal for practical education of their people.

Symmes' *Utile Dulci* ("The Useful with the Pleasant"), excerpted in the following pages, is an utterly remarkable document. Not only does it contain a wealth of information about early attitudes toward music, but it is a richly entertaining piece of argumentation in itself. Symmes uses the dialogue form effectively—although the right-thinking "Minister" naturally has much more to say than his erring "Nei'bour"—and the witty, colloquial style is imbued with a spirit that is modern as well as Puritan, particularly in the jaunty and irreverent manner in which the author debunks the superstitions and entrenched attitudes of the Anti-Regular-Singers (or "A.R.S.'s," Symmes' favorite method of referring to the opposition). The passages given here begin with the Dialogue itself—there is a lengthy prologue in the original tract—and are chosen to demonstrate the personal style and attitudes of the author, as well as the major features of this cultural conflict. Symmes was a close observer as well as a lively combatant, and for all his exasperation, he shows himself to be sensitive to and occasionally even sympathetic with the ways and the fears of the Usual Singers.]

Utile Dulci

DIALOGUE

Min. [Minister] How d'you *Nei'bour?* I'm glad to see you. What occasions your looking so *sad, & uneasy?*

Nei'b. Alas! Sir, I have met with a great deal of Affliction in my time; I've had a great deal of Sickness, *been exercised with many* Crosses *and* Disapointments, *but indeed never met with any thing in all my life, that made me so uneasy, as this* New Way *of* Singing, *that's forced in upon us.*

M. Truly *N.* I'm heartily *sorry* for your Uneasiness about that matter, and the more so, because I'm satisfyed *Satan* has got a great *Advantage* against you, or you'd never remain so *out of tune,* after all that has been said and done for your satisfaction. But I pray you *N.* to *produce your Cause* and bring forth your *strong Reasons,* and *make out* your Charge, that Singing by Note is a *New-way,* or *obtruded upon you;* and I'll be your easy *Proselite,* and make you a Confession in *Folio,* if you desire it, that I've been deceiv'd and done very much amiss in this matter.

N. Well Sir, but you'll be angry *(they say) if I should be* plain *with you, and it will do no good, to have any Discourse with you about it.*

M. And are none of your *Party* transported sometimes with anger, when they talk about Singing? But—If what you call *Plainness,* be down-right *Rudeness,* and the last *Dogmaticalness,* and if those that should come to *learn of me* and be instructed by me, come rather to *dictate to me:* and instead of (as the *Apostle* directs) *Entreating me as a Father* (supposing they think me out of the way) *arraign* my Administrations, and treat me with the last *Scurrility,* or at best, as if I were the *Pupil,* and they the *Tutor;* (I say, if so) I've *just reason* to be angry, and I do well to let them know I am so. I should sin against God, and betray the Authority I'm vested with, and vilify my office, if I should

tamely suffer my self to be *insulted,* and not manifest my Resentments, with due discretion, *Rebuking with sharpness* where there may be occasion for it, as the Apostle directs. Tho' I hope I do not forget, that the *Servant of the Lord must not strive, but be gentle unto all men: not a brawler, but apt to teach, patient, and in meekness instructing those that oppose themselves.* And let me assure you, *N.* if you'l *modestly* produce your Allegations & Objections, I'll (by the help of God) use you, with all the *patience & Calmness,* with all the *Goodness and Gentleness,* you can desire. And this, I think, is fair.

N. Truly *Sir, I think so too. And if any say otherwise, I must own they'r very unjust. If then you'r at leisure, Sir, and will give me leave to speak freely, and hear me patiently, I'll tell you what sticks with me.*

M. Well N. I dare promise nothing in my own strength; and I must confess, there's scarse any thing apt to put me out of patience so soon, as to hear the *Unsufferable Impertinces* of some of you *Anti-Regular-Singers;* However (as I told you) I'll endeavor to hear you patiently, at least while you keep within the bounds (I don't say of good sense! but) of Modesty and good Manners. Let me then, hear your Objections: Only, let them be reduc'd to a proper order, that I may'nt be oblig'd to answer ten times to the same thing, but may know when I've done, and that our coming together and this our Confabulation may be *for the better and not for the worse.*

N. Why truly Sir, I don't know whether I've skill eno' to range my Objections to your mind. I believe you've heard all the Objections I have to produce, and if you'll please to dispose them in an agreeable Method, I'll endeavor, as my Memory serves me, to keep to that Method.

M. You speak well N. and give me good hope, (tho' you look'd so Unpleasantly at first) that you come hither with a Teachable Disposition; and if so, I doubt not, but I shall give you full satisfaction in every Article, e'r we've done. However, I'll promise you *N.* in this Conference, to act not only the part of a *Respondent,* but of a *Moderator* also, and will agreeable assist you, in stating and prosecuting your Objections, that you may have no cause to complain, *You can't be heard.*

N. Sir, *I thank you for your* Civility. *I'm sorry I ran away with the* Popular Clamour *against you. I must needs own you treat* me *very Candidly.*

M. Well, N. I'm thankful, and rejoyce greatly, if I can give you content; for *that's* my Ambition & hearty Desire; and since you ask it of me, I'll tell you how you may Range your Objections, to make them look most *Formidable* and fit for business. Those that I've heard of, (tho' no doubt some of you

A.R.S. that have such an *incomparable talent* at raising *Objections* against *Mathematical Demonstrations,* may have many more in store, against the Day of Battel) but those they've been pleas'd to favour us with the *Knowledge of,* are reducible to *Three* Heads. *First,* Some against the *Thing it self,* which you'r pleas'd to call a *New Way* of Singing, and the *Consequents* of it. And they are these *Seven.* (1) That it is a *New Way,* an *Unknown Tongue.* (2) That it is not so *Melodious* as the *Usual Way.* (3) That there are so *many Tunes,* we shall never have done learning. (4) That the Practice of it *gives Disturbance;* Roils & Exasperates men's Spirits; grieves sundry good People, and causes them to behave themselves indecently & disorderly. (5) That [it] is *Quakerish & Popish,* and introductive of *Instrumental* Musick. (6) That the *Names* given to the Notes are *Baudy,* yea *Blasphemous.* (7) That it is a *Needless way,* since their *good Fathers* that were strangers to it, are got to Heaven without it. *Secondly,* Some are against the *Persons,* that are the Promoters, Admirers & Practitioners of this way. And they are Three. (1) It's said to be a *Contrivance* to get *Money.* (2) They spend *too much time* about learning; they tarry out a Nights Disorderly, and Family-Religion is neglected by the means. (3) They'r a Company of *Young Upstarts* that fall in with this way and set it forward: and some of them are *Lewd & Loose Persons.* *Thirdly,* The other Objections are against the *Manner of bringing* Regular Singing *into the Church:* And these are peculiarly level'd against my self. These are your *Principal* objections; a'nt they, *Nei'bor?*

N. Yes *Sir, They are so. But for my part, I don't father all of them; yet since we'r upon the Head; I should be glad to hear what you can say, (as the time will allow) to these several Objections, or any other that in Discourse may come to mind.*

M. Well N. I am willing to speak *particularly* to them; but there's so many of them, you can't expect I should say much to them, but I'll endeavor to speak to the purpose and eno' . . . Come, let me hear your first Objection; and done with Preambles.

N. *Why Sir, my first Objection is this, That it is a* New Way, *an* unknown Tongue.

M. . . . this you call a *New Way,* was study'd, known and approv'd of in our College, from the very *Foundation* of it; (*and tho' for some years of later time it was unhappily neglected, yet (blessed be God) it is again revived, I hope will be ever continued in that School of the Prophets.)* . . . the *Notes* of the Tunes were plac'd in our *New-England Psalm Books* from the *Beginning,* with general *Directions* for Singing by *Note,* and that there are many of the *Children,* and *Grand-Children* of the first Setlers of *New-England,* who are now living, that well *remember* their *ancestors* Singing by *Note;* I say, besides all this, It's evident, that Singing by Note is no Novelty, since Musick is one of the *Liberal Sciences,* (or, (as *Alsted* terms it) a Mathematical Science subalternate to Arithmetick, and may be call'd a special Arithmetick,) has been so accounted in all Ages, and amongst all learned Nations; and was doubtless Coaeval to, if not more ancient than Instrumental Musick; of which *Jubal* was the *Inventer,* as *Moses* tells us, *Gen.* 4. 21.

Moreover, the very Tunes prick'd in our *Psalm books,* are with little or no variation in Mr. *Ravenscrofts* Psalm-Book, printed above a *Hundred* Years ago. . . .

Furthermore, (as is evident from a Psalm-Book of Elder *Chipman's* now in my hands) The Church of *Plymouth* (which was the *First* Church in *New-England*) made use of Ainsworth's version of the Psalms till the Year 1692 . . . and till about 1682 their *excellent* Custom was to Sing *without* Reading the Line [that is, "lining out" the Psalm]. . . .

Briefly, all that know any thing to purpose about Singing by Note, know as certainly, as they can any thing, that what is now call'd the *Usual Way,* in opposition to Singing by Note, is but a *Defective Imitation* of the Regular Way. And in some Places, they've kept nearer to the Rule, and in others, they've varied more from it. And wherever they differ any thing considerable, their Singing, as to the external part of it, is so far Defective and Irregular. And,

Finally, Singing Skilfully or by Note is expressly & by just consequence requir'd in the *Word of GOD;* as in *Psal.* 32.2 & 47.7. 1 *Chron.* 15.22. 1 *Cor.* 12.31. *Mal.* 1.14. . . . and many other Scriptures; several of which you've heard me Expound. So that your *Usual Way* of Singing is *but of Yesterday,* an upstart Novelty, a Deviation from the Regular, which is the only *Scriptural good Old Way of Singing;* much elder than our Fathers, or Fathers Grandfathers; as we could easily further evince were it needful; But they that won't be satisfyed with what I've now offer'd to consideration, . . . *neither would they be perswaded, tho' one arose from the dead!* What say you *N?*

N. Say! *Why truly Sir, I'm* amaz'd *I should be so long deluded & Hood-winck'd. I* must own, *You have* Antiquity *on your side, or I shall forfeit the Character of a Reasonable Creature, if things are as you tell me.*

M. I aver what I've said to be so; and I'm ready to produce the Books to prove what I've asserted.

N. Sir; *I'm obliged to take your Word in some things of greater Consequence than this, and therefore I can believe you as to the History you've given me of this Matter.* . . .

But *what do you say, Sir, to it's being an* unknown Tongue?

M. I say there is in it, an *Allusion* to the *Apostles* expression of Praying or Preaching in an Unknown Tongue: . . . It is a comparison without any similitude, as the Objector supposes there is. Indeed, if we propos'd to Sing in *Latin,* as the Papists do, this comparison would be just. But tho' we possibly Sing Tunes that some in the Congregation can't sing, yet we sing the same Psalms we ever us'd to sing. Yea, if we throw by our Psalm Books and Sing only *F. S. L.*[*] in the Meeting-house, as some have been so weak, as to suppose we intended . . . there had been some room for such a *cramp Objection.* But verily, this Objection will hold against Singing any Tune, for *there is no one Tune, that all* in the Congregation that try to sing and do well to do so, are *Masters* of, and consequently in your sense they'r an *Unknown Tongue* to them. And surely Persons may sing the Words, the Matter to be sung, in a Congregation when there is eno' to lead the Tune, tho' they were never acquainted with one Note of the Tune before, and that very acceptably to God, if their hearts are right with Him. But, let me hear your next Objection, and try if there's any more force in *That,* than in *This.*

N. My *second Objection is This,* That this Singing by Note is not so Melodious & Pleasant, as the Usual Way: *Some have call'd it* Yelling. *Others have said, they'd as leeve hear the* Wolves *howl. And for* my own *part, I can't* fancy *it. One good man said,* He never had heard *Christ's* Voice *in this way of Singing since it came up.*

M. . . . I'll honestly confess to you that before I was pretty well acquainted with the Rules of Singing, I rather *fancy'd* the *Usual,* than the Regular way: But my *Judgment* satisfy'd me the Regular must be best. And I know, one reason why my Fancy for the present was most gratify'd with my singing the Usual way, was, because I was used to *that,* and not Master of *the other.* And hence it is, that *Home is Home, be it ever so Homely.* And even so the miserable *Hottentots* (pardon the Comparison!) who think to adorn themselves with the *Guts of Beasts,* with all the Garbage in them; prefer these Guts to a *Chain of Gold,* because it's what they'r used to, and it pleases their Fancies. But surely if they'd exercise *Reason,* the Ornaments us'd by other People, are more beautiful and becoming; or else all the Civiliz'd & Polite part of the World are deceiv'd and those Dregs of Mankind are in the Right of it.

Furthermore, I've said to some of my Hearers, that if any of you *A. R. S's* would take the pains to

[*Fa Sol La]

acquaint your selves with the *Rules* of Singing, so as to be able to Sing 6 or 7 Tunes tolerably by Art, *If they did not then say as I do,* that singing by Note is Unspeakably preferrible to singing the Usual way; *I'd give up the Cause as to them.*

Besides, There are *few* of you *A. R. S's,* that ever heard Singing, in the several parts of Musick; and some of you don't know the *Difference* between the Treble & Bass. Hence I heard one, (that your Fraternity set much by) say, that *the Treble & Bass must be sung with the same Voice!* And another was pleas'd to say in my Hearing, That one Sabbathday in a certain Meeting-House, there was *Four sorts* of Singing! for some sung *Rowly Way;* and some sung the *Usual Way;* and some sung the *New Way;* and some sung *Bass.* Whence I learnt that the Usual Way at one Town, and the Usual Way at another, were very *Different: Fas est—.* Now there is no man can judge aright of the Melody of Singing by Note; that has not heard Tunes sung in the several parts, or in Consort; and that not by Beginners only, but by *Adeptists,* or at least persons *well skill'd* in the Science of Musick; any more, than a man can judge of *Reading,* by Hearing one Read that *just begins* to put his *Syllables* together.

Again, Consider *N.* that the *Beauty* and Harmony of Singing consists very much in a just *Timing & Turning* the Notes: every Singer keeping the exact *Pitch* the Tune is set in, according to the part he Sings. Now you in the *Usual* Way, are very *faulty* on this account. Hence you may remember, that in our Congregation we us'd frequently to have some People Singing a Note or Two, *after the rest* had done. And *you* commonly strike the Notes not *together,* but *one after another;* one being half way thro' the second Note, before his Nei'bor has done with the First. . . .

Once more, I put it to your Conscience *N.* who are the *Best Judges* of Melody, Such as can Sing *both* the Usual Way and by Note; or they that can Sing *neither;* or only the *Usual Way?* . . . the *Chief Musicians* in our Country & Nation, recommend the Regular Way, as Unspeakably most Melodious; and our Reason and Sense tell us so likewise: Whereas it is only an Ungovern'd Fancy tells you the contrary. This several amongst us, declare upon Experience.

But suppose your way is after all, by you esteemed most Melodious; yet surely the Consequents of People's learning to Sing by Rule, should prevail with all that love God, to deny their own Fancy, rather than in the least discourage such a Method of Singing. For, I trust we'r all agreed that Singing the Praises of GOD is a Duty incumbent on us Christians. And if it be a Duty to Sing, it is a Duty to use our endeavors to learn to Sing. For we don't come *Singing,* but *Crying* into the World. And tho' some have a more Musical Genius than others, yet Men don't Sing as *naturally,* as Pigs Squeak, or Children Cry; but their Genius must be *cultivated,* e're they can Sing with skill & understanding. Now if we are to learn any Art we shall surely take the *Easiest* and most *Speedy* way to learn it; and this generally speaking is by acquainting our selves with the *Rudiments & Rules* of that Art. If we would teach our Children *to Read,* we don't set them first into *Chronicles,* but to their *Hornbook* or *Primmer.* And so if we would learn to Sing, we must first learn to *raise our Notes.*— . . . And this we know, that there are Multitudes, can learn to Sing no *other way,* than can learn *by Rule.* And will you shut out so great a part of Mankind from joyning in the Worship of GOD, for a *meer* Fancy, and a *Groundless* one? When if you turn the Tables, all that can learn the Usual way easily, can if they will learn the other.— I might here (by the way) say something to a *Silly Objection,* I've heard, that it can't be right to Sing by Note; because it's so *easy to learn it.* Surely no man need go Seven years to *College* to know how to answer this! Won't you suffer your Children to learn to *Read,* or *Write,* or *Cypher,* because some, yea the generality of *Children* and *Young Men,* learn all these things with a great deal of *Facility;* whilst such as did not learn them when Young, can never learn them, without the greatest *Difficulties,* if at all.

Besides, sometimes you object It's so *Difficult* to learn to Sing by Rule, that it's more *pains* than *profit:* more cost than worship. Thus do your Objections *Militate* with one another; and I'll leave you to reconcile 'em: or e'n let 'em fight it out! So then your *Usual Way* of Singing, (wherein you Sing commonly the Treble only, not keeping your Pitch, not keeping Time; or turning your Nots alike) is as much less Melodious (to a Musical Ear & proper Judge of Harmony) than our Singing a Tune in the several parts of Musick with great Exactness, as a Tune play'd by an *Unskilful* Hand, or an *Untun'd Instrument,* is less Melodious than the same Tune play'd on a *Well-tun'd* Instrument, with great Accuracy, by a *Skilful Musician.* And this I think you may Conceive of, or you'r mighty dull of Apprehension.

And, whereas you tell me, One Good man said, *He had not heard* Christ's *Voice in this way of Singing by Note,* or to that purpose—: I speak solemnly, The man that talks so, has just reason to consider, and others to suspect, whether *He knows* Christ's Voice. Sure I am that the same person, as good as he is, (if I am rightly inform'd) betray'd so much ignorance of that *Sacred Voice,* that I could scarce have suspected a well-grown *Lamb,* much less a *Sheep* of Christ's Flock, could have been guilty of; in asserting three things; (1) That *Instrumental* Musick was an Invention of *David,* and not of Divine

Institution, even under the Law: tho' the Royal Prophet tells us, *Psal.* 81.4. *This,* i.e. Instrumental Musick was a *Statute in Jacob and a Law of the God of Israel.* (2) He asserted, that if Instrumental Musick were of Divine Appointment, *Organs* were not. Whereas the Jewish Church, *however,* are expressly exhorted, *Psal.* 150.4. to Praise God, with *Organs.* (3) He was pleased to say, that if Instrumental Musick and particularly *Organs,* were of Divine Institution, yet the *Jews* did not play on them, upon the *Sabbath-Day.* Whereas, in the 150 Psalm the People of God are directed to Praise Him in the *Sanctuary* with *Organs.*[*] . . . Now unless, your good man, knew Christ's Voice better in his Word, that has an Immediate relation to Musick; I'd advise him, never to Utter any more such complaint, lest he oblige us to conclude, he's as *shy* of his *Bible,* as some *A. R. S's* are of some *other* Books printed for their Instruction.

N. Sir! I can't but say, you've convinc'd *me, there's no manner of sense in this Objection; and if you as fully answer the Rest, I'll never open my mouth more against Singing by Note. . . . my next Objection is,* That there are so many *Tunes* we shall never have done learning 'em. *If you'd set any bounds, that we might know when we should have done, there would be some sense in it. But some tells us, there's an 150 Tunes, and we need do nothing else but learn to Sing. And I hear that one of our New Singers, (that is a* Pillar *among us) says, That* there are *Six* Excellent Tunes, and if a Man fall into any one of them, he may make Principal Melody.

M. A goodly saying indeed! You'd best get it annex'd to the sayings of the seven wise men of *Greece,* in the next Edition of 'em. Suppose *N.* when the Man *falls into* one of those *Gimm Tunes,* he should unhappily *Turn out* again, as they tell me, he does, on some occasions; whether *that* won't spoil the Harmony?— But to the Formidable Obj. (which no doubt is sufficient to puzzle *Aristotle* and all his Followers, to solve,) I'll tell you *N.* That as all the *English* Books in the World are composed of 24 [sic!] Letters, and when a Child has learn't those Letters thorowly; and learn't to spell and put his Syllables together, he can read, in *another Lad's Book,* as well as *his own:* and does not complain,—O! if there were but 10 or 12 Books, I could learn to read with some Courage; but when I hear of so many Thousand, I'm utterly disheartn'd, I shall never have done, I must do nothing else but learn to read! So, in Musick, all Tunes are composed of 7 Notes, and when a per-

[*In attacking these assertions Symmes indirectly attacks the anti-instrumental music position of fellow Regular Singer Cotton Mather. See the selection from Mather's *Magnalia Christi Americana.* Symmes did himself distrust instrumental music, but on social rather than religious grounds.]

son has learn't perfectly to *Name & Raise* his Notes and *Turn* his Thirds; He may with a little Practice, if within the *age of Discipline,* and apt to learn, Sing any Tune he sees prick'd at first sight, or with a little Conning over, or hearing another Sing it; and here's no occation to complain of the Multiplicity of Tunes; for he's still at his liberty to Sing what he pleases.

And, as to their being Sung Publickly; It's time-eno' for People to *complain,* when they'r *hurt.* How many Tunes soever there are (and indeed there may be Ten Thousand made by the same Rule that one is) yet, there has hitherto but Five been Sung in our Congregation, more than were wont to be Sung. . . . And I never propose to set any Tune Publickly, but what I'm assur'd *there's enough to lead* the Congregation in the Singing of it; and if they won't *follow,* you may guess who's to blame.— Besides, *Variety delights.* And it's strange that People, that are so *set against stated Forms of Prayer,* should be *so fond of Singing half a Dozen Tunes,* nay *One* Tune, from Sabbath to Sabbath; till every body *Nauseates* it, that has any Relish of Singing. In short, *Ministers* are Debtors, not to the *Weak* only, but to the *Strong.* They must give strong Meat to strong men, as well as Milk to Babes.

· · · · ·

And whereas you say, Many *good* People are griev'd about it. I answer, *That's none of their goodness,* I'm sure; but their Pittiable *weakness* at best. And for any to be angry at it, is to be angry *without Cause,* if ever men were so. And you remember, what *Christ* has said of such, *Mat.* 5.22 [" . . . whosoever is angry with his brother without a cause shall be in danger of the judgment. . ."]. And tho' we'r Commanded not to *give* offence, we'r not Commanded, not to let People *take* offence. And if Good People are offended with us, when we give them no reason to be so, that's our *unhappiness,* and not our *Sin.* The *wo* belongs to such as *take* offence, where there is none *given.* And if many Good People are griev'd; I'm perswaded as many and as Good as they are, are rejoyc'd at this matter, and look upon the revival of the *study & Practice* of the Art of Musick, as an happy Omen that *the time of the singing of Birds is coming on.* . . . There are many *Thanksgivings* to GOD, for bestowing this Good Gift on his People, notwithstanding all the Disturbance occasion'd by it. And whether is *better,* to please GOD, or *Men,* judge ye! . . . *In short, N.* Do you love *Peace,* so, as to purchase it with the loss or practical *Denial* of *Truth?* I tell you truly, It's a *Cursed* peace you get upon those terms! It's bought too dear! No! follow Peace and *Holiness. Love the* Truth & Peace, *Zach.* 8.19. Both are best. But better Truth without Peace, then Peace without

Truth. . . . And now please to produce your 5th Objection, and let's try the weight of that.

N. *It was this, That this way of Singing is* Quakerish, *and* Popish, *and introductive of* Instrumental *Musick.*

M. Well, N. And what's your *Sixth?* I think (if I remember right) they'r pretty near of kin, and therefore let us answer them together.

N. Sir, *I find already you'll* Non-suit me in these Objections, and therefore *I'll only mention them: I shall never plead to 'em. My* Sixth *Objection was, that the* Names *given to the* Notes *are* Baudy, *yea* Blasphemous.

M. Verily, my Friend, *Apollo* himself, that Laugh'd but once a Year, could never forbear Giggling again, at such *Comical* Objections. . . . These Objections certainly labour of the Malady, of *Obscurum per* Obscurius, to prove a dark point by that which is more dark. In plain English, *N. A Broad Laugh,* is all the Answer such *Whimsical* Objections deserve: or rather a hearty *Scoul;* or, Deep *Sigh,* to observe the Doleful Effects of Man's Apostacy. To be oppress'd with such Objections would *make a wise man mad, Eccl.* 7.7.

However, to *gratify* you N. I'll say in a few words! Tho' we understand *Quakerism* and *Popery* as well, and hate them as much as you do; yet, I'll never *despise* what is *Laudable* in them. I admire the Quakers *neat* and *modest Dress,* and condemn nothing in it; but the wearing it, with *Affected Singularity.* And if the Papists sing a better *Tune,* or with a better *Air,* than we do, I'd as soon *imitate them,* and a thousand times sooner, than the *Honestest* man among you, that has *no Skill* in Singing. You've heard frequently, That *Truth is as precious in the Church of* Rome, *as in the Churches of* New-England. And verily, the *Papists* in many Articles, and particularly in their Bodily Devotion, are a *shame* to many Protestants! If Papists will come Early to Meeting, and behave themselves in the Worship of GOD with *Gravity* and *Wakefulness,* must I (under a pretence of abhorring Popery) make a Trade of *Coming,* when *Prayer* is just *done;* or *run out,* needlessly and unexemplarily, before the Exercise is ended; and go away *without the Blessing;* . . . *Away, Away!* The Papists themselves will rise up in judgment against Protestants, that act at this Rate, and will condemn them!

And since you make a Noise (tho' no *pleasant* one) about *Instrumental Musick,* I'll give you an unanswerable argument, that may put you out of all pain about it: And that is, That, truly, it's too *Chargeable* a peice of Worship ever to obtain amongst us; and you may depend upon it, that such as are not willing to bear the Cost of a *Bell,* to call the People together on the *Lord's Day,* and of a *Man* to *ring* it (as it is with too many amongst us) will never be so *Extravagant* as to lay out their Cash, (especially, now Mony is so scarce) to buy *Organs,* and pay an *Artist* for playing on 'em.

· · · · ·

N. Sir, *It's said* (1) *That the bringing up of this way is a Contrivance to* get Money. (2) *That there's* too much time *spent in learning. That People* Tarry out *Disorderly, and Family-Religion is* neglected. (3) *That they'r a Company of* Young Upstarts *that fall in with this way, and set it forward, and some of them are* Lewd & Loose *Persons and guilty of Prophaness in Singing Psalm Tunes in Barns and at* Plow & Cart: *will make nothing to Sing part of a Psalm Tune, and then, Cry,* St'r up Darby—*Nay, they'll Sing* Fa, Sol, La, *in the* Tavern.

M. Now take an answer N.—As to getting *Money* by it; this were a *Better* Contrivance (allowing the Objection) and more justifyable, than many *approved* of, by some that Object this. And why the *Singing Master,* is not worthy of his Reward for his pains in teaching our Children to *Sing,* as well as the *School Dame* and School *Master* for Teaching our Children to *Read,* Write & Cypher, I can't Devise. For, *Musick* is as Real & Lawful & Ingenious as *Art,* as either of the other. I don't say indeed as *Useful & Necessary.* But to put you, in this place, out of pain about your *Purses;* I'll undertake, if you'll learn to Sing, you shall all be taught on *free* Cost.

And, as to spending too much *Time,* or neglecting *Family Religion,* (if there be any ground for such an Objection) we'r very *sorry* for it. I'll *countenance* no such things. But I won't therefore condem the *Practice,* and *discourage* any from learning to Sing; but will Exhort them to *reform* such things, and *cut off occasion,* from such as seek it, *to speak evil of the things they understand not.* For my own part, as Iv'e the Honour of Conducting this Flock of *Christ,* I shall recommend it to *Heads* of *Families,* that, when they go out in an *Evening* to Sing, theyd set their Houses in order *before* they go from Home. And as for *being out late,* it can't well be *avoided,* where People go so *far,* as some must do; and I wish *some that make the Objection* (tho' *this* I confess is only *Argumentum ad Hominem)* did not drive a Trade of tarrying out unseasonably, on *less* Justifyable Occasions.

And, as to Singing in Barns and Fields — . . . tho' there may possibly be some *Deference* to be paid to Common *Psalm-Tunes;* yet it's wonderful to hear *those* talk at this rate, that deny the *Holiness of Places.* For surely the *Meeting-House* is as Holy as any *Tune.* Is the *One* improv'd in the *Worship* of GOD? so is the *other.* But this Objection arises from a *Superstitious* Notion, some have Imbib'd, That there is some *Sacredness in Tunes.* But I assure you, & can easily demonstrate to you, there is not the *least Jot.* If any would suppose there's a *Relative Holiness* in some Psalm-Tunes, I affirm, there is no more *Real Holiness* in the most Celebrated Psalm Tune, than in the *Tune of, Pepper is Black.* And if People have taken up any other notion, it's *high time* they should be better inform'd, and convicted of their Error. *Psalm-*Tunes & *Song-*Tunes are *all* made by the *same* Rule: and those that *made* the Psalm-Tunes were not Divinely inspir'd; nor had they *Authority* to *consecrate* any Tune to the Worship of GOD. I remember, as I was talking with one good Man on this Head, he cry'd out, *I'm convinc'd; for* (said he) *tho'* the Bible *is Holy, the* Covers *are not so.*—And further I affirm, the *most* of the *Psalm-Tunes,* as Sung in the *Usual way,* are much more like *Song-*Tunes, than as Sung by *Rule;* because you've more *Supernumerary* Notes & Turnings of the voice your way, than in ours. An Ingenious Gentleman, who has prick'd *Canterbury,* as some of *you* Sing it, finds (as I remember) no less than 150 Notes, in that Tune, in *your* way, whereas in our's, there are but 30. Did we propose so many *Crotchets,* and *Quavers,* and *Semi-*quavers and *Demi-*semi-quavers, in every Tune, I should not wonder if you were *discouraged* from endeavoring to learn to Sing. But alas! *This* is what you've generally *no Notion* about: And yet think your selves sufficiently *accomplish'd* to judge in the Affair—. Yea some *Rage* again in their Confidence. And yet sometimes *their own Mouths condemn* them. I was told by a very *worthy Man,* That he was not long since arguing with one of your *Fraternity,* and at length us'd this *Similitude,* —*You are a* Planter Nei'bour. Now suppose, while you'r Planting, there comes a *Sailer* athwart you. *Well!* crys he; *What are you doing,* Friend?—A doing (say you)? Why, I'm *Planting.*—What at *this time* of Year? quoth the *Sailer.* The *Planter* replys, *Yes;* when should I Plant?—Why (says the Sailer) in *August;* if you intend to have a Crop,—*No* (says the Planter) you'r *deceived:* Iv'e been a Planter this 20 Year, and my Father was a Planter before me, and I know certainly, I should have no Crop if I should Plant in August. You know better how to Rig and Sail a *Ship,* than how to raise Corn.—You talk like a *fool* (cryes the *Sailer*) I know, *you* and your *Father* before you, were *deceived:* I tell you, you should Plant in *August* —. *What would you say to him?* says my *Friend.*—Say? Cryes he: *I'd up with my Fist* (which he did at that Instant) *and hit him a Dab in the Chaps,* (and he gave the Man a good Dowse.) And upon the whole I say, *Ne sutor ultra Crepidam.* Let not the Shoe-maker go beyond his Last. And *every Man to his Trade,* wherein he's to be believ'd.

Briefly, Whereas you say, it's by some objected, they'r *young Upstarts*—. I answer, It's an unparellel'd

(I'd almost said *unpardonable*) piece of *Ignorance,* or *Impudence,* for any to say so. I remember indeed, that one of my Reverend Brethren, told me, That some of his Hearers made Objection, at the Beginning of this Ridiculous Controversy. Whereupon, he took occasion to ask the Judgment of several *Aged* Ministers, and of several of *middle Age;* and finding they all *agreed* in their Sentiments about this matter (and whatever he is for a *Christian,* I'll be bold to say, He's a *poor Tool* of a *Scholar;* and may either be Saluted,—*Salve* Doctor, *sine Libris!* or, if he has a Library, His *Books* may be Complemented, *Salvete Libri sine Doctore;* that does not *know,* that *Musick* is as proper a *Science,* as *Geometry* or *Arithmetick:* I won't *English* it to you, but I say, finding *all* the Ministers he discours'd, highly *approving* of singing by Note) He tells his Friends, *Tho' you were pleas'd to say there were no Ministers for it, but some* Young Men; *yet I find this and the other* Aged *Minister of the same Judgment—, Yes,* say they, but those Ministers are *superannuated.* Well says my Friend, but I've discours'd with these and those, *middle-ag'd* Ministers, and they'r of the same mind—. Yes, cry they, *Ministers will hang together right* or *wrong!—*

Horribile dictu! I'm amaz'd to think of the *Perverseness* not to say, *Atheism,* some discover, when under the power of inveterate prejudice.

Furthermore, There was an Excellent Man of our Church, that told me, about a Year ago, that some of your Party said, if Old Dr. *Mather* approv'd of it, they should then *suspect* they were *out of the way* in opposing it. Upon which I *wrote* to that venerable Doctor. And he very kindly sent me his Son's (Dr. *Cotton Mather's*) *Accomplish'd Singer* [See previous selection], and upon the last Page of said Book, He wrote with his own hand, these Words.

"I DO concur with what is here Published by my Son, and heartily wish, that Young People may be Encouraged to Learn to Sing Regularly."
INCREASE MATHER

[After thus marshalling the support of the man regarded by many Puritans as the ultimate earthly authority, Symmes quotes extensively from the tract of the younger Mather, then returns to the "Objections" of the Usual Singers, and finally wins "Nei'bor" over—of course—to the camp of the Regular Singers.]

IV

William Billings
Prefaces to *The New-England Psalm-Singer*
(Boston, 1770) and *Singing Master's Assistant*
(Boston, 1778)

[William Billings (1746-1800), the gimpy, one-eyed son of a Boston shopkeeper, began as a tanner early in life, apparently had his own tannery on Frog Lane (now Boylston St.) for a time, and was good enough at his trade to be official Sealer of Leather (inspector) for Boston from 1787 to 1796. In order to support himself and a large family, he also worked as a street cleaner and a "hogreeve" (roughly speaking, enforcer of the local stray-swine laws).

All this struggle to make ends meet notwithstanding, Billings was primarily a musician, perhaps our first native-born, full-fledged professional musician, and he was a genius, a largely self-taught master of psalmody, our first great composer. In 1770 the young man published his first collection:

The New-England Psalm-Singer: or, American Chorister. Containing a number of Psalm-tunes, Anthems and Canons. In four and five parts. Never before published. Composed by William Billings, a native of Boston, in New-England.

The specifics of birthplace which Billings proudly includes on the title page signaled an event of great cultural importance: With this one publication, containing over 120 original works, Billings increased the total number of published American compositions by tenfold, and in the process also published the first collection devoted entirely to the art of one American composer. The frontispiece of the book was by Paul Revere, and Billings was a close associate of many of the Boston leaders of the Revolution. The composer of the rousing "Chester," the unofficial national song of the Revolution, Billings was a friend and singing partner of Sam Adams, and his music contains many references to the American cause. The most famous examples are "Chester" and "Lamentation over Boston," a parodic Jeremiad inspired by the British occupation of Boston in 1775-76: ("By the Rivers of Watertown we sat down and wept . . .").

Billings was apparently a skillful singer, and from 1769 or earlier, he intermittently taught singing schools in Boston, Weymouth, Stoughton, and elsewhere. The Singing School movement was a grass-roots educational institution of national importance; its founders were the Regular Singers of the first part of the century (see the Symmes listing above), and their creation was for over a century the principal means of musical education in this country. Psalmody was social music at least as much as it was church music, and the school sessions convened by the singing masters (often in taverns and meeting-houses) were an important part of the social life of the community. Indeed, in many communities the singing school provided the only socially acceptable means for the young of both sexes to gather in the same place. Billings' second published collection, the *Singing Master's Assistant* (1778), contains a strictly practical list of rules and instructions for the benefit of fellow singing masters. That list is included here because it tells something of the social as well as the musical behavior of the sometimes not altogether musically devoted singing students.

Also included from the long and variegated preface to *Singing Master's Assistant* are its opening remarks, a passage imbued with deeply humorous self-knowledge as well as self-confidence; and also a famous example of Billings' satirical style, a rough and witty way of confronting the critics who attacked his music on the grounds of its failure to observe the rules of classical harmony. "To the Goddess of Discord" is a mock address written to accompany its author's horrific and very funny exercise in discord, "Jargon," a piece designed to provide the critics with all the seven- and passing-chords at once which they missed in his third- and open-chord-dominated music.

The first Billings selection here is the most famous, the opening to his first publication. It is a resounding declaration of musical independence and faith in his muse. Billings' music exercised an unparalleled dominance in American psalmody for more than a generation, and some works never lost a place in the hearts of many. However, Billings became the most obvious target of those who rejected the native musical art in the process of crusading for the appreciation of the classical European tradition (see the Hubbard listing below). Even in his own lifetime Billings encountered considerable opposition, and he certainly failed to reap any adequate financial benefit for his labors. Still, the spirit of the man was indomitable, and the preface to his final collection, *The Continental Harmony* (1794—the entire work has been reprinted in facsimile by the Belknap Press) expresses his vibrant, ecstatic devotion to his art, his unabashed love of music for its own sake, rather than for purposes of worship.

> It is an old maxim, and I think a very just one, viz. *that variety is always pleasing,* and it is well known that there is more variety in one piece of fuging music, than in twenty pieces of plain song, for while the tones do most sweetly coincide, and agree, the words are seemingly engaged in a musical warfare; and excuse the paradox if I further add, that each part seems determined by dint of harmony and strength of accent, to drown his competitor in an ocean of harmony, and while each part is thus mutually striving for mastery, and sweetly contending for victory, the audience are most luxuriously entertained, and exceedingly delighted; in the mean time, their mindes are surprizingly agitated, and extremely fluctuated; sometimes declaring in favour of one part, and sometimes another.—Now the solemn bass demands their attention, now the manly tenor, now the lofty counter, now the volatile treble, now here, now there, now here again.—O inchanting! O ecstatic! Push on, push on ye sons of harmony, and
> > Discharge your deep mouth'd canon, full fraught with Diapasons; / May you with Maestoso, rush on to Choro-Grando, / And then with Vigoroso, let fly your Diapentes / About our nervous system.

After a century and a half of neglect and abuse from a good part of the professional musical community, Billings' art is at last being rediscovered and performed, and the cultural significance of this uniquely colorful man and his work is being evaluated and appreciated by some of our finest musicologists and historians. In 1975, two of the best of them published the very best book about Billings, and in fact one of the very best books about early American musical culture as a whole: David P. McKay and Richard Crawford, *William Billings of Boston*

(Princeton). Also, most of Billings' major publications are now being or have been reprinted, and there are recordings of much (if not nearly enough) of his music.]

The New-England Psalm-Singer

TO ALL MUSICAL PRACTITIONERS:

Perhaps it may be expected by some, that I should say something concerning rules for Composition; to these I answer that Nature is the best Dictator, for all the hard dry studied Rules that ever was prescribed, will not enable any person to form an Air any more than the bare Knowledge of the four and twenty [sic] letters, and strict Grammatical Rules will qualify a Scholar for composing a Piece of Poetry, or properly adjusting a Tragedy, without a Genius. It must be Nature, Nature must lay the Foundation, Nature must inspire the Thought. But perhaps some may think I mean and intend to throw Art entirely out of the Question, I answer by no Means, for the more Art is display'd the more Nature is decorated. And in some sorts of Composition, there is dry study required, and Art very requisite. For instance, in a Fuge, where the Parts come in after each other, with the same Notes; but even there Art is subservient to Genius, for Fancy goes first, and strikes out the work roughly, and Art comes after and polishes it over. . . .

For my own Part, as I don't think myself confin'd to any Rules for Composition laid down by any that went before me, neither should I think (were I to pretend to lay down Rules) that any who came after me were any way obliged to adhere to them, any further than they should think proper. So in fact I think it is best for every Composer to be his own Carver. Therefore upon this Consideration, for me to dictate, or pretend to prescribe Rules of this Nature for others, would not only be very unnecessary, but also a great Piece of Vanity.

It would be needless in me to attempt to set forth the Usefulness and Importance of Psalm-singing, which is so universally known and acknowledged, and on which depends no inconsiderable Part of the Divine Worship of our Churches. But this much I would say, That he who finds himself gifted with a tunable Voice, and yet neglects to cultivate it, not only hides in the Earth a Talent of the highest value, but robs himself of that peculiar Pleasure, of which they only are conscious who exercise that Faculty. . . .

Boston, October 7, 1770.

· · · · ·

ADVERTISEMENT

TO THE GENEROUS SUBSCRIBERS FOR THIS BOOK:

The Author having to his great loss deferred the

Publication of these Sheets for Eighteen Months, to have them put upon American Paper,[*] hopes the delay will be pardoned; and the good Ladies, Heads of the Families into whose hands they may fall, will zealously endeavour to furnish the Paper Mills with all the Fragments of Linnen they can possibly afford: Paper being the Vehicle of Literature, and Literature the Spring and Security of human Happiness.

. . . . .

If you fall in after a rest in your part you must fall in with spirit, because that gives the Audience to understand another part is added, which perhaps they would not be sensible of if you struck in soft. In 'fuguing' music you must be very distinct and emphatic, not only in the tune but in the pronunciation; for if there happens to be a Number of voices in the Concert more than your own, they will swallow you up. Therefore in such a case I would recommend to you the resolution (though not the impudence) of a discarded actor who after he had been twice hissed off the stage, mounted again and with great assurance thundered out these words, 'I will be heard.'

Singing Master's Assistant

No doubt you (do, or ought to) remember that about eight years ago, I published a Book entitled, The New England Psalm Singer, etc. And truly a most masterly and inimitable Performance I then thought it to be. Oh! how did my foolish heart throb and beat with tumultuous joy! With what impatience did I wait on the Book-Binder, while stitching the sheets and putting on the covers, with what extasy, did I snatch the yet unfinished Book out of his hands, and pressing it to my bosom, with rapturous delight, how lavish was I, in encomiums on this infant production of my own Numb Skull? Welcome; thrice welcome; thou legitimate offspring of my brain, go forth, my little Book, go forth and immortalize the name of your Author; may your sale be rapid and may you speedily run through ten thousand Editions, may you be a welcome guest in all companies and what will add tenfold to thy dignity, may you find your way into the Libraries of the Learned. Thou art my Reuben, my first born, the beginning of my strength, the excellency of my dignity, and the excellency of my power. But to my great mortification, I soon discovered it was Reuben in the sequel, and Reuben all over; for unstable as water, it did not excell. But since I have begun to play the Critic I will

[*Billings was a staunch supporter of the boycott of all British imports which was in effect as part of the colonial reaction to the Townshend Acts of 1767. In early 1770 Lord North repealed all but the tea duties, and most of the colonies settled back contentedly—but Boston (and Billings) remained troublesome.]

go through with my Criticisms, and endeavor to point out its beauties as well as deformities, and it must be acknowledged, that many of the pieces are not too ostentatious, as to sound forth their own praises; for it has been judiciously observed, that the oftener they are founded, the more they are abased. After impartial examination, I have discovered that many of the pieces in that Book were never worth my printing, or your inspection; therefore in order to make you ample amends for my former intrusion, I have selected and corrected some of the Tunes which were most approved of in that book and have added several new pieces, which I think to be very good ones; for if I thought otherwise, I should not have presented the book to you. However, I am not so tenacious of my own opinion, as to desire you to take my word for it; but rather advise you—purchase a Book and satisfy yourselves in that particular, and then, I make no doubt, but you will readily concur with me in this certification, viz., that the Singing Master's Assistant, is a much better Book, than the New England Psalm Singer. And now Reader I have no more to say.

. . . . .

Observe these Rules for regulating a Singing-School

As the well being of every society depends in a great measure upon GOOD ORDER, I here present you with some general rules, to be observed in a Singing-School.

1st. Let the society be first formed, and articles signed by every individual; and all those who are under age, should apply to their parents, masters or guardians to sign for them: the house should be provided, and every necessary for the school should be procured, before the arrival of the Master, to prevent his being unnecessarily detained.

2d. The Members should be very punctual in attending at a certain hour, or minute, as the master shall direct, under the penalty of a small fine, and if the master should be delinquent, his fine to be double the sum laid upon the scholars.—Said fines to be appropriated to the use of the school, in procuring *wood, candles, &c.*

N.B. The fines to be collected by the Clerk, so chosen for that purpose.

3d. All the scholars should submit to the judgment of the master, respecting the part they are to sing; and if he should think fit to remove them from one part to another, they are not to contradict, or cross him in his judgment; but they would do well to suppose it is to answer some special purpose; because it is morally impossible for him to proportion the parts properly, until he has made himself acquainted with the strength and fitness of the pupil's voices.

4. No unnecessary conversation, whispering, or

laughing, to be practised; for it is not only indecent, but very impolitic; it being a needless expence of time, and instead of acquiring to themselves respect, they render themselves ridiculous and contemptable in the eyes of all serious people; and above all, I enjoin it upon you to refrain from all levity, both in conduct and conversation, while singing sacred words; for where the words *God, Christ, Redeemer, &c.* occur, you would do well to remember the third Commandment, the profanation of which, is a heinous crime, and God has expressly declared he will not hold them guiltness [*sic*] who take his name in vain; and remember that in so doing, you not only dishonor God and sin against your own souls; but you give occasion, and very just ground to the adversaries or enemies of music, to speak reproachfully. Much more might be said; but the rest I shall leave to the Master's direction, and your own discretion, heartily wishing you may reap both pleasure and profit, in this your laudable undertaking.

· · · · ·

TO THE GODDESS OF DISCORD

DREAD SOVEREIGN,

I have been sagacious enough of late, to discover that some evil-minded persons have insinuated to your highness, that I am utterly unmindful of your Ladyship's importance; and that my time, as well as my talents, was wholly taken up in paying my divoto to your most implacable enemy and strenuous opposer, viz. the GODDESS OF CONCORD, which representation is as false as it is ill-natured; for your Ladyship may believe me without hesitation, when I assure you on the word of an honest man, that knowing your Ladyship to be of a very captious disposition; I have always been very careful of trespassing on your grounds for fear of incuring your displeasure, so far as to exite you to take vengeance (which is well known to be your darling attribute).

I have likewise been informed, that some of my most implacable enemy's are some of your Majesty's privy council, and that your Majesty's Secretary at war, viz. Lord Jargon, was about to send some of your other Lords in waiting, viz. Lord second, Lord 7th, Lord 9th, alias Lord 2d, junior, with some others, to beat a tattoo upon the drum of my ear, with so great a number of contra-vibrations without the intervention of a single coincidence, and with so much Forte as to dislocate my auditory; upon which information I called a court of Harmony, the result of which was, to repel force by force, and we had even proceeded as far as to order Lord Consonance, our Secretary at peace to furnish our life guard with an infinite number of coincidences, without the intervention of one contravibration; and although we have the majority on our side, yet we held it in scorn to take any advantage from our numbers, therefore we had selected an equal number of those who had attained unto the first three, viz. Lord Unison, Lord Diapente, Lord Octave, alias Lord Unison, jun'r, and for their Aid de camps, we had chosen two twin brothers, viz. Major and Minor Trio, together with Major Sixth, &c we had proceeded thus far when in turning over a very antient history I met with the following passage, viz. *"by wise council thou shalt make thy war, and in multitude of counsellors there is safety."* Upon reading this passage I was resolved to enlarge the council, therefore we made choice of king Solomon, the son of David (but as he nor his father was never known to traverse your territories I suppose you have no knowledge of them). The result of our second council was to lay aside this enterprize and proceed in a very different manner; for by consulting this great councellor we were convinced *"that wisdom is better than weapons of war."*

Therefore it was resolved, that I singly should begin the attack in the common form of dedications, and besiege you with flattery, and if that should fail, as we have brib'd over a number of your nobility, we are determined to turn their force against you, and then we assure ourselves of success; but perhaps I trespass on your patience in this ambiguous preamble: Know then dread Sovereign that I have composed the following peice, out of such materials as your kingdom is made up of, and, without vanity, I believe you will readily grant that it is the best peice that ever was composed: this I chearfully offer at your shrine; and I must take the liberty to tell your Majesty, that I expect this one piece will fully compensate for my former delinquency and remissness to you ward; and that you will not be so unreasonable as to insist on another oblation from me; neither through time nor eternity; and let me tell you, that in this offering I followed the example of our native indians, who sacrifice to the angry God much oftener than to the good-natured one; not from a principle of love, but of fear; for although you could never excite my love, you have frequently caused me to fear and tremble; and I solemnly declare that I dread your extempore speeches more than I do the threats and menaces of all the crowned heads in Europe; and now madam, after this candid and honest confession, I must insist on your signing the following Receipt which for your honour and my security I shall always carry about me.

A RECEIPT.

Received of the Author, a peice of Jargon, it being the best peice ever composed, in full of all accounts from the beginning of time, to and through the endless ages of eternity. I say received by me,

GODDESS OF DISCORD.

GIVEN from our inharmonical Cavern, in the Land of CHAOS: from the year of our existence, (which began at Adam's fall.) Five Thousand Seven Hundred and Eighty Two.

DEMON DREAD, Speaker.
ATTEST, HAMAN HORROR, Secretary.

And now Madam Crossgrain after informing you, that this receipt shall be my discharge, I shall be so condescending as to acquaint your uglyship, that I take great pleasure in subscribing myself your most inveterate, most implacable, most irreconcilable enemy.

THE AUTHOR.

In order to do this peice ample justice, the Concert must be made of vocal and instrumental Music. Let it be performed in the following manner, viz. Let an ass bray the Bass, let the fileing of a saw carry the Tenor, let a hog who is extream hungry squeal the Counter, and let a cart-wheel, which is heavy loaded, and that has been long without grease, squeek the Treble; and if the Concert should appear to be too feeble you may add the cracking of a crow, the howling of a dog, the squalling of a cat, and what would grace the Concert yet more would be the rubing of a wet finger upon a window glass; this last mentioned instrument no sooner salutes the drum of the ear, but it instantly conveys the sensation to the teeth; and if all these in conjunction should not reach the cause you may add this most inharmonical of all sounds, *"pay me that thou owest."*

V

John Hubbard
An Essay on Music (Boston, 1808)

[Although he was principally a Professor of Mathematics and Natural Philosophy at Dartmouth, John Hubbard (1759-1810) was a devoted musical activist throughout his life. In the service of the cause of raising the standards of appreciation and performance, he gathered a musical library which was one of the best in the nation; he helped found the Dartmouth Handel Society; and he made a collection of church anthems adapted from the music of European masters, which was published after his death and very well received. In the words of the important early music historian Nathaniel Gould, Hubbard's personal crusade was unfinished because "God saw fit to take him to himself, in the prime of life, to sing anthems on high."

One of the most articulate and effective leaders of the musical reform movement, Hubbard most clearly expressed the central assumption of this crusade, that the only criteria which applied to music were the "scientific" standards of harmony and counterpoint which found their greatest practitioners in seventeenth- and eighteenth-century Europe. The objects of reform were, therefore, to spread the music of the masters among Americans (specifically, for Hubbard, American church congregations, although the movement's major roots were in early American concert life), and to get Americans to turn away from their home-grown psalmody and learn to create as well as appreciate music in the mode of the sophisticated European product.

Hubbard's essay, excerpted here, was originally a lecture delivered in Massachusetts in 1807; indeed, Hubbard and the other reformers found their greatest numbers and strongest support in Massachusetts and the Boston area in particular. A good many of the professional musicians who had migrated to the New World since the Revolutionary War ended up in this city of thriving commerce and growing cultural sophistication, and the concert activity rivaled and sometimes surpassed that of New York and Philadelphia. The year of the publication of Hubbard's essay was also the year of the founding of the Pierian Sodality at Harvard (see Dwight); in the next year the extremely important pioneering orchestral organization, the Philharmonic Society, was founded by Gottlieb Graupner, the most valuable of the musical immigrants; and in 1815, Graupner and others founded the Handel and Haydn Society, the nation's most important medium for the presentation of great European music for much of the first half of the century.

Hubbard's essay stands as perhaps the most important statement to emerge from the early years of this movement, and as such it exhibits both the strengths and the weaknesses of the hard-line "classical" outlook. On the one hand, it reveals its author's deep love of music and his commitment to bringing to American ears the masterpieces of Handel, Haydn, Mozart, and other glorious figures of the Baroque and Classical periods of European music; on the other hand, the tract is a sometimes violent expression of narrow-minded distaste and misunderstanding of our rich native art of psalmody, a music which Hubbard regarded as a clumsy attempt to imitate his beloved masters, but which actually grew out of the traditions of rural English psalmody and the American singing schools and had nothing to do with the "classical" models. There were many American composers and singers who were able to appreciate both Handel and Billings, the European art and the American—in fact, the great psalmodist Daniel Read named his son George Frederick Handel Read. However, to a young nation seeking an identity and yearning after the cultural approval of its elders, the arts and critical standards of Europe represented an awesome cultural weight, and this balanced appreciation was not to last, indeed was never widespread.

Hubbard and those who followed the same path

(chiefly Lowell Mason and Thomas Hastings) were guilty, then, of stunting a valuable native growth, but they also accomplished wonders in musical education, raising standards of performance and appreciation throughout the country. Hubbard shows himself to be very much a product of his time, even as a uniquely effective musical pioneer. His arguments reveal a strong consciousness of both European cultural superiority and the traditional Puritan view of music. He attacks domestic psalm-tunes on the grounds of what he regards (mistakenly) as their profane origins, and his chief concerns are moral and religious; however, he aims his argument directly at the cultural insecurity of Americans by basing it upon the classical standards of style: our native music is, to him, not only morally dangerous; it is bombastic, stylistically gauche, the product of little learning. Hubbard presents a remarkable argument, based upon a commanding grasp of the then-current conceptions of the origins, the growth and the power of music. He puts his wide knowledge to skillful use, even managing to summon Voltaire to his aid in his closing religious argument—no mean feat.]

An Essay on Music

"Pronounced before the Middlesex Musical Society, Sept. 9, A. D. 1807, at Dunstable, Mass., by John Hubbard, Prof. Math. and Nat. Phil., Dartmouth Coll."

To alleviate the innumerable calamities of life, to soothe and calm the boisterous passions, to light up the emotions of love and friendship, to elevate and inspire the mind with true devotion, to give us some foretaste of those sublime pleasures enjoyed by the celestial choirs, is the office and effect of music . . .

When music was first introduced into our world, cannot possibly be determined. "When the morning stars sang together, and the sons of God shouted for joy," man, in his state of innocence, must have caught the divine ardor. His soul, elevated with devotion, would naturally express its feelings in the simple music of nature.

What progress was made in this art by the antediluvians, must forever remain unknown to us their descendants. Their improvements are buried with them in everlasting oblivion. If Jubal could construct the complex harp and organ, he must have been considerably skilled in the science of music. Instrumental music is never introduced till vocal has gained a considerable degree of perfection.

Instruments are designed to imitate the voice; the extent, tones, and modulations of the voice must therefore be known before they can be imitated. The most rude and uncultivated savages are not without their songs, though destitute of musical instruments.

In the time of Moses we find Miriam, the prophetess, leading the choir of Israelitish women, in songs of praise to their great deliverer, and accompanying their voices with the timbrel. We likewise find, that the song of Moses was written in poetry, undoubtedly for the purpose of being sung by the choirs of Israelites. But the Jewish music does not appear to have attained its greatest perfection till the inspired son of Jesse assumed the harp. In his and his son's reign, it arrived at its highest degree of perfection. Here we find it employed in uttering the devout effusions of the heart, and rendering praises to the great JEHOVAH. Nor were the heathen ignorant of this noble art. From the holy altar of the Jews, they snatched a spark of the sacred fire, and prostituted it to the service of their gods. But even in this servitude, her powers were considered as almost unbounded. Orpheus, while celebrating the praises of his false deities on his harp, could move the inanimate world with his music.

In treating upon music, we shall consider it both as an art and a science. As an art, it depends upon the powers, abilities, and genius of the writer. As an art, it cannot be limited, or restricted within any particular rules. The genius, the feelings, and the improved taste of mankind, must regulate every good writer. Like the painter, the sculptor, the architect and the poet, nature and propriety must direct the effusions of his mind. As a science, it is regulated by measure, harmony, cadence, accent, mode, etc. Science may invent good harmony, agreeable measure, flowing and easy cadence; but genius only can give force and energy to music.

[Hubbard then discusses "the essential parts or divisions of music, as consisting of *melody, harmony, expression,* and *accent.*"]

. . . In the writers of music we find the same variety of style, as in poetry or prose, viz.; the *sublime,* the *beautiful,* the *nervous,* the *concise,* the *dry,* and the *bombastic.*

Few writers have given us specimens of the sublime. Amongst these, Handel undoubtedly stands first. His Grand Hallelujah, and his Chorus, *"Break forth into joy,"* in the Messiah, are excellent specimens of this style. Giardini has likewise given us some specimens in "Cambridge;" especially on the words, *"Father, how wide thy glories shine,"* etc.: and on these, *"But when we view thy great designs,"* etc. In performing such strains, the mind is lost in admiration. It is almost incapable of contemplating the great ideas thus presented. Like the sublime in nature, our astonishment incapacitates us for reflecting upon the object before our eyes. The sublime in music knows no medium. The writer who attempts this, must either reach sublimity, or sink into indifference. Sublime compositions must be simple, unstudied, expressive, and connected with some great and important idea.

The specimens we might produce of the *beautiful,* are very numerous. They ravish, they charm, they transport us beyond conception. In this style Handel is excellent. His air in the Messiah, *"I know that my Redeemer liveth,"* is, perhaps, equal to any now extant. Pergolesi, in his air, *"Eja, mater, fons amoris,"* in his "Stabat Mater," is beautiful beyond description.

Passing over other styles, a discussion of which would afford very little amusement, we come to the *bombastic.* This style, in poetry and in prose, consists in attempting to magnify those subjects which are trifling and indifferent; or in using high sounding words and epithets without any great or noble ideas. In music it consists in laboured notes and strains, disconnected from any exalted ideas; or in attempting to communicate some low idea which cannot be expressed by notes. In this style, our unfortunate country has been peculiarly fruitful. Almost every pedant, after learning his eight notes, has commenced author. With a genius, sterile as the desarts of Arabia, he has attempted to rival the great masters of music. On the leaden wings of dullness, he has attempted to soar into regions of science, never penetrated but by real genius. From such distempered imaginations, no regular productions can be expected. The unhappy writers, after torturing every note in the octave, have fallen into oblivion, and have generally outlived their insignificant works. To the great injury of true religion, this kind of music has been introduced into our places of worship. Devotion, appalled by its destructive presence, has fled from the unhallowed sound.

Among the most prominent faults of this style, we may reckon the common fuge. ["Fuge" is the old spelling for "fugue," and is the term which Billings and those who followed him used for their contrapuntal music; in origin and in intention it actually had nothing to do with the classical "fugue," although Hubbard and many others down to the present have regarded the "fuge" as nothing more than a clumsy attempt at a "fugue."] As the intention of vocal music is to communicate ideas, whatever renders those ideas indistinct or obscure, must be a perversion. Let us now examine music of the style last mentioned. We shall here find four parts, in harmonic order, each, at the same time, pronouncing different words. . . . To catch any idea from such a chaos of words, uttered at the same instant of time, a hearer must be furnished with ears as numerous as the eyes of Argus. Such fuges must be a perversion. They cannot affect the heart, nor inform the understanding. Though the performers may be admired for their dexterity, they can never excite any devout feelings in their hearers. Such music can never be of more consequence than an oration pronounced in an unknown language.

But modern innovators have not stopped here. From the midnight revel, from the staggering bachanal, from the profane altar of Comus they have stolen the prostituted air, and, with sacrilegious hands, have offered it in the temple of JEHOVAH. [Here a footnote claims, "If any person will take the trouble of examining the songs in the Beggars' Opera, he will find from what sources many of our modern tunes are derived."] The air of a catch, a glee, a dance, a march, or a common ballad is very improper for the worship of the MOST HIGH.

As the taste and practice of music have great influence on our religion and morals, every person is under the most solemn obligations to use all his exertions for the suppression of that which is improper. "Let me," said Voltaire, "write the common ballads for any nation, and I will make their religion what I please." If the common songs of a nation can thus influence their religion, how much more their sacred music? Many respectable clergymen in New England, have been almost determined to omit music in public worship. To their great sorrow, they have observed, that the effects of a most solemn discourse were often obliterated, by closing with improper music. We cannot doubt the correctness of this idea. Let every friend of religion use his utmost exertions to remove this Achan from the sacred camp. Let not this Dagon of impiety be permitted to stand in the presence of the holy ark.

VI

John Rowe Parker
The Euterpeiad; or Musical Intelligencer.
Devoted to the Diffusion of Musical
Information and Belles Lettres
(Boston, 1820-22)

[*The Euterpeiad* first appeared April 1, 1820, and is thus the first periodical devoted to music published in this country. Its creator and editor was John Rowe Parker, proprietor of the Franklin Music Warehouse, No. 6 Milk Street, Boston. Parker was an enterprising merchant, a wide-ranging observer of the arts of his city, an amateur musician and zealous laborer for the cause of classical music—and in later life also well known as an authority on semaphoric signals. The purposes of the magazine, as expressed in the first issue, were to offer the public

> a brief history of music from the earliest ages, Cherish a classical taste, watch progress of the art, Excite the emulation of genius, record the transactions of society, Examine and impartially review new works, Stimulate professional gentlemen to explore new traces in the regions of science, etc.

In fulfillment of these aims, Parker wrote some of the liveliest and most informative criticism available in any contemporary American journalism, and he drew widely upon other sources, including correspondents in other cities as well as Boston, and foreign (chiefly English) journals—and for about two years he ran, as promised, "A Brief History of Music," which was baldly plagiarized from the history by the famous English chronicler, Dr. Charles Burney. Included were countless anecdotes of people and events and reviews of both American and foreign publications, as well as lectures and dissertations from fellow educators of the public taste, such as Thomas Hastings. Through it all it is Parker's vivid personality and considerable skill that unites the paper and makes it a uniquely fascinating whole.

After a year of publication it apparently dawned on the editor that art and "belles lettres" did not exert enough drawing power, and he added a "Ladies' Gazette" to the magazine, containing articles on such extra-musical issues as getting a husband and "Pleasures of a Married State." This department eventually became a separate publication, *The Minerviad* (naturally), concentrating on women's entertainment and advice (including an article on blushing, for instance, which dilates upon the physical reasons for "the irritation of the face," and locates the cause of such irritation in "the noxious qualities of certain words and phrases of an addressor"—a woman blushes because the breath of her flatterer contains "acute and alkaline particles," or so we are told with apparent sobriety). The separation of the two periodicals proved only that, if art alone wasn't enough for early nineteenth-century Boston, neither was woman's entertainment alone, and they both folded within six months (although *The Euterpeiad* was later revived by another editor in New York).

Parker's magazine was published semimonthly in four quarto pages and included an example of sheet music with each issue. The following selections are all from a four-month period toward the end of *The Euterpeiad's* brief life, April to July, 1822. They are chosen from a relatively short period and printed in order of appearance to give some sense of the continuity of Parker's coverage of his subject. Included are reviews and reports of concerts and of music publications, as well as essays and a letter to the editor. The notices of Lowell Mason's *Boston Handel and Haydn Society Collection of Church Music* and of the collection by the wonderful, eccentric immigrant Anthony Philip Heinrich (who was famous while in Boston as "Father Heinrich," and who was otherwise known as "the Beethoven of Louisville") are of special historical interest (see the Mason selection below). The central preoccupation of the magazine is apparent in all of the examples: the propagation of classical music and the raising of musical standards in Boston and America.

Despite his ultimate lack of journalistic success, Parker did contribute mightily to this cause and in the process laid the foundations for an American music criticism of real quality and independence.

H. Earle Johnson's *Musical Interludes in Boston: 1795-1830* (Columbia University Press, 1943) contains an arresting account of Parker and his journal.]

The Euterpeiad, April 11, 1822

THE ROXBURY CONCERT OF SACRED MUSIC.

On Sunday Evening 31st inst. [sic] a very spirited performance of several classic pieces of music, was got up at a considerable expense under the direction and superintendance of Mr. John Fuller, at the Rev. Dr. Porter's Meeting House, Roxbury: accompanied by a full orchestra with Messrs. Graupner, Granger and Mr. S. P. Taylor at the Organ. This elegant instrument is of a very superior structure, and was recently erected by Mr. Thomas Appleton, of this City; its tones are very heavy and powerful, and in every particular, redounds to the credit of this ingenious artist.

This exhibition of Sacred Music, commenced with *"Lord of all power,"* by Mason, and was followed by *"Come sweet Spring,"* from Haydn's Oratorio of The Seasons, after which Mrs. Rowson's *"Child of Mortality,"* was succeeded by Luther's *"Judgment Hymn,"* Granger's *"Star of Bethlehem,"* was followed by Kent's Anthem *"Give the Lord the Honour,"* after which *"The Vesper Hymn,"* and Beethoven's *"Halleluiah,"* from the Mount of Olives, closed the first part.

The second part opened with Haydn's *"Andante"* from the Surprise, after which *"Almighty God,"* by Mozart, was succeeded by Haydn's *"Heavens are telling,"* followed by *"Peace and Holy Love"* by Bray, Pucitta's *"Strike the Cymbal"* was followed by Whitaker's *"O thou whose power,"* after which, Handel's grand *"Halleluiah Chorus"* closed the Evenings performances.

We have often expatiated upon the advantages resulting from exhibitions of Music of this description, taking place in the country towns, and that the countenance and support derived from the Reverend Clergy patronizing such performances, are as necessary as they are useful. On this occasion, we must be permitted to observe, so large a number of Instrumental and Vocal performers as were present, attempting music of this high style of conception, *without rehearsal,* together with the manner and execution which we witnessed, must be considered as a circumstance of more than ordinary character, and redounds not only to the credit of the individuals engaged therein, but is an additional evidence and proof of the usefulness, effect and influence, of the Musical Institution of the City.

The audience assembled, was very numerous, and in no instance within our recollection has an exhibition of Sacred music of this classic style, out of the metropolis, given greater or more universal satisfaction, and we may add, none ever was heard, wherein the public so fully received their *money's worth.*

THE
BOSTON HANDEL AND HAYDN SOCIETY
COLLECTION OF CHURCH MUSIC;

being a selection of the most
approved
PSALM AND HYMN TUNES;
Together with many beautiful extracts from
the works of
HAYDN, MOZART, BEETHOVEN,
AND OTHER EMINENT MODERN COMPOSERS.
The whole harmonized for three and four voices,
with a figured Base for the Organ or Piano Forte
calculated for public worship or private
devotion.
Published by RICHARDSON & LORD, Boston.

The lovers of Metrical Psalmody will doubtless be somewhat anxious to have an account of this Collection of Church Music. We noticed the original design of this work sometime since, and that its harmonies would undergo a critical revision by Dr. G. K. Jackson of this City, whose science and learning, as well as the entire devotion of his mind to the subject, must have their due weight with respect to Church Music. This venerable musician is ably qualified to judge with respect to the presiding gravity which ought to prevail in compositions intended for devotional exercises, and while we agree in the principle fully and entirely while we except completely as any writers who have considered the subject, against all light and profane treatment of the music of the church, there yet appears to us to be an allowance for the various associations connected with the worship and praise of the Creator, as well as for the intellectual progression of ages, which perhaps demand a somewhat greater latitude than it has been customary to admit. The first question for consideration, is, whether the fervour of religious praise—whether the elevation of religious joy, for instance, may not be raised and exalted by music of a florid & figurate nature! 2d, whether such affections may not be more completely roused and excited through the instrumentality of such means; and lastly, whether in the present state of musical knowledge, attainments, and habits, compositions, (although they be of great learning, gravity, and strict propriety,) are capable of raising in the mind any desired emotions at all? To assert that a new style, which admits modern improvements in art generally, is not indispensable to the ends we seek, appears to us to be to maintain, *that Church Music shall remain stationary, while every other circumstance of our nature and habits is undergoing change and modification.* The truth seems to us to be, that a sympathy in the application of the rule that must obtain here, as in everything submitted to public feeling, that success is the test, and that what has the most beneficial effect is the best. At the time Haydn and Mozart wrote, there can be no doubt that the extended acquaintance with musical resource the world had attained, demanded not only grandeur and gravity, but force, variety and beauty of style, to engage the affections in any eminent degree. For in proportion as the affections are oftener or more strongly moved on ordinary occasions by music, a competition is established that acts involuntarily upon the hearer; and unless the music of the church keeps at least an equal progression with the improvements going on in every other branch of musical composition and execution, it must be obvious, that its extended agency will fail. While therefore we except against any innovation that can be associated with unworthy feelings, we can but acknowledge the necessity of enlisting into the musical science of the church every power of the mind that the art continues to add to its resources, if we mean to give music any agency really beneficial.

(To be Continued.)

[In subsequent issues Parker expanded his defense of progress in sacred music while detailing his approval of this important collection, which was essentially the work of the young Lowell Mason, although it was launched upon the musical world with the aid of Dr. Jackson, brilliant English-born organist and composer whose reputation was as great as his 300-pound avoirdupois.]

CRITICISM.

"The dawning of Music in Kentucky."
By A. P. Heinrich, published in Philadelphia.

In attending to other duties, we fear we have too long neglected the pleasing task of recommending the above *American production* to the favorable notice of the public. The fantastical drapery of this work, and not a few difficulties in which it is intrenched, furnish no tempting invitation for a practical perusal; and many, who judge only from appearances and local prepossessions, may have persuaded themselves that such a perusal would not only be a waste of labour upon the mere coinage of

a disordered brain; It is therefore, with great satisfaction that we feel ourselves authorized to say, that whoever has the will and ability to overstep the fence and unveil the hidden treasure, will be no less surprised than delighted with his discovery. With what success the first attempt of this kind was made in Boston, and to whom the honor of it belongs, has already been stated in our former numbers; and we can only add now that the vigour of thought, variety of ideas, originality of conception, classical correctness, boldness and luxuriance of imagination, displayed throughout this voluminous work, are the more extraordinary, as the author but a few years since, was merely an amateur and a prosperous merchant whom sudden misfortune transformed into a professor, the only character in which he expected to gain honest livelihood; and as this transformation had not taken place till he was verging on the age of forty. His genius however triumphs over every thing. —There is enough in his well-stored pages to gratify every taste and fancy. There is versatility for the capricious, pomp for the pedant, playfulness for the amateur, learning for the scholar, business for the performer, pleasure for the vocalist, ingenuity for the curious, and puzzle for an academician. He seems at once to have possessed himself of the key which unlocks to him the temple of science and enables him to explore with fearless security the mysterious labyrinth of harmony. He may, therefore, justly be styled *the Beethoven* of America, and as such he is actually considered by the few who have taken the trouble to ascertain his merits.

We think ourselves particularly bound to pay him this tribute, as he has been lately treated with undeserved, though we hope, accidental neglect as regards the beautiful spectacle of *"La Belle Peruvienne."* This ballet which has so delighted the public of New York, is much indebted for its attraction to the charming music which accompanies its action. A. P. Heinrich has been made one of the chief contributors to this department, yet he alone was passed over in silence by the New York criticks, who failed not to notice the other foreign celebrated authors that were, not like him, in want of a name. The very first piece which opens the ballet with such characteristic magnificence is the march of "Kinsky" taken from "The dawning of music." The sweet expressive strain that describes the Princess in the act of administering aid to the shipwrecked stranger, is also to be found in the same work under the title "From thee Eliza I must go." Passing over other fragments borrowed from the same source and used in the service of that popular spectacle, we must particularly notice the pathetic and sublime melody which may be said to give utterance to the European's prayers and protestations of innocence in the beginning of the 3d act. This melody is a part of the Ode composed and dedicated by our enthusiastic author, to the memory of Commodore Perry, as inserted in the above mentioned work. It is a strain which would do credit to the Beethoven of Europe, and we can not do better than give here an epitome of it, and thus conclude our remarks by appealing to the judgment of the reader himself. Our limits will not allow us to do the author full justice in presenting this specimen of his talents as it stands, in the original, but we may perhaps succeed in awaking some interest and curiosity which may easily be gratified by a reference to the work itself where the accompaniment exhibits all that rich combination of harmony, which can only emanate from true taste and profound knowledge.

The Euterpeiad, May 11, 1822

EXTRACTS FROM AN ADDRESS DELIVERED BEFORE
THE PSALLONIAN SOCIETY, AT PROVIDENCE.
CONCLUDED.

The first adventurers to America were in no situation to cultivate music. They had sufficient employment to guard against cold, hunger and extermination. A new country must long be a stranger to refinements. They cannot thrive without opulence, or, at least, competence. The United States are but just arriving at the possession of both. Though, since we attained a national existence, our progress in things useful and profitable has been without a parallel; tho' in the important science of government, we have left the world behind us; tho' we already rival the oldest and wisest nations in poetry, philosophy, eloquence and fine writing; yet we have only read and heard of sculpture and painting: architecture and music are but beginning to exist in our country. It is true that in our capital cities, that species of music which attains no other object than pleasure has been often heard from the stage and from the orchestra in considerable perfection. Songs of every description, amatory, sentimental and frivolous, have been imported from Europe and sung by our accomplished ladies. But that sublime species of music which is suited to impress the eloquence of inspiration has been but lately introduced among us. Such music adapts itself to the subject, and carries the subject to the heart. Having united itself with the pathos of Heaven, it acquires a sort of omnipotence. It can melt the soul into the deepest contrition; gently raise it to humble devotion; inspire it with a calm and serene confidence, and elevate and expand it in contemplation of the power, majesty and glory of God.

But what has been the prevalent character of sacred music in this country? Long after the landing of our fathers, at Plymouth, it was a sort of tremulous groan of a whole congregation of discordant voices, by way of response to the nasal twang of the deacon. This state of musical science was succeeded by what passed for a vast improvement, under the name of "new fashioned singing."—Every village chorister who had learned his gamut well, understood all the modes of time, could explain to his astonished pupils the whole mystery of finding the *mi* amidst a cloud of flats and sharps, and shew them what an amazing number of semi-quavers were necessary to fill a bar, became an eminent composer.

The whole country was inundated with "Village Harmonies" and "Columbian Collections," filled with ranting melodies and doleful ditties.—These were sung by the choir, with the leader at their head, joining in every part and beating out the "exact time," with all the skill imaginable.—As the old tunes went slow, the new ones must, of course, go quick; and furious fuges of chasing crotchets were driven through the last strain at full speed.[1]

The old people strenuously opposed all this as unsuitable to the solemnity of worship. It certainly was so. Struggles ensued in almost every parish between the votaries of the old and the new psalmody. This harmonious warfare was prosecuted with various success on both sides. The new style, however, generally gained ground. In some places, they even went so far as to introduce an abomination into the gallery, the name of which was not generally understood, at that time, but it was something deservedly odious, on account of its exact resemblance to a smaller musical instrument with which every excess of levity was associated in the rustic mind.[2] Many good people, and even some clergymen, were thus forcibly driven from the house of worship. Some left it with conscientious indignation; others with sincere sorrow and regret. And can we censure them? As lovers of sacred music, we certainly cannot.

A complete revolution was finally effected, which, like many others, was from bad to worse. This, with few exceptions, continued to be the state of psalmody in New England, until within ten or fifteen years past. Before that period, our tune makers, in general, knew no more about the laws of harmony than the peckers of a mill-stone knew about Italian sculpture.

Since that period, European publications of chaste and classical church music and the finest Oratorios

[1]This is an expression of the powerful prejudice against the art of Billings and the other masters of our home-grown counterpoint.]

[2]The offending instrument was probably the bass viol, which many progressive choirmasters found useful for filling out the lower harmonies.]

in the world have been reprinted in this country. These have been studied, understood and admired. Upon these models, our taste has been formed, and our native genius excited.

We have already one composer who so far excells every other, in this line, which our country has produced, that his musical writings, after running through several editions in this country, have been re-published in London. They have been there much sought, and much admired.*

Our progress of late in sacred music has been truly wonderful. The first society which was formed in our country for the cultivation of correct and classical sacred music, was the Psallonian Society, in Providence. This society originated in the voluntary association of eight gentlemen of this town in the year 1809. The object of this association as expressed in the record of it, was "the performance of classical sacred music, both vocal and instrumental." In the year following, this association assumed its present name and adopted a code of bye-laws. The late Col. Thomas Smith Webb was then elected the first president of this society. In 1816, we received a very considerable accession of numbers and talents.

The addition of a number of fine female voices at this time gave a sweetness to our melodies, and operated as a sort of new creation to the society.—The two gentlemen who filled the first and second offices at this period, have been continued by unanimous annual elections to the present time.

A charter of incorporation was granted to the society by the General assembly of this state, at their October session, 1816. By this charter the government of the corporation is chiefly vested in nine directors, including the president, vice president, secretary and treasurer, who are members of the board *ex officio*.

In February 1820, the society performed a select Oratorio for the purpose of aiding in the benevolent exertions, then made throughout our country for the relief of the sufferers by fire in Savannah.

As it has ever been a primary object of the Psallonian society to promote a correct style of performing a most interesting part of public worship; they have admitted members from all the religious societies in town, and have frequently assisted in the dedication of churches and other solemn and interesting occasions.

While we trace the progress of our association, and call to mind the satisfaction we have enjoyed in expressing the most divine sentiments clothed in the most appropriate harmony, these pleasing recollections bring with them the melancholy reflection that more than one† of our original number "have gone to that country from whose bourne no traveller

returns." Their voices, with which we have been accustomed to unite with so much satisfaction, are now silent. They have left a void, not soon to be filled, in that fraternity over which Washington delighted to preside; in that fraternity alike venerable for its antiquity and the benevolence of its principles. These principles, they explained and enforced;— nay more—these principles they reduced to practice. Their conduct was squared by the line of rectitude; their feelings were attuned to the finest harmony.

THE PROGRESS OF SACRED MUSIC.

Public exhibitions of the progression of an art now gradually winning its easy way into the amusements, habits and affections of the community, afford us at intervals, interesting topics for discussion, and we doubt not laudable examples for illustration, as times go on. Exhibitions of this description deserve record and commemoration, not only on account of the concentration of the powers of the art, but also for the influence over the minds of the public, and the general praise inherent in such displays, and for the admirable uses to which that influence may be applied. Each and all of their properties afford subjects of agreeable and useful contemplation to the artist, the investigator of musical science, and the philanthropist.—We are among those who delight to follow out these causes and consequences to their results upon society, because from them may be deduced the moral happiness as well as the scientific perfection which is communicated to a people, and attained by them through the sedulous cultivation of the fine arts. Such appears to be the philosophical view, which it should be the earnest endeavor of all who, like ourselves, are employed in analysing the principles and settling the pretentions of these pursuits, to inculcate as they proceed.

In noticing the several public exhibitions of sacred music of the higher class of compositions among our *brethren in the country towns,* we generally observe a propensity to attempt the performance of pieces, far beyond the powers and ability of their respective choirs; so frequent are the instances to which we allude, that the custom has become universal. When we hear Handel's solos attempted, by those who do not possess a single qualification of tone, emphasis, expression or even articulation, and Haydn's *"Heavens are telling,"* jumbled through, without an instrumental accompaniment, our feelings are shocked; disappointment is general, and the attempt becomes an object of censure and disgust. Nor can we pass unnoticed, an equally erroneous practice which per-

* Mr. Oliver Shaw of Providence, one of the prime movers in establishing the Psallonian Society.

† Col. Thomas S. Webb, and Amos M. Atwell, Esq.

vades many of our *city brethren* by a self conceited opinion of their own qualifications, in affecting a superiority, and disdain to practice plain psalmody, after having feasted upon the charms of music of the highest style of composition. While we condemn the towering ambition of our country friends, we are constrained to check the vanity of our city brethren. We would wish to call the attention of all classes to the late Book of Psalmody published by an institution, of which as a member, we feel a degree of pride in belonging. [The Handel and Haydn Society.]

The rehearsal on Tuesday evening last, from the new collection, at Boylston Hall, was fraught with many of the most chaste and sublime specimens of Psalmody ever composed.

The performance of the several pieces, gave us a most striking illustration of the effects produced by a correct arrangement, particularly in the inner parts; and while the ear was delighted with a concord of harmonies, the mind realized a conviction, of the great affinity displayed between sense and sound.

There needs no argument at this period, to prove the general proposition, that to add to genuine refinement is to humanize the mind and to improve the highest and best pleasures of our existence; we shall however impart new accessions of strength and the most endearing confirmation this beneficent principle, if we take care to shew its operation, enforce by instances its direct influence, and to connect the most beautiful of its effects with the causes, whenever opportunity is allowed us in such narrations.

A persevering zeal in the pursuit of so laudable an object, as the cultivation of a taste for sacred music in particular, will tend to the edification and consequent happiness of the whole community, and to the softer sex do we appeal for encouragement in this undertaking; nothing further than the suggestions of their own hearts will be necessary to induce them to concur in a work, which in our opinion may be called of national importance.—Most earnestly do we hope that the female part of the community generally, will not be backward to lend their aid in so good a cause. The diffusion of musical knowledge among them, must add to the prodigious influence which they have on all that relates to manners, morals and religion.—Therefore as it is from them that we generally obtain our first religious principles, as it is from their lips that our own are taught to utter prayer and praise. To the glory of the female sex, it has been frequently observed that they are "naturally inclined to religion;" and when we see a woman seriously and unaffectedly engaged in devotional exercises, we are tempted to cry out, with the Psalmist, "Thou hast made HER but a little lower than the Angels."

PSALMODY.
"Palmam pui merust ferviat."[3]

MR. EDITOR,

I have perused with much satisfaction, a late Book of Psalmody, published by the Handel and Haydn Society of Boston, with the harmonies revised and corrected by Dr. G. K. Jackson; and while the most invidious critic cannot but bestow the meed of approbation upon this classical collection of Church Psalmody, I am constrained to acknowledge, as an individual, my obligations to the *true source,* from whence this book emanated. Feeling a deep interest in promoting the circulation of a *standard work,* (so much wanted,) I shall venture a few remarks upon the general character of Psalmody, as well as an opinion of this meritorious compilation of ancient and modern airs.

The learned Dr. Mason says, "Our first Reformers were clearly of the opinion, that a Christian congregation should sing with the spirit and with the understanding also, and that what first gave rise to metrical psalmody, was, that simple metre was chosen because it facilitated the general memory; simple melodies, because they were the easiest to be performed by the general voice.

"In harmonie, the very image and character of vertue and vice is perceived, the mind delighted with their resemblances, and brought, by having them often iterated, into a love of the things themselves. For which cause, there is nothing more contagious and pestilent than some kinds of harmony; than some, nothing more strong and potent unto good. And that there is such a difference of one kind from another, we need no proof but our own experience: in as much as we are at the hearing of some more inclined unto sorrow and heaviness; of some more mollified and softened in mind; one apter to stay and settle us; another, to move and stir our affections: there is that draweth to a marvellous, grave, and sober mediocrity; there is also that carryeth, as it were, into ecstasies, filling the mind with a heavenly joy, and for the time in a manner severing it from the body, so that, although we lay altogether aside the consideration of dittie or matter, the very harmony of sounds being framed in due sort, and carried from the ear to the spiritual faculties of our souls, is, by a native puissance and efficacy, greatly available to bring to a perfect temper, whatsoever is there troubled; apt as well to quicken the spirits, as to allay that which is too eager; sovereign against melancholy and despair; forcible to draw forth tears of devotion, if the mind be such as can yield them; able both to move and to moderate all

[3sic, although what was meant was "Palmam qui meruit ferat" ("Let him bear the palm who has won it")]

affections. The prophet, David, having therefore singular knowledge, not in poetry alone, but in musique also, judged them both to be things most necessary for the house of God, left behind him, to that purpose, a number of divinely indited poems; and was farther the author of adding unto poetrie melodie in publique prayer, melodie both vocal and instrumental, for the raising up of men's hearts, and the sweetning of their affections towards God."

This beautiful passage, if it was unsupported by other testimony, might well stand as authority for the introduction of music into the service of the church; but there appears to be less difficulty to sustain the practice, than to decide upon the manner and the species of composition best fitted for devotional purposes.

Differences which learned authors entertain upon the species of composition most naturally, most usefully to be employed, resolve themselves in our minds into one single fact, viz. that the untaught many will most certainly unite in the air, and adhere to no other part, while the instructed few, will according to their advancement, combine with the rest, and take such part as they are accustomed in their musical amusements to perform.—That the ear will prefer, and the memory more easily seize upon and retain an agreable than a dull heavy melody, is not to be denied, and that a certain quantity of variety would be beneficial, will not be refused to us by those who at all consider the difference of science and the progress of taste as among the causes which operate upon our sense of the way in which the act of devotion ought to be celebrated, as well as upon our manners in other respects.

The gentleman by whom much the largest portion of this valuable book was compiled, originated in our County. Mr. Lowell Mason, now resident in Savannah, Georgia, was several years engaged in collecting this truly erudite epitome of refined and tasteful melodies. Feeling a deep interest in the subject of Church Psalmody, Mr. Mason, on a late visit to his native county, produced the manuscript copy of the above work, and waited upon Doct. G. K. Jackson, of Boston, with the same, for his opinion as to its contents, and for his advice in regard to its publication. This venerable and much respected Professor, immediately suggested the propriety of submitting the work to the government of the Handel and Haydn Society, who made several additions, and with the consent of Mr. Mason, employed the learned Doctor to revise, correct and arrange its harmonies. With this patronage, and under such auspices the public are now in possession of the work.

From these premises, we are induced to infer that such a selection of melodies & harmonies as those contained in *The Boston Handel and Haydn Society's Collection of Church Psalmody,* may be advantageously employed in Divine service, according to the capabilities of the congregation, and they will be found to embrace *all* the requisites proposed.— The subjects are popular and beautiful, and they are arranged in a way to afford every possible desideratum to the man of taste, the profound musician, or the inexperienced tyro.   MIDDLESEX.

From the New Hampshire Gazette, Portsmouth.

"It is with pleasure we learn that a society for the performance of sacred music has recently been organized in this town. It has our best wishes for its success. This success however, we are aware good wishes can do but little in securing, without *the most persevering exertions* on the part of its members. We are aware too of the many discouragements to such exertions to be encountered by such a society, in the frequent interference of personal avocations with the duties of the society, the indifference and coolness of many whose aid may have been expected, and not least, in the slow and almost imperceptible progress to be perceived from the most diligent efforts, even when attended with ordinary success.

"From the names which appear upon the roll of this society, we have confidence the members will not be turned from their pursuit by trifling difficulties, or abandon the object because labor and attention may be necessary to its accomplishment.— Those who have long stood at the head of the choirs in our several churches are among the officers of this institution."

We cannot too strongly urge the expediency of the Clerical part of the community affording their countenance and support to institutions of this nature, with their patronage. The musical portion of their respective congregations, will not only learn "to sing with the spirit, but with the understanding also."
                                                        Ed. Euterpeiad

NEW ORATORIO.

THE DELUGE, a new Oratorio from the pen of Mr. Bochsa, was lately brought out at Covent Garden Theatre, London; of its merits, the Literary Gazette says "It certainly did not give satisfaction, and we entirely concur in the public verdict against it. Music has no means of expressing what Mr. Bochsa here attempted: the very imagination shrinks at the idea of the rushing of mighty waters; and can that be adequately told by a few fiddles which the soul of man can only contemplate in imperfect vision."

From the New London Advocate:
NEW INVENTED MUSIC.
We have recently viewed with pleasure, an ele-

gant piece of Music, just invented and put in operation by our ingenious and enterprising townsman, Mr. RICHARD C. POTTER, which he correctly names the *Columbian Harp*. It is of a trianglar form, containing 66 strings, raising three octaves, performing two parts;—the frontispiece representing the beautiful castle of Lumley and the adjoining avenues. For style of architecture, harmonious sound, &c. it is acknowledged by several of our first amateurs, to be equal, if not superior, to any thing of the kind now in vogue.

MADAME CATALANI.

One of the Liverpool papers describing the powers of Madame Catalani's voice says, such was the torrent of sound she emitted at one moment, that the glass globules pendant from the central chandelier, were powerfully agitated, and struck against each other.   WHEW.

The Euterpeiad, June 2, 1822

THE ORATORIO.

The occasional performance of Oratorios at Boylston Hall, affords us at certain intervals, opportunity to record the exhibition of music in the metropolis, and is a necessary appendage to our publication, because the progress of science and of practice will be indicated by such an exposition. All that we dare promise our readers to attempt from time to time, is an occasional essay towards the elucidation of this desirable purpose, a full and adequate description is beyond our means. The acknowledged imperfection to which our limits bind us, shall not deter us from offering such a speculation as our acquaintance with the state of public music in the City, enables us to draw up for the amusement of those whom distance may remove from the theatre of emulation, contention and talent, the centre from whence improvement must be projected.

The prominent feature of the times appears to us to be an overweening disposition for *Instrumental accompaniments*. Expression seems gradually yielding to execution, the pure commanding eloquence of earlier composers is melting away before the voluptuous, not to call them meretricious graces of more modern composers, and declamation, sentiment, and pathos are superceded by passages of agility and florid ornament. The music, which we may be permitted to call music of the mind and of the soul, still indeed continues to be heard, tho' almost banished by the great body of the public, who evidence a tedium and heaviness whenever

intense are substituted for voluptuous feelings, whenever music aims to call up the bliss which is intellectual, instead of desiring to produce that soft dream of extacy which follows the excitement of the tenderest passions.

The Oratorio on Tuesday Evening 31st ult. was composed of an appropriate selection of airs, duets and chorusses. The opening consisted of the first part of King's Intercession, after which Beethoven's *"Eternal God,"* was succeeded by an air and chorus from Gardiner's Oratorio of Judah, the latter was executed in a highly animated and spirited style. The duet *"O Lovely Peace"* was well expressed by two Sopranoes, whose precision and happy conception was exceeded only by a most correct intonation. *"The Smile"* by a Tenor voice, accompanied by the Organ alone, deserved commendation. Beethoven's *"Hallelujah"* closed the first part of the Evening's performances.

The second part commenced with a favorite Recitative, followed by an Air and Chorus from Haydn's Creation. This gentleman's Bass solos are highly appreciated, his conceptions and manner of executing accompanied Recitatives, have awarded him an exclusive right to this most highly descriptive style of composition.

An Aria by Haydn, from the Oratorio of Judah, *"When I think of thy goodness"* is feelingly expressive, the close, at the words *"When in grief my heart was broken"* was given with considerable pathos by a favorite Soprano. *"To thee Cherubims"* from the Dettingen te Deum, was incomparably well sung. *"In native worth,"* and *"In rosy mantle"* with the duet *"By thee with bliss,"* and the Semi Chorus *"For ever blessed be his power,"* were well conceived, and were followed by *"The Heavens are telling,"* which chef d'oevre of the Creation closed the performance.

There is abundant proof that the delights of music are daily propagating to an extent far beyond former precedent. Is there not, however, some danger that its very excellence should be its bane, since the time and expense required for its cultivation to the point of perfection, which the diffusion of taste and knowledge renders indispensible, are likely to deter multitudes of parents from making it a part of the education of their children. Good sense will, however, measure the occasion, and we trust, that no one will suffer an ambition, painful, even when possessed of the eminence it covets, and alike unreasonable for and unattainable to the million, to deprive them of a gratification which moderately desired and courted, will never fail to repay those who seek its satisfactions with a pleasure that will be permanent, because it must be always progressive.

It is to the establishment of these nurseries, that we are to expect the dissemination of taste for the practice of this delightful art: Of all the fine arts, there are none which so universally move the heart, none which are so delightful a relaxation, none so easily within the reach of every individual, none so intimately blended with the finest feelings and most amiable sympathies of our nature. In the other arts, the emotions which we experience are the feelings produced by the art alone; and are renewed, as if for the first time, whenever they are presented to the mind. But the beauty of music is felt with increased force as we advance in years, and while every other enjoyment palls by repetition, music alone comes with renewed delight, fraught with the remembrance and the endearments of past existence.

We have noticed a few weeks past sundry meetings for exhibiting performances. The following are among the numerous establishments created within a few years, for the improvement in the science, and practice of the art of singing:

Performances have occurred at Springfield, Spencer and Waltham, Mass.—the Pleyel Society, Nantucket—Jubal Society, Hartford, Conn.—Phil Harmonic Society, New Haven, Conn.—Beethoven Society, Portland, Maine—Psallonian Society, Providence, R. I.—Neponset Society, at Milton, Mass.—Beethoven Society, Taunton, Mass.—New Hampshire Musical Society, Concord—Haydn Society, Baltimore—and within a few days past the Musical Fund Society of Philadelphia, have for the first time attempted the Oratorio of the Creation, which from the following account, contained in the National Gazette, must have afforded a truly delectable treat, to the rare and curious in music.

"The Oratorio of the Creation, performed yesterday evening at the Washington Hall, was executed in a manner that surpassed the expectations even of those who were most sanguine as to its success. The number of the audience was from 1800 to 2000—the largest ever known at a musical performance in this city; and we may venture to add, that on no similar occasion has so much delight been generally experienced. The scene was altogether brilliant, and eminently gratifying to the portion of the company particularly concerned about the popularity and progress of the musical art. Mr. B. Carr, to whose indefatigable pains in preparing the Oratorio, the highest praise is due, presided at the organ with his usual skill and exquisite judgment. Mr. Cross, as the principal bass voice, was heard throughout with the utmost attention and pleasure. His final exertions with Mrs. French had a surprising effect, and may be truly said to have enchanted every listener. That lady never displayed her fine powers to more advantage than in the Duo "Graceful Consort." To her we

understand great obligations are acknowledged by the Musical Fund Society. She volunteered her assistance in a most liberal manner, and if she did not sing more than the part of Eve in the concluding duett, it was owing to debility of frame, occasioned by a severe indisposition from which she had scarcely recovered. We have not room to-day, for more particular commemoration, which we think the exhibition of yesterday fully deserves. We propose to speak of it again; but cannot refrain from adding at present that we trust the Oratorio will be repeated in the autumn or winter."

From such classical, scientific and erudite talents, as were concentrated on this occasion, we hope to receive a more detailed analysis, than the above mentioned paragraph: the idea of the Poet must have been most truly exemplified,

"Then did the keys their bold mutations ring,
"And bards immortal, sweet chromatics bring."

The Euterpeiad, July 20, 1822

ON SINGING.

The most interesting as well as material part of music, is singing. The human voice may be denominated an instrument, capable of producing the most delightful and affecting sounds. The voice, however, of itself is a gift from Providence, and the excellence of its nature is owing to no merit in the possessor; therefore, to say that a person is a fine singer, for no other reason, than that he or she may have a fine voice, would be as absurd as to say a man is good, because he has great strength. If the tones of the voice are in their nature pleasing and expressive, the voice is good; but if those tones are produced in an unnatural manner, the voice becomes imperfect, and the singer has no skill in the art of singing, notwithstanding they may be uttered by a good musician, and in various modes of execution.

It has been a question in the minds of many professors and amateurs in music, why the meetings of musical societies should be suspended during the summer season, when "all nature is dress'd in her gayest attire," and when the voice is in better tune, the air in better condition, and greater vibrations of tone and reverberations of sound, are produced, than at any other season? The grand anniversary of the charity children of St. Paul's Church, London, where nine thousand are assembled, takes place in the *summer season*. Haydn declared, that the strongest musical impression he ever received, was made on him by that exhibition, which, he said, affected him so powerfully, that he was confident he should remember it to his latest hour. Vauxhaul Gardens are generally thronged to hear music *in the summer season.* The Summer Theatres furnish light operas and other musical pieces.

We know of no plausible reason why our musical Societies should suspend their meetings in the summer season, when the mind, body, and whole system, are physically, as well as more musically disposed, as every thing conspires to a relish for the concords of sweet sounds; and even when among the feathered tribes,

"The joyous birds, shrouded in cheerful shade,
Their notes, unto the voice attemper'd sweet,
Th' angelic trembling voices made
To the instruments divine, respondence meet."

HANDEL AND HAYDN.

It is not a little surprising, that a society bearing the names of these exalted personages, should so frequently lose sight of the principles which led to its formation, as to justify a neglect of some of the finest productions which the world has witnessed. As a lover of the sublime compositions of these great men, and with a fervent desire that their productions may become familiar to the lovers of sacred melody, these observations are naturally suggested.

It is not the intention of these remarks, to arraign the motives of the executive part of the Handel and Haydn Society. On the contrary, we believe they deserve much credit for their zeal and exertions in promoting the advancement of sacred music, and creating a taste for genuine harmony, divested of many of the faults, which have existed a long time in its execution. We conceive, however, that it is due both to the Society and the public, that the works of these great composers should command a primary and exclusive attention, and that while any of their productions are yet unnoticed, they should be produced as soon as practicable. This seems both due to the society and the public.

To present to the ear the effusions of authors who never have arrived to the beauty and sublimity of either of these great men, seems deviating from the objects which should be considered of the first magnitude, and which nothing would justify but the want of power to give them their proper influence. That this want of power has, and does frequently exist, is very probable; but that it occurs so frequently as to justify the neglect of due exertion and means for its accomplishment, seems quite problematical.

It is much to be regretted, by the admirers of the sublime compositions of Handel and Haydn, that several of their masterly productions lie neglected by a society, which professes to bear the names of these eminent men, and whose principal object is to cultivate a knowledge of their works. We would ask whether it would not more essentially sub-serve the interest of musical science or of this society, that a more strict adherence to these mighty masters should be observed, and less attention shown to the effusions of others, which have nothing of the influence which belongs to their beautiful productions.

Among the works of these sublime composers, which we think too frequently neglected, and which should command a primary consideration, is that most masterly production of Handel, *"The Dettingen Te Deum,"* a production we conceive to be unparalled in sublimity of style, and awfully majestic on all who have a head to conceive, or a heart to feel, the influence of its powerful execution. This composition alone, to a society bearing the name of its author, we humbly conceive should be as familiar to every member, as frequency of repetition and diligent study of its beauties can make it. Other productions of these authors might be mentioned, which we think have been neglected, and which claim an exclusive attention, but enough, we trust, has been said to incite an interest which belongs to the subject, and which we are apprehensive is not sufficiently kept in view. In offering these remarks, it is far from the wish of the writer, that any thing censurable should be considered in their construction. On the contrary, no one feels a more lively interest in the prosperity of The Handel and Haydn Society, and the objects which it embraces, and no one has experienced more pleasure from the exhibitions which it has given, than the author of these remarks, and is more willing to acknowledge the gratification experienced at the occasional displays of both taste and talent which it has elicited.

ORTHODOX.

VII

Lowell Mason
Manual of the Boston Academy of Music for Instruction in the Elements of Vocal Music on the System of Pestalozzi, Chapter I (Boston, 1834)

[Lowell Mason (1792-1872) began his professional life as a bank employee in Savannah, Georgia. He had shown considerable musical talent and enterprise while growing up in Medfield, Massachusetts, but the idea of his becoming a professional musician was at first remote, largely because of still-potent middle-class and Puritan prejudices against music as a profession (a century earlier, Thomas Symmes was already at war with the popular distrust of singing masters—see the selections from *Utile Dulci*). It was not until 1827 that Mason, already 35 years old and a family man, made the plunge and left the Savannah bank to lead church choirs professionally in Boston and, shortly after his arrival, to assume the presidency of the Handel and Haydn Society. In the meantime he had, of course, become a major figure in American music in spite of his nonprofessional status. In 1821 he had published, jointly with the organization named in its title, *The Boston Handel and Haydn Society Collection of Church Music,* an enormously popular and influential selection of hymns. It was based upon a large English collection, William Gardiner's *Sacred Melodies,* and it consisted of hymns which were set to eminently singable arrangements (distortions, one might say) of Mozart, Handel, Haydn, Beethoven, and others, even a few American psalmodists—there are even thoroughly homogenized versions of Billings. The purpose of the collection was to raise the level of the repertory of American congregations, and it succeeded in meeting a great need of the musical reformers, now a thriving and widespread lot, for a generally available and technically convenient source of great music for chorus.

Mason was a cultural reformer in the line of John Hubbard (*q.v.*), and he possessed in large measure both the positive and negative qualities of that line; his real strength, however, lay in the area of education: he was an extremely effective and innovative teacher. As a classroom teacher, as a public lecturer, and as a choir leader, as well as a writer, he carried his belief in music and in educational reform to thousands of people, and through his many disciples —among them, George F. Root (*q.v.*)—he reached millions more. Within a few years of his arrival in Boston he was teaching elementary vocal music to small classes of children, something he had successfully begun in Savannah. He made such progress with Boston children that he was soon teaching and giving concerts with great numbers of them. He had a national reputation as a superb church choir director, but all of his pedagogical labors with children were accomplished without pay, out of a desire to demonstrate that a great potential for music was to be found in all children. In the early '30's Mason was converted to the dynamic educational theories of the Swiss reformer J. H. Pestalozzi, which he applied brilliantly to the teaching of music. In 1833, he and "an association of gentlemen" founded the Boston Academy of Music in order to carry out these theories on a large scale. The Academy soon became a national focal point for musical pioneers. Teachers and students came from all over the country to learn from Mason and his cohorts, and the Academy's orchestra, although a struggling band at best, gave the first American performances of Beethoven's Second and Sixth Symphonies, among other works. (See the chapter from Thomas Ryan's autobiography, below, for a personal account of the efforts of the Academy's orchestra.)

As a part of his work with the Academy, Mason devoted himself to another project that was to have far-reaching consequences: by means of five years of patient argument, demonstration and (again unpaid) experimental teaching, Mason, with the help of his colleague, George J. Webb, convinced the Boston Public Schools to take the totally unprecedented step of making music an official part of the curriculum. In 1838, Lowell Mason became the world's first superintendent of music in the public schools.

Mason became something of a national institution within his lifetime, as a composer as well as an educator. Many of his hymns were very popular, and a small number of them are probably immortal ("Nearer my God to Thee," "From Greenland's Icy Mountains"). The criticisms of some aspects of his cultural legacy are serious and valid, in particular his intolerance of music that did not conform to his standards; however, he also exerted an enormous positive influence, spreading musical knowledge and skill to countless people who would otherwise have received little or none of it. He laid the groundwork for modern musical training for children, and his traditional position as "Father of Singing among the Children" is secure.

Mason's 1834 *Manual of the Boston Academy of Music* was an instructional work used by the Academy and also by teachers elsewhere who were trained at the Academy or in one of the great number of "music conventions" held in nearly every part of the country. These "conventions" were actually gatherings of teachers and those desiring to become teachers, sometimes including student choirs, which took place for the purpose of further training, for the exchange of ideas and methods, and for the opportunities they afforded for mutual display of talent and accomplishment. Mason was essentially the originator of the convention movement, and for more than half a century they were the most important national rallying points for music educators. The introductory chapter of the *Manual* serves to present the central ideals which governed Mason's educational approach. It offers a lucid statement of the author's belief in the moral, social, intellectual and physical benefits to be had from music training and performance. Mason was a powerful personality, very sure of himself and his goals; there is much in this chapter that reflects that personality and its informing idealism.

The only modern biography of Mason is *Lowell Mason,* by Arthur Lowndes Rich (University of North Carolina Press, 1946), although he is given considerable coverage in all the standard general histories of American music.]

Manual of the Boston Academy of Music

INTRODUCTION.

Chapter I.
General Observations.

§ 1. *The* DESIGN *of the Manual,* is to afford such facilities for the cultivation of vocal music, as to place instruction in the elements of this useful and delightful department, on the same footing with instruction in the other branches of common elementary education. Vocal music *can* be taught in families, common schools, and other seminaries of learning, in the same manner as other elementary branches; and any teacher who can sing, and who has a knowledge of the common rules of music, can, with the aid of such a manual, successfully introduce it. The same general course must be pursued in singing schools for adults, as in those for children. If adults have never learned to read, they must, like children, commence with their letters and syllables; so, like children, they must commence learning to sing, by acquiring a knowledge of the elements of vocal music. Hence, the manual is designed not exclusively for teachers of children. Nor is it designed exclusively for schools. Individuals, who have some knowledge of music, will be able to pursue privately the course here pointed out; and, by practising thoroughly the examples as they occur, may become quite correct and expert singers. Parents too, who can sing, can in the same manner, successfully teach their children to sing.

§ 2. *The* PECULIARITIES *of the system,* consist in its being strictly elementary and systematic. *One* thing is taken up at a time, and thoroughly examined and practised, before another is commenced. The knowledge, aside from the mere definitions, is acquired by the pupils themselves, and not from the dictation of the teacher. He seldom directly tells them any thing, which by a series of questions, he can lead them to find out themselves. His object is so to *lead* them to the desired information, as to excite their curiosity, and fix their attention. Knowledge acquired in this manner, is deeply impressed on the mind, and therefore durable. The scholars too are highly gratified, as may be observed by the smile frequently excited, when they come to the desired and often unexpected conclusion, by a course of reasoning which is their own. This is what we understand by the *Pestalozzian system* of instruction, which has recently been introduced into other branches of education. It always pleases scholars *to find out things themselves;* and what is thus learned is not only remembered but understood. By pursuing this course, an interest may be kept up for years in the study and practice of the elements of vocal music, which is usually regarded by scholars as dry and uninteresting; such an interest too as scarcely any other study can produce; because no other has such an influence on the feelings. This is not imagination, but fact; as is abundantly proved by the experience of those teachers, who have thus pursued it. Another peculiarity of the system is that the teacher sings very little with the scholars; and thus, as they are guided by their own ear and skill, they can go on improving after their teacher has left them. In the common method of teaching, a large part of the singers are guided solely by the predominant voice of the teacher; and when he leaves, the singing gradually declines.

§ 3. SOURCES OF INFORMATION. These are various; but always derived from personal experience, or the written experience of others, and never from mere theory. The system must be traced to Pestalozzi, a Swiss gentleman of wealth and learning, who devoted his life and fortune to the improvement of the young. He spared no pains nor expense, in procuring teachers of talents and acquirements, and in providing other necessary means for promoting his favorite plans of education. He obtained the services of Pfeiffer and Nägeli; who, under his patronage, drew up a very extensive work on elementary instruction in vocal music. Other works on the same general principles, were afterwards published by Kübler, and other distinguished German teachers, in which much improvement was made on the original treatise of Pfeiffer and Nägeli. These German works have been introduced into this country by Wm. C. Woodbridge, the well known geographer and editor of the "Annals of Education;" and these have been made the basis of the following work. Useful hints have also been derived from several works on vocal music recently published in England.

§ 4. REASONS WHY VOCAL MUSIC SHOULD BE GENERALLY CULTIVATED. I. *It* CAN *be generally cultivated.* It is the universal testimony of those who have had experience, that, as a general fact, all have organs adapted to produce and distinguish musical sounds. Every child can vary the tones of his voice; and if he receives early instruction, it will be as easy for him to learn to sing, as to learn to talk or to read. If we had not learned to talk in early life, our organs would have become so rigid and unmanageable, as to render it impossible ever to learn to speak correctly, and perhaps not at all. It is a well known fact, that adults seldom acquire any sounds in a foreign language, which are not in their own. But put a child into a foreign family, and he will soon get all their peculiar tones. He can learn by imitation, while his organs are flexible and pliant. This is true not only of the voice, but also of the ear. What is technically termed a *musical* ear, is chiefly the result of cultivation.* It is by experience that infants learn to distinguish sounds; and when their attention is early arrested by musical sounds, the ear becomes sensitive and active. But neglect the ear, and it becomes dull, and unable to discriminate. 'By practice, the discriminating powers of the ear may be carried to the highest degree of perfection.' 'In the improvement or rather the actual formation

of an ear, we may mention William Cotlman, of Leicester, (Eng.) who blind from his birth, had so dull an ear at six years old, that he could not distinguish the tones of a violin from those of a flute. At this period, he was presented with a piano forte; which, at first, amused him only by its curious structure. At length, his ear was caught by the sounds, and he soon began to lay aside his other amusements, and show an increasing fondness for music. The rapidity with which his ear was formed, is certainly without a parallel. On first hearing the "Seventh Symphony" of Haydn performed by a full orchestra, he instantly comprehended the different modulations in that piece, and played them on the piano forte with the greatest accuracy.' 'The formation of the musical ear depends on early impressions. Infants who are placed within the constant hearing of musical sounds, soon learn to appreciate them, and nurses have often the merit of giving the first lessons in melody.' 'Children brought up in musical families and often entertained by musical sounds, so soon acquire a musical sense, as, in some instances, to be regarded as prodigies."† Such were Mozart, Crotch, &c. To show that this is the result of cultivation, those children who are taken care of in infancy by singers, usually become so themselves, whether the parents sing or not. It has also been found by teachers of infant schools, that almost all children can sing. In the Boston alms house, in which place, if any where, we should expect to find children neglected or having defective organs, only three out of about 75 were found, who could not, on the first trial, sing the first four notes of the scale; and two of those three had been in the establishment but a few days. These were allowed to take their seats with the others, and practise as they were able; but no particular attention was paid to them. After a few weeks, they were examined, and one of them was found to have become one of the best singers among them, and another had made considerable progress. The organs are seldom so defective as to preclude cultivation. Attention and perseverance will usually overcome all difficulties. To accustom ourselves to *listen* with attention, is the first step to vocal improvement. The lamented professor Fisher, of Yale College, could not distinguish different sounds, until he took a string and divided it according to the mathematical proportions for the successive sounds; and in this way tuned his voice and his ear. Yet before he left this country on his fatal voyage, he had made great advancements in the cultivation of music, and written a valuable treatise on musical temperament. He had also made considerable progress in the construction of an organ according to those

*Gardiner's "Music of Nature."
†See Musical Cyclopedia, art. 'Ear.'

40

principles; which certainly required a most delicate ear. By close attention, we may soon acquire a musical ear; and ultimately find no difficulty in determining the finest gradations of sound. 'There are few persons indeed so destitute of natural qualifications as to be unable to sing agreeably, by resolute perseverance in a judicious course of practice. And I believe that the impediments to great excellence, lie more frequently in the want of other attributes, than in deficiency of physical powers of organ. There are instances even of distinguished performers, that commenced their musical education, without the slightest hope of gaining any strength sufficient to qualify them for the profession, who have, nevertheless, attained a most respectable rank in art. Such examples indeed are rare, but there are multitudes in private life who have *literally made a voice.'** The musical talent is wanting then in only a few. Most who suppose themselves to be destitute of it, have only let the time in which the talent, small in itself, was capable of developement, pass by unimproved. But if this talent has been conferred by the Creator on so many, and indeed with few exceptions on *all,* then vocal music is an object of *universal cultivation.*

§ 5. II. *Vocal music* OUGHT *to be generally cultivated.* If we have established the point that it *can* be, few will doubt that it *ought* to be cultivated. Whoever acknowledges the high rank, which music demands, and deserves to hold in christian devotion, will not consider its cultivation of little moment. If a service is acceptable, it is our *duty* to use every exertion to render it worthy of acceptance. If the sacrifice send up a grateful incense to the throne of God, it should be, as much as possible, 'without spot or blemish.' The musical talent is one given us by our Maker. It is a responsible and sacred talent; and can we do otherwise than yield to the constraining obligation, 'to stir up the gift that is in us!' Few can plead incapacity, and no one has a right to do it, until he has subjected his powers to a rigid examination. No talent however vigorous, springs spontaneously into action. Some labor is necessary to unfold its latent energies, as well as to improve it. Many talents remain actually unknown to their possessor, until circumstances bring them to view. It is not only our duty to improve on our own talents, but also to develope and cultivate those of our children. 'Not only should persons make conscience of learning to sing; but parents should conscientiously see to it, that their children are taught this, among other things, as their education and instruction belong to them.'* The business of common school instruction generally, is nothing else than the harmonious developement and cultivation of all the faculties of children; hence, music as a regular branch of educa-

tion, ought to be introduced into schools. The musical talent ought to be, in the same natural manner, incited, developed, cultivated, and rendered strong. Further reasons will be presented in the following sections.

§ 6. ADVANTAGES OF THE EARLY AND CONTINUED CULTIVATION OF VOCAL MUSIC. I. *It improves the voice,* in speaking and reading, by giving smoothness, volume and variety to the tones. The voice, like every other faculty, is strengthened by use. If a child lifts a given weight every day, we all know his strength will be gradually increased, provided he is not forced to exert himself beyond his strength. So the voice by constant exercise, will continually improve, provided it is not strained beyond its natural tone. The voice, it is true, *may* be greatly injured or even destroyed, by thus *forcing* it, particularly on the high notes; but under proper and judicious direction, it will daily improve by use. This is in strict analogy with the common laws of exercise, applicable alike to the physical, intellectual, and moral powers of man. Children, in their amusements, are often exerting their voices to their utmost extent, and this without injury, because they do not go beyond their natural tones. Criers in the streets of our large cities, acquire an astonishing volume of voice and force of intonation, by this daily practice; yet who ever heard of such persons or any public criers losing their voices, in consequence of such exertion? It is dangerous to use the voice in singing, only when it is dangerous to use it by much talking; that is, when the lungs are affected by a cold or by the consumption. This is the common cause of a ruined voice. Persons who are fond of music, often force the lungs in singing when in a diseased state, and by excessive irritation, bring on permanent disease. Singing not only tends to strengthen the voice, but also gives smoothness and variety to the tones in speaking. It is as necessary to give a pleasing variety to the tones in order to produce good speaking as good singing; and the musical intervals should be as much under the control, in the former case as in the latter. The tones in speaking should have that gradual swell and vanish which give beauty to singing. If our public speakers had early been taught to sing, and continued the practice, we should not hear their too often drawling tones, particularly those of clergymen. A speaker who cannot sing, is generally monotonous and dull. This can be remedied only by teaching our children generally to sing.

§ 7. II. *Vocal Music conduces to health.* It was the opinion of Dr. Rush, that singing by young ladies whom the customs of society debar from many other

---

*Bacon's "Elements of Vocal Science."
*Pres. Edwards.

kinds of healthy exercise, is to be cultivated, not only as an accomplishment, but as a means of preserving health. He particularly insists, that vocal music should never be neglected in the education of a young lady; and states, that besides its salutary operation in soothing the cares of domestic life, it has a still more direct and important effect. 'I here introduce a fact,' says the doctor, 'which has been suggested to me by my profession; that is, the exercise of the organs of the breast by singing, contributes very much to defend them from those diseases, to which the climate and other causes expose them. The Germans are seldom afflicted with consumption: nor have I ever known more than one instance of the spitting of blood amongst them. This, I believe, is in part occasioned by the strength which their lungs acquire by exercising them frequently in vocal music, which constitutes an essential branch of their education.' 'The music master of our academy,' says Gardiner, 'has furnished me with an observation still more in favor of this opinion. He informs me, that he had known several instances of persons strongly disposed to consumption, restored to health by the exercise of the lungs in singing.' 'In the new establishment of infant schools for children of three and four years of age, every thing is taught by the aid of song. Their little lessons, their recitations, their arithmetical countings, are all chanted; and as they feel the importance of their own voices when joined together, they emulate each other in the power of vociferating. This exercise is found to be very beneficial to their health. Many instances have occurred of weakly children of two or three years of age, that could scarcely support themselves, having become robust and healthy by this constant exercise of the lungs.' These results are perfectly philosophical. Singing tends to expand the chest, and thus increase the activity and powers of the vital organs.

§ 8. III. Vocal music in its *elevated* form, *tends to* IMPROVE THE HEART. This is its proper and legitimate and ought to be its principal object. It can and ought to be made the handmaid of virtue and piety. Its effects in softening and elevating the feelings, are too evident to need illustration. There is something in the nature of musical tones, viewed in their pure and simple, not unnatural state, which is truly heavenly and delightful: and if music of such a character could become universal throughout the nation, it would be a sure and excellent means of national improvement. We speak expressly of music in its elevated and natural form, and not that screaming or screeching at the very extent, and highest pitch of the voice, which is sometimes heard, and called vocal music. Such is not the *music of nature,* and such not the music we hope to be instrumental of diffusing by the publication of this Manual. It

is to be regretted that music which is accompanied with vulgar and indelicate associations, as has been too often the case, should find its way into our nurseries and juvenile schools, and even into the drawing rooms of young ladies. The effects of a suitable style of music in connection with judicious words, is now to some extent well known. It tends to produce love to teachers, love to mates, love to parents, and love to God; kindness to dumb animals, and an observance of the works of nature and of the events of Providence; and leads the mind 'through nature up to nature's God.' Such are its legitimate tendencies; and such we hope to be instrumental in making its ordinary tendencies. In this way, amusement may be blended with instruction; and cheerfulness, happiness, and order introduced into the family and into the school. This is not theory or imagination, but fact; testimony to which has reached our ears, from both teachers and parents. We will give a few examples of words, to illustrate the reason of this; the effect of the association of the music with the words of course we cannot give. The children, while at play, sing to a pleasing air:*

1. O come to the garden, dear mates of the school,
   And rove through the bowers so fragrant and cool.
2. We'll gather the lilly and jessamine fair,
   And twine them with roses to garland our hair.
3. We'll cull all the sweetest to make a boquet,
   To give to our teacher this warm summer day.
4. Then hie to the school room, with joy and with glee;
   And sing our sweet ballads, so happy are we.

Now who does not know that such an exercise tends to unite the hearts of the children, and to make them love and obey their teachers. In the same way, love to parents and kindness to animals are inculcated. To show how the thoughts may be turned to God from scenes and events in nature, we quote the following, on hearing the whippoorwill:

1. Hear the birds singing so sweet and so clear,
      'Fear thy God!' 'Fear thy God!'
   'Tis the whippoorwill cries in your ear.
   In green bushes warbling, with leaves all concealed,
   He warns the tired reaper who comes from the field,
      'Thank thy God!' 'Thank thy God!'
   For he is so bounteous and kind.

*See 'Juvenile Lyre.' [A songbook, pub. in 1831, by Mason in collaboration with Elam Ives. Described by Mason as "the first school song book published in this country."]

2. Hear him again with his varying song,
      'Praise thy God!' 'Praise thy God!'
'Tis he that has blest thee so long.
Behold the full harvest and fruits of the field,
And taste the rich pleasures and comforts they
    yield.
      'Love thy God!' 'Love thy God!'
For he is so gracious and good.

Thus, whenever the voice of the whippoorwill is heard, the thoughts both of the children and of the parents, if they sing with or listen to their children, will always through life be turned by association to the goodness and faithfulness of God. It is all-important that the youthful mind should be well stored with useful associations, to preoccupy the ground, otherwise seized upon by the adversary to nourish evil passions. The very nursery may and often does become a school of piety; the mother winning the child's attention to the simplest, and, at the same time, the richest truths, by means of sacred song. And those only, who have had the advantage of such an artless mode of instruction in their childhood, can estimate its value; when in the turbulent scenes of life, though many an intermediate association for good or for evil has passed away, the little hymn chanted by a fond mother, comes rushing upon the mind, in all the freshness of juvenile emotion. So seldom is the proper cultivation of music admitted into the general plan of education at home or abroad, that the advantages resulting from it, are in a great measure conjectural; yet the subject is worthy of consideration, in proportion to its importance as a stimulator of youthful feeling. We can affect the moral character, only through the medium of the feelings. When they are interested, the attention can be fixed, and the mind turned to the most important truths. Most of our feelings are habitual, and connected with our ordinary associations. Hence, a most important part of education is to control and direct the associations. No instrument for this purpose is more powerful than vocal music; hence, parents ought to spare no pains to have their children properly instructed in it. There is a criminal neglect on the part of parents, as is evinced by the character of the music and of the poetry not unfrequently found on the piano forte. Surely they should allow their children to learn none but intelligent pleasing melodies, and *good* valuable poetry; of which, owing to the corrupt taste, we find a want, notwithstanding we have a multitude of songs and ballads. This defect will be remedied, we doubt not, as soon as the public taste demands it. Only the most choice songs and melodies must be admitted into our families and schools; if, after being learned in youth, they are to live and be sung in a later age. LET ME HAVE THE MAKING OF THE BALLADS OF A NATION AND YOU MAY MAKE THEIR LAWS.

§ 9. IV. *Vocal music tends to produce social order and happiness in a family.* Those parents and children who sing together, have a stronger attachment for each other. The family circle is prized; for here can always be found amusement, and such as does not lead into temptation. They can truly sing, 'Home, sweet home.' Nothing tends more to produce kindly feelings. It is almost impossible to sing with one, towards whom we indulge unkind feelings; and if we do, such feelings will soon be forgotten. Singing is naturally the overflowing of kind and joyful feelings. Who ever saw children singing together, or parents and children, that were not apparently happy? When singing is employed in the family devotions, it tends to produce a proper frame of mind, and to calm the feelings. It throws a delight and interest into the exercises, which calls up and fixes the attention. In the pious families of the Scotch, singing is as necessary a part of the devotions of a family, as reading the Bible; and in no families in the world, do all the members more heartily unite in these exercises.

When vocal music is properly attended to in schools and in families, its effect will be seen in the house of God; and we then shall not be pained with the profanity we now too often are compelled to witness, both in the choir and in the congregation.

§ 10. V. *The course of instruction pursued in the Manual, is eminently* INTELLECTUAL *and* DISCIPLINARY. The mind is exercised and disciplined by it, as by the study of arithmetic; and the voice as by reading and speaking. It tends to produce habits of order, both physical and mental. Considered then merely in a literary point of view, and as affecting our habits and manners, it ought to be introduced into every system of education. Sometimes a mind naturally dull, like that of the blind boy, has been awakened by the excitement of music, and thus stimulated to action in other pursuits. The excitement of one dormant faculty may be made the instrument of the excitement of others. We rarely find a singer of a dull disposition; although some, who yielding themselves entirely to an improper indulgence of music, are rendered unfit for almost every thing substantial or useful. This, however, is not the fault of music, but is the result of an improper cultivation of the musical talent, and a want of a proper balance of mind. A man may give himself up entirely to any exciting subject, and be unfit for the common business of life. But in a well balanced mind, music can never do injury. Parents and friends of children will thus see, that by urging the importance of introducing vocal music into our schools, we are not advocating a waste of time, or the introduction of a study merely ornamental.

§ 11. It is almost the only branch of education, aside from divine truth, whose direct tendency is *to cultivate the feelings*. Our systems of education generally proceed too much on the principle, that we are mere intellectual beings, not susceptible of emotions, or capable of happiness. Hence, we often find the most learned the least agreeable. There is no necessity for this. The feelings may and ought to be cultivated in connection with the intellect. Before our race can be much improved, the principle that the human soul is all mind and no heart, must be discarded; and human beings must be treated as possessing feelings as well as intellects. The feelings are as much the subject of training as the mind; and our happiness depends more on the cultivation of the former than of the latter. The chief object of the cultivation of vocal music is to train the feelings. How this is done, has been exemplified in the preceding sections.

§ 12. *The error of supposing* vocal music can be *taught in a few months;* or that it is an easy task to learn to sing. This is a fatal mistake; and ruinous to correct execution. No one can learn to sing without active, persevering, and long continued effort. You may as well expect a child to learn to talk or to read, by being taught a few lessons. No: a child should commence learning to sing as soon as he does to read, and should continue to learn as long as he continues in school; and after that, advance to perfect himself by his own exertions. Adults must begin and learn like children. If we have never learned to read, we must begin and go on like children, though not with as much repetition. So in learning to sing, we must begin and persevere through life in the same manner. All that a teacher of a class can do, is to direct the scholar into the proper course, and then leave him to pursue his way himself, or with the help of associates, if he desires to arrive at excellence.

VIII

John Sullivan Dwight
"The Concerts of the Past Winter"
and Other Selections*
(1840-1881)

[John Sullivan Dwight (1813-1893) is the central figure of this anthology, as he is arguably the central figure of nineteenth-century Boston music. This is not because of any outstanding personal musical ability—he was a worse than indifferent flute player with a shaky grasp of music theory—but because of his many significant accomplishments as an amateur (in the best sense) working to establish a deep and lasting musical culture. The son of a Boston physician, Dwight went to Harvard and joined the Pierian Sodality, the only musical organization in the school at that time (1829). Members of that little club were later to form the Harvard Musical Association, which, with Dwight as its spiritual leader, became one of the most valuable pioneering musical organizations in the country. Meanwhile, in 1832 Dwight entered Harvard Divinity and was caught up in the advanced social and religious thought that was then shaking that bastion of Unitarianism to its roots— these were the first heady years of the Transcendentalist movement. Dwight's graduate dissertation, "The Proper Character of Poetry and Music for Public Worship," sounded a theme which fell uneasily on conservative American ears, but which was to be basic to Dwight's whole life: music should be accepted on its own merits "as a means of genuine culture."

Dwight's circle of friends included most of the leading lights of the Boston-Concord intellectual avant-garde; Theodore Parker was friend and advisor during Dwight's three-and-one-half-year wait for a pulpit, and when he was finally accepted at Northampton, it was George Ripley and W. H. Channing who presided over his ordination. The support of these leaders notwithstanding, Dwight did not last long at Northampton, where the spirit of Jonathan Edwards still hovered over the congregation, making it somewhat distrustful of the young Transcendentalist and music lover. It appears that he was not really suited to the ministry anyway, for most of his energy went into his love of music and into various literary and social activities on behalf of the advanced cultural causes of himself and his friends, including Emerson, Margaret Fuller, and Elizabeth Peabody, as well as Ripley and Parker. In 1838 he wrote and published the first American review of Tennyson; he was also active as a translator of German poetry, thereby earning the appreciation of Carlyle. Perhaps his most important piece of writing in this early period was the survey, "The Concerts of the Past Winter," written for the first issue of *The Dial,* the famous organ of the Transcendentalist movement. This article, included here, is for the most part a vigorous and perceptive account of various musical events in the city; it is of much more than contemporary interest, however, because its author has supported and deepened his observations with often extremely sensitive remarks on the nature of music in general, certain composers in particular, and musical culture as it was developing in Boston. Upon this last subject Dwight was especially perceptive and even prophetic, as his prescriptions for a healthy musical community (as they are expressed in the last paragraphs of the article) clearly demonstrate.

After he decided to quit the Unitarian ministry, Dwight took a bold step which gave proof of his commitment to profound cultural change: he joined his friend George Ripley at Brook Farm. Brook Farm, carved out of some unpromising land in West Roxbury, near Boston, was probably the most famous and (for a time) successful of the many Utopian communities that grew up in the 1840's in reaction

---

*"The Concerts of the Past Winter," *The Dial* (July, 1840). "Music," *Aesthetic Papers,* Elizabeth Palmer Peabody, ed. (Boston, 1849). *Dwight's Journal of Music:* "Introductory" (April 10, 1852); "Jonas Chickering" (December 17, 1853); "Valedictory" (September 3, 1881). "Music as a Means of Culture," *Atlantic Monthly* (1870).

to the bustling materialism of the young and eager United States. In the words of founder Ripley, the object of Brook Farm was "to insure a more natural union between intellectual and manual labor than now exists; to combine the thinker and the worker, as far as possible, in the same individual." Accordingly, Dwight worked both as a farmhand and as teacher of Latin and music at Brook Farm. He also organized musical events and pageants, generally infecting his fellow Utopians with his own enthusiasm for great music. Among his students was George William Curtis, later a famous *Harper's* editor and himself an important music critic.

When the Brook Farm community reorganized along the lines proposed by the French Associationist Charles Fourier (particularly as they were presented to Americans by Fourier's magnetic disciple Albert Brisbane), Dwight added to his duties those of writer and editor. He devoted himself to *The Harbinger*, the most important early American socialist periodical. It began its short life as a Brook Farm project, and Dwight helped to edit and to manage it, in the meantime contributing well over a hundred articles to it during its four years of existence. The vast majority of them are straightforward music criticism, occasionally intermixed with visionary philosophy, and these musical essays constitute a major cultural achievement. He also wrote about many other Associationist-related issues—including a philosophical approach to cooking—and he spread his social and musical gospel by other means also, most importantly a series of lectures on music in New York.

In 1848 the Brook Farm enterprise failed, its demise brought about more by external disasters (a series of fires and a siege of smallpox) than internal weakness. Dwight returned to Boston, still pursuing his reforming labors, but also suffering from poverty and indecision—he now had failed both as clergyman and as Utopian reformer. In 1849, however, he did publish the essay "Music" as a part of Elizabeth Peabody's ill-fated attempt to issue a series of anthologies of Associationist essays (it was to be a one-issue series, but that issue did contain Dwight's essay). The essay is included here; it is, for all its visionary sweep, the most lucid and effective statement of the Transcendentalist faith in the spiritual power of music.

In 1851 Dwight's life finally began to take a definitive shape. He first married Mary Bullard, herself a singer and frequent Brook Farm visitor, then set about planning that which was to be the great accomplishment of his life: *Dwight's Journal of Music* commenced publication April 10, 1852, and for nearly thirty years thereafter, until September 3, 1881, it reigned as the finest music periodical in America. It never had more than a few hundred

subscribers, but they were widely scattered and included a majority of the most active and able laborers in the American musical vineyard. Contributors were many and important: Curtis, Lowell Mason, the great Beethoven biographer Alexander Wheelock Thayer, William Foster Apthorp (*q.v.*), and others. Despite its critical success, the magazine meant much drudgery and little remuneration for Dwight, although for two decades of its existence the major music publisher Oliver Ditson undertook the publishing of it, giving Dwight a small measure of security. (That arrangement ended when Ditson tried to compel the editor to turn his creation into a house organ of the Ditson Company; Dwight refused to part with any of his editorial independence, and he separated himself and his *Journal* from Ditson, a move involving much sacrifice.)

The Harvard Musical Association (H.M.A.) gave the *Journal* much support through the years, and in turn Dwight upheld the cause of that organization, giving liberal (though critical) coverage to the concerts of its orchestra (which he helped to found) and giving much editorial space to its overriding cultural goals. After a long campaign Dwight and the H.M.A. succeeded in bringing about the acceptance of music as a *bona fide* part of the curriculum in higher education. John Knowles Paine, Harvard's organist and choirmaster, who had long taught informal music courses on a voluntary basis, finally succeeded, with the help of Dwight and his colleagues, in being accepted as a full-fledged Instructor of Music and ultimately, in 1875, as Harvard's and America's first Professor of Music. Another major goal of Dwight and the Association was the creation of a substantial and appreciative audience for great music. This was accomplished by means of the orchestra of the H.M.A. which, despite its shortcomings, had a large following for many years and succeeded in laying the cultural groundwork for Henry Lee Higginson's great contribution to Boston, the Boston Symphony Orchestra. Dwight's "History of Music in Boston" contains (as one might expect) a detailed account of the many accomplishments of the H.M.A.

Dwight was a firm devotee of German music and culture and of "high culture" in general—to the nearly complete exclusion of popular culture and those works of our native musicians which failed to adhere to classical models (his prejudice against Gottschalk is the best example of this). He also resisted mightily the onslaught of "modern" music, which often meant anything after Mendelssohn and most particularly meant Wagner. He thus earned the title of "Autocrat of Music" in many Boston circles, and he was regarded with contempt or fear by some. However, the *Journal* does for the most part reveal the openness and impartiality which its editor claims for it in the introductory essay of the first issue, which is included here. Also included is the final issue's "Valedictory," in part a statement of bitter resignation, in part of pride and pleased retrospection, and—most remarkably—also a confession of its author's sense of his own limitations. One more item from the Journal is included, a memorial piece about the great Boston piano-builder, Jonas Chickering. It was chosen as a glimpse of another dimension of musical culture and an example of Dwight's and Boston's grateful appreciation of a figure who for years played an indispensable part in the city's musical growth.

Dwight's 1870 lecture, "Music as a Means of Culture," was published in the *Atlantic Monthly* and was long regarded as a classic statement of faith in the moral power of music. It is that, and as such it appears at times to be fatally simplistic, at least from the vantage point of a much-disabused age. It earns its place here, however, not only as a statement of bygone attitudes, but as an often beautiful assertion of the profound connection between art and morality—an assertion which our more sophisticated age has not, after all, been able to disprove.

When Justin Winsor was assembling the four-volume *Memorial History of Boston,* to be published in observance of the two hundred and fiftieth anniversary of the founding of the city, it was inevitable that he choose Dwight to write the chapter on the history of music in the city. Although his version of musical history has quite a number of blind spots—the largest being his complete and ignorant rejection of the music of the Puritans and the psalmodists—and although there are distortions and errors exposed by later research, the chapter stands as a work of overall excellence. Dwight's judgment of early American music was shared by nearly every scholar from the time of Hubbard until well into the present century. The distortions brought about by his "high culture" point of view are easy to discover because he states his cultural assumptions quite openly. Thus, with certain allowances made, "The History of Music in Boston" is still the most useful (and most gracefully written) general account of the middle seventy years of Boston musical life in the nineteenth century, and it has the advantage of having been written by one of the chief makers of the history it chronicles. Unfortunately considerations of space and budget prevented inclusion of this piece in the present collection. Winsor's volume is, however, generally available in greater Boston libraries.

Dwight's *Journal* died for lack of support, but this does not mean that Dwight himself was neglected. From his quarters in the building of the Harvard Musical Association in Pemberton Square, the old widower continued to figure prominently in the musi-

cal affairs of the city until the end of his life. He had left behind the early dynamism of the Transcendentalist Club for the cultural Old Guard atmosphere of the Saturday Club (as had his friend Emerson), but his writing and his enthusiastic personality continued to display the same love and commitment that had originally set him on his long crusader's journey.

The only published biography of Dwight is George Willis Cooke's *John Sullivan Dwight: Brook-Farmer, Editor, and Critic of Music* (Boston, 1898), although there is also much information in Cooke's edition of *Early Letters of George Wm. Curtis to John S. Dwight* (New York, 1898). Both of these works, as well as the complete *Dwight's Journal of Music,* have been reissued in scholar's reprints. There is an excellent discussion of Dwight in Irving Lowens' *Music and Musicians in Early America* (Norton, 1964).]

The Concerts of the Past Winter.

MUSIC has made a decided progress in our city this last winter. This has appeared in the popularity of the concerts, compared with other amusements, and in the unusual amount of good music, which has not been wholly thrown away upon us. Of course many a lover of the art could not but look skeptically upon all this; could not fail to see that people were determined to this or that concert by fashion rather than by taste, and that the cheap contrivances of Russell [*] always carried away the crowd, while the artist sang or played to the few. We cannot flatter ourselves for a moment that we of Boston are, or shall be for years to come, a musical people. The devoted lover of the art is only beginning to be countenanced and recognised as one better than an idler. He must still keep apologizing to his incredulous, practical neighbors for the heavenly influence which haunts him. He does not live in a genial atmosphere of music, but in the cold east wind of utility; and meets few who will acknowledge that what he loves has anything to do with life. Still we are confident we feel a progress. There is a musical element *in* the people; for there is certainly a religious sentiment, a restlessness, which craves more than the actual affords, an aspiration and yearning of the heart for communion, which cannot take place through words and thoughts, but only through some subtler medium, like music. It is not nature's fault, if we want the musical sense or organ. Slow, but sure development, under proper culture, will prove this. Singing is taught in schools embracing thousands, without much consciousness,

[*For a more tolerant view of Henry Russell, see the Root selection.]

to be sure, of the higher meaning of music, but with great success in producing quick and correct ears, and pure, flexible voices, and in making the number of those who can sing and read music, and of those who can enjoy and appreciate it, vastly greater than it was. This creates audiences for the oratorios and concerts; there is a looking that way; and the art bids fair sooner or later to have justice done it.

Next to thorough drilling in the rudiments, we want inspiring models. We want to hear good music. In the schools the surface of the soil is loosened: it is time that good seeds should be dropped into it. The Psalmody of the country choir and the dancing master's fiddle, the waltzes and variations of the music-shop, Russell's songs, and "Jim Crow" and "Harrison Melodies," are not apt to visit the popular mind with the deep emotions of true music. Handel should be heard more, and Haydn, and Mozart, and Beethoven. The works of true genius, which cannot be too familiar, since they are always new like nature, should salute our ears until the nobler chords within our souls respond. We should be taught the same reverence for Bach and Handel as for Homer; and, having felt the spell of their harmonies upon us, should glow at the mention of their names. Every opportunity of hearing good music is to be hailed as an angel's visit in our community. It is in this view that we look back with pleasure upon the concerts of the past season.

That music of any kind draws crowds, is encouraging. But we have been more than encouraged, on looking over our old concert bills, which we have kept through the winter as a record of pleasant hours, to see how much genuine classic music has been brought out, with more or less success at the various concerts:—music, which the few devoutly musical had heard of, and longed to hear, with but a faint hope that they should soon be so blest;—music, which introduces us within the charmed precincts of genius, like Beethoven's. In attempting to single out the most significant from such a multitude of performances, we shall of course omit much that was praiseworthy; for our opportunity of hearing was limited, nor is our memory sure, nor our space sufficient.

Most worthy of mention were the Oratorios of the Handel and Haydn Society. We had *The Messiah* twice and *The Creation* several times. Neukomm's *"David"* had the greatest run, as usual. It is brilliant and variegated, and had been more thoroughly practised and learned than the other pieces. But as a composition it should not be mentioned with them. Its interest fades away, when it is repeated beyond a certain point, while that of *"The Messiah"* steadily increases. To the former we owe some bright hours, to the latter an influence for life. We feel tempted to call *"The Messiah"* the only Oratorio, and to doubt if there will ever be another. *"David"* is something halfway between the Oratorio and the Opera; it is too dramatic, too individual and personal, too circumstantial to be sublime. *"The Messiah"* was brought out this winter for the first time in a manner which made it felt, and conveyed some idea or presentiment of its true grandeur, depth, and beauty. Many hearers then, for the first time, discovered what a treasure the world contained, and were moved to try to appreciate it. This effect was owing in great part to the Society's new hall, *the Melodéon,* which gives ample scope to the great choruses. The orchestra, though small, was uncommonly good. Much as we loved this music before, we were not properly aware until now of the surpassing beauty of the accompaniments. They were sketched by Handel, when instrumentation was limited, and filled out with a glorious warmth of coloring by Mozart. To have done it so well his soul must have become impregnated with the very spirit of the original. Handel seems to have monopolized the one subject for an Oratorio, *Humanity's anticipation of its Messiah.* This properly is the one theme of all pure music; this is the mysterious promise which it whispers; this is the hope with which it fills us as its tones seem to fall from the blue sky, or to exhale through the earth's pores from its secret divine fountains. Music is the aspiration, the yearnings of the heart to the Infinite. It is the prayer of faith, which has no fear, no weakness in it. It delivers us from our actual bondage; it buoys us up above our accidents, and wafts us on waves of melody to the heart's ideal home. This longing of the heart, which is a permanent fact of human life, and with which all know how to sympathize, has received its most perfect historical form in the Jewish expectation of a Messiah. The prediction and coming of Jesus stand as a type forever of the divine restlessness, the prophetic yearning of the heart of humanity. Has any poet found words for this feeling to match with those of the Psalmist and the Prophets of old? With wonderful judgment Handel called out the noblest of those grand sentences, and constructed them into a complete and epic unity. They are almost the only words we know, which do not limit the free, world-permeating, ever-shifting Protean genius of music. Words, the language of thoughts, are too definite, and clip the wings and clog the graceful movements of this unresting spirit: she chants forgetfulness of limits, and charms us along with her to the Infinite; she loves to wander through the vague immense, and seems everywhere at once; then only is she beautiful. With the growth of the musical taste, therefore, one acquires a more and more decided preference for instrumental music rather than song;

music *pure,* rather than music wedded with another art, which never can be quite congenial. We prefer a Beethoven's Symphony to anything ever sung, with the single exception of Handel's Messiah. In that the words seem one with the music,—as eternal, as sublime, as universal and impersonal. They set no limit to the music, but contain in themselves seeds of inexhaustible harmonies and melodies. We could not spare a word, or suffer any change. *"The Messiah"* always must have meaning to all men, it is so impersonal. Its choruses are the voice of all humanity. Its songs are the communion of the solitary soul with the Infinite. But there is no Duet or Trio in it, no talking of individual with individual. Either it is the sublime of the soul merged in the multitude, or it is the sublime of the soul alone with God. And then its depths of sadness!—from such depths alone could roll those mighty ocean-choruses of triumph, the *"Hallelujah"* chorus, the *"Wonderful"* chorus, and *"Worthy the Lamb." "The Messiah"* will always stand, in its stern simplicity, as one of the adopted of Nature.

How different *"The Creation"!* We are in another element, with another man, with Haydn, that sunny, genial, busy nature. If with Handel all is unity, grandeur, bold simplicity, universality; here all is variety, individuality, profusion of detail. If with Handel it is aspiration to the Unknown, here it is description of the Known. If one forebodes another world, the other lovingly reflects the hues of this world. Handel with bold hand sketches gigantic shadows, which lose themselves in infinite space. With Haydn everything is happily planned within the limits of certainty, and conscientiously and gracefully finished. It is the perfection of art. A work of Haydn's is a Grecian temple: there it stands complete in itself and fully executed, and suggests no more. A work of Handel's, (still more of Beethoven's,) is a Gothic cathedral, which seems never finished, but becoming, growing, yearning and striving upwards, the beginning only of a boundless plan, whose consummation is in another world. We enjoy with Haydn the serene pleasure of doing things, the ever fresh surprise of accomplishment. With him we round off and finish one thing after another, and look upon it and pronounce it good; but we do not lift our eyes away and yearn for what is beyond. Constant, cheerful activity was the element of Haydn. Hence the Creation was the very subject for the man; his whole nature chose it for him. In *"The Creation"* the instrumental accompaniments are prominent, and the voices secondary. The orchestra weaves the picture; the voices but hint its meaning. Literal description of nature is carried even too far in it. Beautiful and surprising as those imitations are, of Chaos, and the birth of Light, and rolling ocean,

and smooth meadows, and brooks, and birds, and breezes, monsters of the deep and of the forest, and insects sparkling like gold dust in the sunny air, —yet often they seem too mechanical and curious, and out of the province of Art, which should breathe the pervading spirit of Nature, as a whole, and not copy too carefully the things that are in it. Whoever has studied the Pastoral Symphony, or the Pastoral Sonata of Beethoven, will feel the difference between music which flows from an inward feeling of nature, from a common consciousness (as it were) with nature, and the music which only copies, from without, her single features. These pieces bring all summer sensations over you, but they do not let you identify a note or a passage as standing for a stream, or a bird. They do not say; look at this or that, now imagine nightingales, now thunder, now mountains, and now sunspots chasing shadows; but they make you feel as you would if you were lying on a grassy slope in a summer's afternoon, with the melancholy leisure of a shepherd swain, and these things all around you without your noticing them. Haydn paints you this or that by means of various qualities and combinations of tone, and various movements; with wonderful success he calls up images; you admire the ingenuity and the beauty, but are not inspired. We were glad to hear the opening symphony, representing chaos, performed by the orchestra so as to give us some dim conception of what it might be when given by a great and practised orchestra abroad. Here, of course, these things are done upon a small scale. Still they afford the lover of music an opportunity to study the great works, of which he has heard, and thus prepare himself to hear them understandingly whenever he shall be blessed with a hearing of them in their full proportions. We do feel that we grow familiar with *"The Messiah,"* though we have only heard it here. The characteristic and eternal features of the composition as it was in the mind of Handel, seem to come out more and more clearly as we think it over, and remain in our mind long after the accidents of an inadequate performance are forgotten. An ideal of what *"The Messiah"* in itself must be is nourished in us by *"The Messiah,"* as we have heard it under such comparatively poor advantages. For this we thank the Handel and Haydn Society. We congratulate them on the success of their last performances; and we think the interest with which a crowded audience listened, a sign of some significance in a community only beginning to be musical. Would it not have been better to have repeated *"The Messiah"* again and again, and then *"The Creation,"* as long as audiences would come, so that our people might study and get to appreciate this grand music? They require to be heard many times, until their melodies wander through our vacant minds unconsciously as we walk and as we work. A repeated performance of *"The Messiah,"* as good as the two given last winter, would do more to bring out the latent musical taste of the people, than anything else unless it were a very perfect opera, which we cannot have.

Next to the oratorios, we remember with most pleasure the two concerts of Mr. Rackemann, and the two of Mr. Kossowski, the distinguished pianists. These gentlemen are both artists; the former superior in chaste elegance and finish of execution, the latter in fire and energy. The former seems to have accomplished most; the latter promises most,—there is inspiration, as well as skill in his performance. They have introduced us to the new school of Piano Forte playing, and have let us hear some of the wonderful feats of Thalberg, Dohler, Chopin, Henselt, and Liszt. These masters have given a new meaning to the Piano Forte, having, by indefatigable practice superadded to more or less of genius, attained to a mastery of its powers, and bringing out the peculiar soul (as it were) of the instrument, in a way unknown before. Their compositions are peculiarly Piano Forte compositions, and adapted to the display of their new arts of astonishing execution. It was a satisfaction to hear them. They certainly have a great deal of character, and are interesting in their kind. We can enjoy them for what they are, without complaining that they are not something else. They are rich, brilliant, wild, astonishing. They revel in insatiable rapture and rage of all fantastic motions. They are the heaving of the billowy deep, now dark, now lit by gleams of lightning; they are the sweeping breeze of the forest; they are the flickering aurora; they are the cool flow of the summer evening zephyr; they are the dance of the elves by moonlight; they are everything marvellous and exquisite. There is marked individuality, too, in the works of each. There is sweet pathos in the *Notturnes* of Chopin. There is a fond, dreamy home-sickness in the *"Souvenir de Varsovie,"* by Henselt; and in his *"If I were a bird I'd fly to thee,"* how the soul dissolves and floats away!—the instrument becomes fluid. The *"Galope Chromatique"* of Liszt, was altogether the wildest and most original thing of all, and displayed a genius which we might expect from this devout admirer of Beethoven. We can admire too, though without much lasting soul-satisfaction, the massive, gorgeous constructiveness of Thalberg. One of the novelties of this style of playing, which is highly expressive, consists in carrying on an air in the middle of the instrument, with a florid accompaniment playing around it, above and below. The story seems transacted betwixt earth and sky. In this way the whole length of the Piano Forte speaks at once, and it becomes quite an orchestra in itself. It is with pleasure that we record these things, and we hope to have an opportunity to appreciate them better, that we may judge them more discriminatingly. But we should have been much more pleased to have heard the Sonatas of Beethoven, the *"Concert-Stuck"* of Weber, and such true classic works, not written for the sake of displaying the Piano Forte, but for the sake of music. The pianists of the day show too much of ambition, too little of inspiration, of true art-feeling, in their playing and their choice of subjects. These performances were varied by two Trios of Beethoven, for Piano, Violin, &c., given in the best style of our young German professors, who always play as if they breathed an element which we do not. These were rare sounds in our concert rooms. The few artists who cultivate this diviner music, seem to keep it to themselves, and to feel that it would be casting pearls before swine to produce it before audiences, which can be enraptured about Russell. But was not the result in these trials encouraging? There was profound silence in the room, followed by a gleam of pure satisfaction on most faces as we looked round;—or was it only the fancied reflection of our own mood? We think not. Let us have more of this. How can we ever have taste enough to keep musicians warm, if they will risk nothing upon us, and never give us a chance to hear the best?

Mr. Knight's last concert deserves particular notice as being the first and the only promiscuous concert in this place, composed entirely of classic pieces from great masters. It was music for the few, who, we trust, are gradually becoming more; and we were surprised that all the lovers of good music did not come out. Here we had Beethoven's *"Adeläide;"* which, however, we were sorry to hear transposed into an English song, *"Rosalie,"* which is not nearly so beautiful, and is moreover an entire change of subject, not the theme which first inspired the music. Mr. Knight sang it in his usual chaste and true style; though with hardly enough of feeling. The second movement, too, was sung much too rapidly; it did not give the ear time to dwell upon those magnificent chords of the accompaniment, which is as wonderful as the part for the voice. But for a just criticism of this and of the whole concert we would refer to the excellent "Musical Magazine" of Mr. Hach,—a work which we are glad to notice in passing; for, next to good music itself, good musical criticism should be hailed as among the encouraging signs. Mr. Knight also sang with great effect *"The Gravedigger,"* by Kalliwoda, and *"The Erl-King,"* by Schubert, two genuine flowers of German song. Then there was a Canzonet of Haydn, a *"Gratias Agimus,"* by Guglielmi, a Septuor of Haydn's, and another of Mozart's, and several more pieces of that order. Mr. Knight is perhaps the most accomplished musician of all the singers who have visited us. Some of his own compositions are original and highly intellectual. His skill in accompaniment is remarkable. For a promiscuous audience his singing of a common sentimental song is too cold, and fails to move; but his singing of such music as the songs in *"The Creation,"* is more than faultless. If he remains with us, we trust he will continue to presume upon the growing taste of the public, and to labor for Art more than popularity. Such efforts will in time be rewarded by the formation of a sure and appreciative audience.

The "Amateur Orchestra" have cultivated the higher classic music with encouraging success, and by the concerts to which they invite their friends occasionally, do much to create a taste for the best Symphonies and Overtures. On the last occasion they were assisted by the "Social Glee Club." The performances of both were excellent, and the selection of pieces such as would interest an audience of musicians. The house was crowded. The grand and dark Overtures of Kalliwoda, another by Romberg, that of Tancredi, and a Symphony by Ries, the pupil of Beethoven, were given with much effect, and evidently felt by the crowd. Of a similar character, though more miscellaneous, was the complimentary concert gotten up by the members of the musical corps for Mr. Asa Warren, the modest and deserving leader for many years of the Handel and Haydn Orchestra. Enthusiasm for the man brought together the largest orchestra, which has yet appeared in our city. The overture to *"La Gazza Ladza"** was admirably executed; it is worth noticing, that this was the first instance we remember of an Overture's being repeated at the call of an audience. This promises something. We could not but feel that the materials, that evening collected, might, if they could be kept together through the year, and induced to practice, form an Orchestra worthy to execute the grand works of Haydn and Mozart. Orchestra and audience would improve together, and we might even hope to hear one day the *"Sinfonia Eroica,"* and the *"Pastorale"* of Beethoven.

The Boston Academy have been very lately giving a short series of public performances, which should be among the most attractive and popular, if there is any charm in the names of Haydn, Sebastian Bach, Fesca, Pasiello, [**] &c. But the audience was not worthy of the occasion. The general public, those who go to concerts for amusement or from the fashion of the thing, had doubtless been wearied out with concerts long before. Still worse, those who went seemed not to be mainly of the musical class; and a magnificent Organ Fugue of Bach, performed by Mr. Müller, the most accomplished organist who has been among us, was thrown away upon a yawning, talking assembly. The *"Spring,"* from Haydn's *"Seasons,"* was better appreciated because of its sprightliness. The Academy want Solo singers. Moreover, their style of singing seems too merely mechanically precise, without glow, and a common consciousness blending instruments and voices into one. Our people are not yet so musical that they can be attracted by a piece without regard to the performer. They will go to hear Caradori, Rackemann, &c. sooner than they will to hear Mozart or Haydn. But we hope the Academy will persevere in producing what they can of the great music. The audience one day will come round.

Much more might be mentioned. But we have not space. And it was our purpose only to mention what stood out in our memory most prominently as signs of real progress. Looking back over this wide field of concerts, we note the few sunny spots. Our "Dial" does not tell the time of day, except the sun shine. It ignores what is dull and merely of course, and proclaims the signs of hope.

Were this the proper place, we might say much of what has been done in a quieter way in private musical circles. Much of the choicest music, of what the English call *"Chamber music,"* has been heard and enjoyed in various houses by the few. Were all these little circles brought together it would form a musical public, which no artist need despise. This leads us to make a few suggestions in view of a coming concert season.

We want two things. Frequent public performances of the best music, and a constant audience, of which the two or three hundred most musical persons in the community shall be the nucleus. Good music has been so rare, that when it comes, those, who know how to enjoy such, do not trust it, and do not go.

To secure these ends, might not a plan of this kind be realized. Let a few of our most accomplished and refined musicians institute a series of cheap instrumental concerts, like the Quartette Concerts, or the "Classic Concerts" of Moscheles in England. Let them engage to perform Quartettes, &c., with occasionally a Symphony, by the best masters and no other. Let them repeat the best and most characteristic pieces enough to make them a study to the audience. To ensure a proper audience there should be subscribers to the course. The two or three hundred, who are scattered about and really long to hear and make acquaintance with Beethoven and Haydn,

[*La Gazza Ladra (The Thieving Magpie), by Rossini, an 1817 opera adorned with one of that master's most successful overtures.]

[**Alexander Ernst Fesca (1820-1849) and Giovanni Paisiello (1741-1816)]

could easily be brought together by such an attraction, and would form a nucleus to whatever audience might be collected, and would give a tone to the whole, and secure attention. Why will not our friends, Messrs. Schmidt, Hach, Isenbech, &c. undertake this? It might be but a labor of love at the outset; but it would create in time the taste which would patronize it and reward it.

Might not a series of lectures too, on the different styles and composers be instituted under the auspices of the Academy, or some other association, parallel with the musical performances? A biography and critical analysis of the musical genius of Handel, for instance, would add interest to the performance of *"The Messiah."*

D.

Music.

One class of persons seeks the soul of Music, and dwells in it; another, the laws which reign in its creations; and a third, the form in which it is embodied, the actual beauty as it charms the sense. To one it is a feeling, a sentiment, a passion; to another it is a science; to another, a sensible creation and enjoyment. The heart, the intellect, and the senses; the soul, the body, and the everlasting laws; the active prompting motive, the passive substance into which it pours its will, and the impersonal regulating reason mediating between will and action;—what more enters into our existence as a whole, or into any single experience or act of ours? At any moment, there is somewhat prompting us within; some thought, accompanying that prompting, to guide it to its end; and some passive instrument or object, endowed with motion or with form, in obedience to that prompting and that thought. We *will,* from inmost passion; we *see,* by light not our own; we *go,* as the world opens to receive us. Thus in life there are three forces:—Motives, which are first, and spring from within; secondly, guiding principles and laws, independent of us, yet involved in us and in every thing; thirdly, actions or expressions, which are the body or thing moved. And these are the three elements of music, as well as of our lives, presiding over all its grand and primary divisions.

In the history also of music, since music could be called an art, which is only in comparatively modern times, each of these three component elements of music has exercised ascendancy in turn. The scientific phase, that is, the learned style, came first in the order of development, with the Bachs; the music of expression, of sentiment, the grand deep poetry and soul of the art, came next, with Haydn and Mozart, Handel and Beethoven; the music of effect, the music of the senses, the age of Rossinis and instrumental virtuosos, has succeeded. Historic periods and scientific doctrine correspond part to part in a series of three terms.

To the three spheres of sentiment, of science, and of practice, conform three classes of character, in whom each respectively predominates. We feel the spirit of the first; we admire the intellect of the second; we deal only with the actions of the third. We turn to the first for inspiration and for influence; to the second for reasons and methods; to the third for execution, whether in the way of amusement or of use. The highest type of the first class is the saint; of the second, the philosopher; and of the third, the statesman. Their collective organizations, from of old, have been the Church, the University, and the State. A corresponding division holds in every department of life, in every art, in every subject of inquiry. Its keen blade passed through each and all, when Thought began. It is the primary analysis of the universe, which the mysteries of the church have carried even into the inmost nature of the Deity.

These analogies, accidentally started, lead directly into the inmost essence of the science and the art of music. The number Three is the number of science; and there is a certain poetry of science, which consists in tracing the presence of the same great laws, and detecting the same type in all things; so that one sphere becomes an expression and reflection, as it were, of every other; so that the passions and emotions of our soul read themselves acknowledged, and enjoy their own harmonies anew, in every kingdom of nature and the arts. So much it is necessary to glance at in the science of music,—that divine source of enthusiasm, that transcendent medium of expression, that homelike yet mysterious element of passion, of the love that yearns for the human, or that climbs in secret aspiration, flame-like, to the infinite Heart of hearts, centre of light and warmth, in whom all spirits seek their unity.

But science is not the essence of music. It is not the warm, glowing thing itself. It is only the measure of its heart-beats, the law that distributes the ramification of the innumerable ducts and channels through which that heart propels its lifeblood. It is the principle of order in the system, the divider of the one into the many, which resent resemblance in each other, and wander off in every way from uniformity, only that they may be the more completely one; or, in other words, that unity may become universality. Since, however, unity precedes variety, since it is only the whole which can explain the parts, we will not follow the spiral path of the restless analyzer and divider, Science, before we have characterized the whole, which in this case it divides.

Music is both body and soul, like the man who delights in it. Its body is beauty in the sphere of sound,—*audible beauty.* But in this very word *beauty* is implied a soul, a moral end, a meaning of some sort, a something which makes it of interest to the inner life of man, which relates it to our invisible and real self. This beauty, like all other, results from the marriage of a spiritual fact with a material form, from the rendering external, and an object of sense, what lives in essence only in the soul. Here the material part, which is measured sound, is the embodiment and sensible representative, as well as the re-acting cause, of that which we call impulse, sentiment, feeling, the spring of all our action and expression. In a word, it is the language of the heart; —not an arbitary and conventional representative, as a spoken or written word is; but a natural, invariable, pure type and correspondence. Speech, so far as it is distinct from music, sustains the same relation to the head. Speech is the language of ideas, the communicator of thought, the Mercury of the intellectual Olympus enthroned in each of us. But behind all thought, there is something deeper, and much nearer life. Thought is passive, involuntary, cold, varying with what it falls upon like light, a more or less clear-sighted guide to us, but not a prompting energy, and surely not our very essence; not the source either of any single act, or of that whole complex course and habit of action which we call our character. Thought has no impulse in itself, any more than the lungs have. "Out of the *heart* are the issues of life." Its loves, its sentiments, its passions, its prompting impulses, its irresistible attractions, its warm desires and aspirations,—these are the masters of the intellect, if not its law; these people the blank consciousness with thoughts innumerable; these, though involuntary in one sense, are yet the principle of will in us, and are the spring of all activity, and of all thought too, since they, in fact, strike out the light they see to act by. The special moments and phases of this active principle we call emotions; and music, which I hold to be its natural language, has for its very root and first principle, and is actually born from, motion.

Sound is generated by motion; rhythm is measured motion; and this is what distinguishes music from every other art of expression. Painting, sculpture, architecture, are all quiescent: they address us in still contemplation. But music is all motion, and it is nothing else.

And so in its effects. It does not rest, that we may contemplate it; but it hurries us away with it. Our very first intimation of its presence is, that we are moved by it. Its thrilling finger presses down some secret spring within us, and instantly the soul is on its feet with an emotion. Painting and sculpture

rather give the idea of an emotion, than directly move us; and, if speech can raise or quell a passion, it is because there is kneaded into all speech a certain leaven of the divine fire called music. The same words and sentences convey new impressions with every honest change of tone and modulation in the speaker's voice; and, when he rises to any thing like eloquence, there is a certain buoyant rhythmical substratum of pure tone on which his words ride, as the ship rides on the ocean, borrowing its chief eloquence from that. Take out the consonants which break up his speech, and the vowels flow on musically. How often will the murmur of a devout prayer overcome a remote hearer with more of a religious feeling, than any apprehension of the distinct words could, if he stood nearer!

Music is a universal language, subtly penetrating all the walls of time and space. It is no more local than the mathematics, which are its impersonal reason, just as sound is its body, and feeling or passion is its soul. The passions of the human heart are radically alike, and answer to the same tones everywhere and always, except as they may be undeveloped; and music has a power to develope them, like an experience of life. It can convey a foretaste of moods and states of feeling yet in reserve for the soul, of loves which yet have never met an object that could call them out. A musical composition is the best expression of its author's inmost life. No persons in all history are so intimately known to those that live away from them or after them, as are Handel, Mozart, Beethoven, Weber, Schubert, Bellini, and others, to those who enter into the spirit of their musical works. For they have each bequeathed the very wine of his peculiar life in this form, that it sparkles still the same as often as it is opened to the air. The sounds may effervesce in each performance; but they may be woke to life again at any time. So it is with the passions and emotions which first dictated the melodious creations.

Hence it is that great composers have no biography, except their music. Theirs is a life of deep, interior sentiment, of ever-active passion and affection, of far-reaching aspiration, rather than of ideas or events; theirs is the wisdom of love; their belief is faith, the felt creed of the heart; and they dwell in the peculiar element of that, in the wondrous *tone-world,* communicating all the strongest, swiftest, and most delicate pulsations of their feeling to the ready vibrations of wood or metal or string, which propagate themselves through the equally ready vibrations of the air, and of every other medium, till they reach the chambers of the ear, and set in motion chords more sensitive, that vibrate on the nervous boundary between matter and the soul; and there, what was vibration becomes sound, and the hearer has caught the spirit of the composer. Yes: the whole soul of a Beethoven thrills through your soul, when you have actually heard one of his great symphonies. There is no other communion of so intimate a nature possible, as that which operates through music. Intimate, and yet most mystical; intimacy not profaned by outward contact of familiarity, but a meeting and communing of the ideal, one with another, which never grows familiar. Why is it but because in sentiment the tendency always is to unity, while thought for ever differentiates and splits? Feeling communicates by sympathy, or fellow-feeling, the earth round; and music is its common language, which admits no dialects, and means the same in Europe and America. Light corresponds to thought; and light is changed and colored by every medium through which it shoots, by every surface which reflects it. Sound, or, which is the same thing, measured motion or vibration, corresponds to feeling, and its vibrations are passed on through every medium unchanged, except as they grow fainter. Light is volatile; but sound is constant: so it is when you compare thought with feeling, which last comes more from the centre where all souls are one.

Music is religious and prophetic. She is the real Sibyl, chanting evermore of unity. Over wild, waste oceans of discord floats her silvery voice, the harbinger of love and hope. Every genuine strain of music is a serene prayer, or bold, inspired demand, to be united with all, at the Heart of all things. Her appeal to the world is more loving than the world can yet appreciate. Kings and statesmen, and men of affairs, and men of theories, would stand aside from their own over-rated occupations to listen to her voice, if they knew how nearly it concerned them, how much more it goes to the bottom of the matter, and how clearly she forefeels humanity's great destiny. The soul that is truly receptive of music learns angelic wisdom, and grows more childlike with experience. The sort of experience which music gives does not plough cunning furrows in the brow of the fresh soul, nor darken its expressive face by knitting there the tangled lines of Satan. Here, the most deeply initiated are in spirit the most youthful; and Hope delights to wait on them.

The native impulses of the soul, or what are variously called the passions, affections, propensities, desires, are, all of them, when considered in their essence and original unwarped tendency, so many divinely implanted loves. Union, harmony of some sort, is their very life. To meet, to unite, to blend, by methods intricate as swift, is their whole business and effort through eternity. As is their attraction, such must be their destiny; not to collision, not to excess followed by exhaustion; not to discord,

chaos, and confusion; but to binding ties of fitness and conjunction through all spheres, from the simplest to the most universal accords. Through these (how else?) are the hearts of the human race to be knit into one mutually conscious, undivided whole, one living temple not too narrow, nor too fragmentary for the reception of the Spirit of Good. Is not this foretold in music, the natural language of these passions, which cannot express corruption nor any evil feeling, without ceasing to be music; which has no tone for any bad passion, and translates into harmony and beauty whatever it expresses? The blending of all these passions harmoniously into one becomes the central love, the deepest and most undivided life of man. This is the love of God, as it also, from the first, is the inbreathing of God, who is love; to whom the soul seeks its way, by however blind an instinct, through all these partial harmonies, learning by degrees to understand the universal nature of its desire and aim. The sentiment of unity, the strongest and deepest sentiment of which man is capable, the great affection into which all his affections flow—to find, not lose themselves; which looks to the source when little wants conflict, and straightway they are reconciled in emulous ardor for the glory of the whole; which lifts a man above the thought of self, by making him in every sense fully himself, by reuniting his prismatic, party-colored passions into one which is as clear and universal as the light; the sentiment which seeks only universal harmony and order, so that all things, whether of the inner or of the outer world, may be perfectly transparent to the love in which they have their being, and that the sole condition of all peace and happiness, the consciousness of one in all and all in one, may never more be wanting;—that is what the common sense of mankind means by the *religious* sentiment,—that is the pure essence of religion. Music is its natural language, the chief rite of its worship, the rite which cannot lose its sacredness; for music cannot cease to be harmony, cannot cease to symbolize the sacred relationship of each to all, cannot contract a taint, any more than the sumbeam which shines into all corners. Music cannot narrow or cloak the message which it bears; it cannot lie; it cannot raise questions in the mind, or excite any other than a pure enthusiasm. It is God's alphabet, and not man's; unalterable and unpervertable; suited for the harmony of the human passions and affections; and sent us, in this their long winter of disharmony and strife, to be a perpetual type and monitor, rather say an actual foretaste, of that harmony which must yet come. How could there be religion without music? That sentiment would create it again, would evoke its elements out of the completest jargon of discords, if the scale and the accords, and all the use of instruments, were forgotten. Let that feeling deepen in our nation, and absorb its individual ambitions, and we shall have our music greater than the world has known. There *was* an age of faith, though the doctrinal statements and the forms thereof were narrow. Art, however, freed the spirit which the priest imprisoned. Music, above all, woke to celestial power and beauty in the bosom of a believing though an ignorant age. The Catholic church did not neglect this great secret of expression and of influence; and the beautiful free servant served it in a larger spirit than itself had dreamed of. Where it could not teach the Bible, where its own formal interpretations thereof were perhaps little better than stones for bread, it could breathe the spirit of the Bible and of all love and sanctity into the most ignorant and thoughtless worshipper, through its sublime Masses, at once so joyous and so solemn, so soul-subduing and so soul-exalting, so full of tenderness, so full of rapture uncontrollable, so confident and so devout. In these, the hearer did, for the time being, actually *live* celestial states. The mystery of the cross and the ascension, the glorious doctrine of the kingdom of heaven, were not reasoned out to his understanding, but passed through his very soul, like an experience, in these all-permeating clouds of sound; and so the religion became in him an emotion, which could not so easily become a thought, which had better not become such thought as the opinionated teachers of the visible church would give him. The words of the Credo never yet went down with all minds; but their general tenor is universal, and music is altogether so. Music extracts and embodies only the spirit of the doctrine, that inmost life of it which all feel, and miraculously revivifies and transfigures the cold statements of the understanding with the warm faith of feeling. In music there is no controversy; in music there are no opinions: its springs are deeper than the foundations of any of these partition walls, and its breath floats undivided over all their heads. No danger to the Catholic whose head is clouded by dull superstitions, while his heart is nourished and united with the life of all lives by this refreshing dew!

The growing disposition, here and there, among select musical circles, to cultivate acquaintance with this form of music, is a good sign. What has been called sacred music in this country has been the least sacred in every thing but the name, and the forced reverence paid it. With the superstitions of the past, the soul of nature also was suppressed; and the free spirit of music found small sphere amid our loud *protestings*. A joyless religion of the intellect merely, which could almost find fault with the sun's shining, closed every pore of the self-mortified and frozen soul against the subtle, insinuating warmth of this most eloquent apostle of God. The sublime

sincerity of that wintry energy of self-denial having for the most part passed away, and the hearts of the descendants of the Pilgrims having become opened to all worldly influences, why should they not be also visited by the heavenly corrective of holy and enchanting music, which is sure to call forth and to nourish germs of loftier affection? Can the bitter spirit of sectarianism, can the formal preachings of a worldly church which strives to keep religion so distinct from life, can the utilitarian ethics of this great day of trade, give the soul such nourishment and such conviction of the higher life as the great religious music of Mozart and Haydn and Beethoven? The pomp and pageantry of the Mass we have not. But the spiritual essence lives in the music itself; and a mere quartette of voices, a social friendly group, bound alike by moral and by musical sympathies, may drink this inspiration, may pour it out on others. The songs and operas of the day, which take the multitude, become insipid in comparison with such music.

Greatest of all masters in this peculiar line was Mozart,—the *boy* Mozart we might say,—who wrote the major part of his eighteen Masses ere he had reached his twenty-second year; and yet they seem, the best of them, to have been wrung from the profoundest experiences of the long-tried heart of a man, as well as to pour forth the raptures of a bright seraph-soul, which has not yet buried any portion of its heavenly inheritance in the earth.

In music of this kind, there is somewhat that is peculiar to the individuality of the composer; but there is more that is universal, true to the inmost meaning of all hearts. Every sentiment, if it is deep enough, becomes religion; for every sentiment seeks and tends to unity, to harmony, to recognition of the one in all. And every sentiment in music is expressed in its purity, and carried up as it were to the blending point of all the emotions in one, which is the radical desire and feeling of the soul, its passion to be one with God.

If Mozart is perhaps the deepest in this order of composition, he by no means stands alone. The church afforded to genius that sphere, for its highest and holiest ambition, which it found not elsewhere. The Masses of Haydn are more numerous, and more of them elaborate, great efforts, than those of Mozart, many of whose Masses were composed at so early an age; and his genius steadily drew him towards that sphere of music, in which he was destined to reign supreme,—the opera. But, though to Haydn we must grant the very perfection of artistic skill and grace, a warm and childlike piety, and a spirit of the purest joy; and though at times he has surpassing tenderness; still there is an indescribable atmosphere, an air of inspiration, a gushing forth as of the very warmest, inmost life-blood, in Mozart's religious music, which affects us, even when it is simpler than Haydn's, with more power. Religion takes in Haydn more the form of gratitude and joy. The mournfulness of a *Miserere* or a *Crucifixus* of his is a passive mood, often but the successful contemplation or painter's study of such a mood, where the subject calls for it, rather than a permanent and inherent quality in the whole music of his own being. His ground tone seems to be a certain domestic grateful sense of life, in which the clearest order and the sweetest kindliness and thankfulness for ever reign. In Mozart the ground tone is love, the very ecstacy and celestial bliss of the re-union of two souls long separated, at once romantic and Platonic, sensuous, and yet exalting the senses to a most spiritual ministry. In him we have what is nearest to the naked soul of music,— its most ethereal, transparent, thrilling body. One would scarce suppose, that the soul of Mozart ever inhabited any other body than those melodies and harmonies in which it dwells for us. Something of a personal love, however, is felt in his most religious strains: it is the worship of the Holy Virgin; the music of that phase of the religious sentiment, which Swedenborg might call conjugal love.

To Beethoven's three or four great Masses, it comes most natural to add the term *solemn;* for, with him, all is a great effort. It is the very sentiment of the man,—aspiration, boundless yearning to embrace the Infinite. With him the very discontent of the soul becomes religion, and opens sublime visions, which are like a flying horizon of ever near, yet unattainable order and beauty. In the inexhaustibleness of the heart's cravings, he finds revelations; and out of those depths, with gloomy grandeur, with fire now smothered and now breaking out, and always with a rapt impetuosity, the worship of his nature springs, escaping like a flame to heaven.

Then, too, besides this captivating music of the Catholic church, we should think of the plain church, the voices of the united multitude, in simple, solemn, sublime strains, presenting themselves as one before the Lord. Even our modern psalm, as monotonous and artificial as it often is, satisfying scarcely more than the grammatical conditions of a musical proposition, has oftentimes an unsurpassable grandeur. Where thousands sing the same slow melody, the mighty waves of sound wake in the air their own accompaniment, and the effect is that of harmony. On this broad popular basis, Handel built. He is the Protestant, the people's man, in music. In him the great sentiment of a common humanity found expression. The individual vanishes: it is the mighty music of humanity; his theme, the one first theme, and properly the burthen of all music, humanity's

looking-for and welcome of its Messiah. What a prediction and foreshadowing of the future harmony and unity of the whole race is that great Oratorio! What are those choruses, those hallelujahs and amens, but the solemn ecstacy, the calm, because universal and all-sympathizing, everywhere sustained excitement, which all souls shall feel; when all shall feel their unity with all humanity, and with all to God.

And it is not alone in the music of the church of any form, whether mass or plainer choral, that this sentiment is strongest. Perhaps no music ever stirred profounder depths in the hearer's religious consciousness, than some great orchestral symphonies, say those of Beethoven. Even a waltz of his, it has been said, is more religious than a prayer of Rossini's. His symphonies are like great conflagrations of some grand piles of architecture, in which the material substance seems consumed, while the spirit soars in the graceful but impatient crackling shapes of the devouring element, and is swiftly lost in upper air.

Dwight's Journal of Music.

INTRODUCTORY.

We here present, some days in advance of date, the first number of a new weekly Journal of Music and the Fine Arts; which we take the liberty of sending, as a specimen, to some thousands of persons, who may be interested in the discussion of these subjects. And yet it hardly can be called a specimen; since in a single number there is barely room to indicate, still less to treat, all sides and points of our design. Besides, it is a *first* number, a first attempt amid much hurry and distraction, to produce a rough sketch which may serve to give some notion of what we hope to do more perfectly as we become more at home in the outward limitations and conditions of our work.

This time, the accidents of starting have had a large share in the composition and shaping of the number. Our news is necessarily not of the newest; and then the best that we could do was to place one musical region in the foreground and foreshorten all the rest, including Germany, "the land of real music," which another time must occupy the front space and the largest. Our review of our own concert season is diffused over too much ground to amount to much more than a brief, dry abstract. Our Correspondence is scarcely organized. Our best articles and essays, among which we number some choice contributions, have had to yield place for the present to lighter and shorter things; but they will keep. Our talk of other Arts, besides the Tone-Art (as the Germans call it) is a mere intimation that we *mean* to talk about them, and that we invite sincere communications thereon from the lovers and connoisseurs in each of their departments. Of Sacred Music, as such, and of that formidable business in our land, music-teaching, we have this time not a word; but will not those texts claim their full share of us, as the annual Pentacost [sic] of psalm-book makers and Conventions comes round? Take this, than, as a sample only of the outward "form and pressure" of our journalism, of our good printer's clever way of making us "presentable," and for the rest turn to our Prospectus on the first page.

Our columns overflow, and we could barely save ourselves this little space for the unfolding of the motives and the spirit of our undertaking. Without being in any sense a thoroughly educated musician, either in theory or practice, we have found ourselves, as long as we could remember, full of the appeal which this most mystical and yet most human Art, (so perfectly intelligible to feeling, if not to the understanding,) has never ceased to make to us. From childhood, there was an intense interest and charm to us in all things musical; the rudest instrument and most hacknied player thereof seemed invested with a certain halo, and saving grace, as it were, from a higher, purer and more genial atmosphere than this of our cold selfish, humdrum world. We could not sport with this, and throw it down like common recreations. It spoke a *serious* language to us, and seemed to challenge study of its strange important meanings, like some central oracle of oldest and still newest wisdom. And this at a time, when the actual world of music lay in the main remote from us, shooting only now and then some stray vibrations over into this western hemisphere. We felt that Music must have some most intimate connection with the social destiny of Man; and that, if we but knew it, it concerns us all.

A few years have passed, and now this is a general feeling. Music is a feature in the earnest life and culture of advanced American society. It enters into all our schemes of education. It has taken the initiative, as the popular Art *par excellence,* in gradually attempering this whole people to the sentiment of Art. And whoever reflects upon it, must regard it as a most important saving influence in this rapid expansion of our democratic life. Art, and especially Music, is a true conservative element, in which Liberty and Order are both fully typed and made beautifully perfect in each other. A free people must be *rhythmically* educated in the whole tone and temper of their daily life; must be taught the instinct of rhythm and harmony in all things, in order to be fit for freedom. And it is encouraging, amid so many dark and wild signs of the times, that this artistic sentiment is beginning to ally itself with our progressive energies and make our homes too beautiful for ruthless change.

Our motive, then, for publishing a Musical Journal lies in the fact that Music has made such rapid progress here within the last fifteen, and even the last ten years. Boston has been without such a paper, and Boston has its thousands of young people, who go regularly to hear all good performances of the best classic models in this art. Its rudiments are taught in all our schools. The daughters of not the wealthy only pursue it into the higher branches; and music teachers count up well amid the other industrial categories. Think of fifteen hundred people, listening every week to orchestral rehearsals of the great symphonies and overtures! Think of those August "Conventions," when thousands from all parts of the country spend whole weeks together in lessons and rehearsals of great Choral and Oratorio music! Think how familiarly and how exactingly we talk of the opera singers, before whom our early admirations have entirely vanished! Think of the ovations of the LIND, and our whole nation's homage paid to Art, the moment that it came to us incarnated for once in so pure a living form!

All this requires an organ, a regular bulletin of progress; something to represent the movement, and at the same time help to guide it to the true end. Very confused, crude, heterogeneous is this sudden musical activity in a young, utilitarian people. A thousand specious fashions too successfully dispute the place of true Art in the favor of each little public. It needs a faithful, severe, friendly voice to point out steadfastly the models of the True, the *ever* Beautiful, the Divine.

We dare not promise to be all this; but what we promise is, at least an *honest* report, week by week, of what we hear and feel and in our poor way understand of this great world of Music, together with what we receive through the ears and feeling and understanding of others, whom we trust; with every sidelight from the other Arts.

The *tone* of our criticisms will, we hope, be found impartial, independent, catholic, conciliatory; aloof from personal cliques and feuds; cordial to all good things, but not too eager to chime in with any powerful private interest of publisher, professor, concert giver, manager, &c. This paper would make itself the "Organ" of no school or class, but simply *an* organ of what we have called the musical *movement* in this country; of the growing love of deep and genuine music. It will insist much on the claims of "Classical" music, and point out its beauties and its meanings;—not with a pedantic partiality, but because the enduring needs so often to be held up in contrast with the ephemeral. But it will also aim to recognize what good there is in styles more simple, popular, or modern; will give him who is Italian in his tastes an equal hearing with him who is German; and will print the articles of those opposed to the partialities or the opinions of the editor, provided they be written briefly, in good temper and to the point.

JONAS CHICKERING.

The grave has closed over what was mortal of that good man. The funeral was from Trinity Church, on Monday morning. Long before the appointed hour, the galleries, porches, and purlieus of the church were thronged with persons of all classes, eager to join in this last sad tribute of respect, and many a tear told how sincere the general sorrow. All met on common ground, for all had lost a *friend.* For Jonas Chickering was a representative man; he stood for the general tie of *friendship,* so far as this entered as a living element into the multifarious life of this large community. The terms friend, neighbor, fellow-citizen, *meant more* to us when we met his face and took his hand.

The funeral cortége was very large, consisting, besides the immediate family and friends of the deceased, of the members of the Handel and Haydn and of the Musical Education Societies, the Massachusetts Charitable Mechanic Association, several Masonic bodies, the workmen of his factory, to the number of some two hundred, and other bodies of piano-forte manufacturers and their employees. These, with nearly all the resident musical professors and principal amateurs, and many of our most distinguished citizens, occupied the body of the church. There were crowds who could not find entrance. The solemnities consisted of the Episcopal service read by Bishop Eastburn and his assistant, and of solemn music by the organist and choir of the church. The societies above-named escorted the procession to Cambridge bridge, where carriages were provided for the many who wished to follow his remains to their last resting-place at Mount Auburn.

Beautiful as well as sad has been this unanimous expression of feeling called forth by the sudden departure of a plain and unpretending good man. It is safe to say that no man's loss in this community would have been felt so universally. Yet he was not a public man, nor one possessed of brilliant, outwardly-commanding qualities. In person and in manner he was meekness and simplicity itself. Of humble origin, remembered without shame, he was humble always, humble in prosperity, but in the true, Christian, positive sense of the word humble. He was, emphatically, one of the people, meeting all persons, his own workmen, and the objects of his thousand nameless acts of charity, as equals. By his own mechanical genius and industry, and by his integrity and social sincerity and kindliness, which

is the best part of social tact, he had risen to the place he occupied as the head of the great business of piano-forte making in this country. Industry, sincerity, and kindness were the only credentials that he asked in others. In matters of church and state he had taken his place, and with the more "conservative" so-called; but always it seemed that friend and neighbor and fellow-citizen and fellow-being were of much more account to him than follower of the same creed or party. He had his opinions, and perhaps his prejudices, but a refreshing liberality told in his conversation and his conduct. He loved to talk—of music *best,* to be sure—but heartily of all things interesting the attention of the community; and he judged thoughts and statements by the two tests of a sound intuitive common-sense and a good heart, rather than by traditions and prevailing ways of thinking. This, we believe, will be the universal testimony of the friends, old and young, who used to "drop in at Chickering's" of an afternoon, after the day's business was done, to have a little neighborly, refreshing chat with the mild and genial proprietor.

Mr. Chickering's superior intelligence and really great moral force of purpose almost suffered, in the general impression, from the remarkable development of all the kind and generous and gentle traits in him. Yet those who knew him well know that, without what is called an education, and with no claim to extensive general information, he was really a most intelligent, if not precisely an intellectual man, and that with the most willing and habitual deference to other's thoughts and wishes, he, through all his gentleness, maintained a clear and stedfast purpose of his own. But it was his goodness of heart, his never-ceasing acts of charity, his uniform cordiality and sweetness, that endeared him to all who came within his reach. In the musical world, especially, he was the best and largest representative of all our hospitality. Every artist came to him, sure of hearty welcome and disinterested advice, and, if need were, of active aid in time and money in the furtherance of his artistic success or the lightening of his failure. Many have been the cases of young and struggling talent, where he has furnished the means of education, and where he has since been looked up to almost as a father. To none that needed and deserved was his hand closed; and if his good nature was sometimes imposed upon, was not the loss a thousand times made good to him in such a sentiment as his death shows to have long existed towards him in this whole community?

The whole cause of music in this city owes much to Mr. Chickering. Every worthy enterprise for the promotion of musical taste and culture has numbered him among its most efficient friends and patrons. He was for many years president of the Handel and Haydn Society, and always exercised an important voice in its affairs. He was one of the readiest and largest venturers in the Boston Music Hall enterprise. His pianos and his rooms for rehearsal have been freely at the service of all concert-giving societies or individuals, amateur clubs, &c. He was chairman of the music committee in Trinity Church, and sang there himself in the choir on the last Sunday of his life, volunteering to fill the vacancy occasioned by some difficulty among the regular singers. Our own little journalizing enterprize, too, owes some of its earliest and best encouragement to him.

This public-spirited activity of his was by no means limited to musical matters. He contributed his part largely and in all ways to the industrial, moral, and charitable prestige of our city. He had been three years president of the Mechanic Association when he died; and it was his unwearied personal devotion to the business of its last autumnal fair, which added, perhaps, the grain too much to the weight of care upon his brain, already overtasked by the large and complicated plans for re-arranging and improving his own business, after the destruction of his factory by fire, and brought on the first of the series of paralytic attacks that resulted in his death. He was a member of the Legislature one or two years. He was eminently a society-man, and an active member of many charitable and fraternal institutions. Death found him in the midst of these good works, too heartily and unselfishly engaged in them to heed his sudden coming, for which, however, he was at any time prepared. He was at the house of a neighbor, assisting in a meeting of the government or council of a new college for female medical education, and was expressing his views, when his head sank upon his breast, and earthly consciousness returned no more.

If we have been repeating facts and impressions which for the week past have been the fond themes of every newspaper and private circle, it is because we are not willing that this Journal of Music should be without some record of a life so purely spent and so affectionately esteemed throughout this whole community of music-lovers—some monument, however humble, to his memory. We can say nothing that has not been better said, nothing that is not known to all in this vicinity, and certainly not the hundredth part of what is felt by all who knew him.

Were we to state what always impressed us most in Mr. Chickering, we should say it was the sweet, harmonious, gentle sphere he carried with him. It would seem as if music, which he so dearly loved and so truly appreciated in its highest forms of art, had so harmonized and tempered the whole inner man,

as gradually to mould the naturally plain features of the outward man into a permanent expression of positive beauty. His face and presence in all pleasant companies contributed a certain ideal charm. The glow of heart and goodness made the air mild and genial about him. Such beautiful simplicity seldom meets us in mature years. Our friend was not a highly cultivated man; his education had been plain and practical; yet goodness of heart so shone through him with ever riper, milder, purer light, and music, which he not only heard and loved, but re-enacted daily in good deeds, had wrought such genuine refinement in the whole man, that he was fit society for the best.

The life of Jonas Chickering was what is called an uneventful one. His father was a farmer and blacksmith in the village of New Ipswich, N. H., where he was born in April, 1797, and brought up with a good common-school education. At the age of seventeen he was apprenticed for three years to a cabinet-maker in his native town. He had a natural love for music, and spent much of his leisure in learning to sing by note, and to play on such instruments as were most in use. There was one solitary piano in the village, and one maiden that could play; and we have heard how the bashful lad, eager to drink in the dulcet sounds, would go and linger by the gate, but could not be prevailed upon to enter the house of his musical fair schoolmate. Was she not a sort of St. Cecilia to him? and was not that piano, discoursing simple and old-fashioned music, a rarer revelation and delight to that boy's wondering soul, than many a most artistic concert to the satiated ears of amateurs in cities? In course of time the piano got out of tune and *"out of kilter,"* and the ingenious Jonas must be called upon to try his hand at putting it in order. He succeeded, after much experimenting, in restoring the wondrous machine to usefulness. He was then nineteen, and this was the germ of the great piano-making business which now bears his name. He came to Boston on the 15th of February, 1818, and sought and found employment that very day, where he continued at work for one year. He then entered the employment of Mr. Osborne, the only piano-forte manufacturer in Boston. In 1823 he commenced the business for himself in partnership with Mr. Stewart, who had introduced many improvements in the piano, and had acquired some fame. His old associates tell how the "green youth from the country" soon put himself *en rapport* with the musical doings of the town; how he has been seen playing a clarionet in the streets, to the accompaniment of bass-drum, &c., the old-fashioned military music of the day; and how he sang alto in the choirs of various churches. Such were the plain New England beginnings of the man who afterwards became the centre of musical art and artists in this city. On the twelfth anniversary of his arrival in Boston, he became associated with the late Mr. Mackay, a thorough business-man and capitalist, with whom he continued ten years. The business has since rapidly and steadily expanded to its present magnitude, well known to all. It will still go on, together with the vast improvements which Mr. Chickering was completing, under his three sons, who have all had practical experience in the establishment.

The funeral of Mr. Chickering was a very solemn and imposing occasion, in itself a tribute of the whole community. But we believe it is a very general feeling among our music-loving citizens, that some public musical solemnity in the Music Hall ought soon to take place in token of our respect and sorrow. *Not,* as we have seen suggested, a *concert,* to raise money and erect a monument; but an artistic solemnity, an expression of the general feeling by music, and perhaps by fit words spoken. Let the oldest musical society, the Handel and Haydn, of which he had been president, take the initiative; let all the musical societies, resident professors and artists, music-dealers and music-lovers generally, raise a committee and contribute their energies to make it all it should be. Some of Handel's solemn choruses and lofty songs of faith, one of the orchestral dirges of Beethoven, &c., readily suggest themselves as fit expressions. And why may not one of our choral societies master some portions of Mozart's "Requiem," the grandest funeral music ever written, which is performed once a year in every considerable town in Germany?

VALEDICTORY.

This is the last appearance of the *Journal of Music* which has so long borne our name. For needed rest, as well as to gain time for the solution of certain practical problems (out of which however, nothing has yet come), this *post mortem* number (so to speak, considering how many obituary eulogies and lessons it has called forth) has been delayed beyond our original intention. In the last number (July 16) we frankly gave the reasons for the discontinuance: namely, that the paper does not pay, but actually entails a loss upon its editor, and that said editor, conscious of his own shortcomings, is heartily weary of the struggle to keep the thing alive within such economical limits as render it impossible to make *such* a journal as he has desired.

The truth is, we have for some time been convinced that there is not in this country now, and never has been, any adequate demand or support for a musical journal of the highest tone and character. The last experiment of any promise, the *Musical Review,* established in New York less than three years ago,

was unable to complete its second year. The musical papers that live and flourish financially are those that serve the interests of music trade and manufacture, and which abound in endless columns of insignificant three-line items of intelligence or news; the slang term "newsy" is a description which they covet. A journal which devotes itself to art for art's sake, and strives to serve the ends of real culture, however earnestly and ably, gets praise and compliment, but not support.

Besides, such is the spirit of competition, that the moment a paper seems to be beginning to succeed, instead of concentrating forces upon it to build it up to self-sustaining strength, others, roused by its example, start some new and rival enterprise, dividing the support which might have gone to one really good, important journal, or to two or three good ones. When we began in 1852, there were barely three or four musical journals in this country. Now they count by the hundred, almost every important music-dealer publishing his own organ.

Again, when we began, musical literature of any consequence, in the English language, was extremely meagre. We had to translate largely from the German and the French, to furnish valuable matter for our readers. All this is changed. Musical writers, criticisms, biographies, histories, analyses of great musical works, abound. Especially has the attention paid to music in the daily and weekly press increased of late, while in their quality the newspaper criticisms show a very marked improvement. Musical journals as such, therefore, such as may have been indispensable to culture and the public taste some years ago, now naturally seem almost superfluous. So long as the average music-loving, or music-curious, citizen can read the notice of the last night's concert, fresh and early, as he takes his buckwheats, smoking hot, over his breakfast-table, he is not apt to trouble himself to look into a specialist paper once or twice a month to keep him up to the true pitch of opinion. Of course it is useless for a slow, fortnightly journal, limited to eight pages, to compete with the daily newspaper in *its* speciality of *news.*

Then, too, there is no putting out of sight the fact, that the great themes for discussion, criticism, literary exposition and description, which inspired us in this journal's prime, the masterworks and character and meaning of the immortal ones like Bach and Handel, Mozart, Beethoven, Schubert, and the rest, although they cannot be exhausted, yet inevitably lose the charm of novelty. We have said our say about them all so often, and so fully, have preached so many sermons on these glorious texts, that it is hard to find anything new to say. What more can one write, for instance, about the five and sixtieth Christmas performance of the *Messiah?*—except to compare the singers, or to criticise the execution, and those are matters of but momentary consequence. In a few years it will be the same with the *Passion Music* of Bach. The thoughts we then insisted on from inmost conviction, with a zeal for inciting others to seek, and helping others to appreciate the divine power and beauty and great meaning of those inspired art creations, are now become the common property of all the world. Of course we never owned them, but we felt them and endeavored, somewhat successfully within a narrow, slowly widening circle to make others feel their truth. All true thought, truly stated, inevitably crumbles in the course of time into the smallest current coin. Lacking the genius to make the old seem new, we candidly confess that what now challenges the world as new in music fails to stir us to the same depths of soul and feeling that the old masters did and doubtless always will. Startling as the new composers are, and novel, curious, brilliant, beautiful at times, they do not inspire us as we have been inspired before, and do not bring us nearer heaven (in fact "the other place" is where some of them seem most at home!) We feel no inward call to the proclaiming of the new gospel. We have tried to do justice to these works as they have claimed our notice, and have omitted no intelligence of them which came within the limits of our columns, but we lack motive for entering their doubtful service; we are not ordained their prophet. If these had been enthroned the *Dii majores* of the musical Olympus, and there had been no greater gods: if the contributions of the past thirty years to musical production were the whole of music, we never should have dreamed of establishing a musical journal, nor would Music have been able to seduce us from other paths, in which, by persevering, we might possibly have done more good. It may be all a prejudice; perhaps we are one-sided; perhaps too steady contemplation of the glory of the great age has seared our eyeballs for the modern splendors; but we prefer to leave these and their advocacy to "whom it may concern." Doubtless here is one secret of much of the indifference to this journal: the "disciples of the newness" feel that it has not been in sympathy with what they would call the new musical spirit of the times, and innocent inquirers take the cue from them. But we revenge ourselves with pointing to the unmistakeable fact, that in the concert-giving experience of to-day, at least in Boston, the prurient appetite for novelty (new fashions) seems to have reached its first stage of satiety, and that programmes must in the main be classical to secure good audiences in the long run. If we in any humble way have helped to bring about this good result, we may at least feel that our labor has not

been entirely thrown away.

But whatever may have been the causes of our failure to make this journal what it should be, we are disposed to find them mostly in the editor himself. We cannot endorse the too kind suggestion of the sympathizing writer in the *Springfield Republican,* that Boston, or that the musical public anywhere, has been "ungrateful" to us. Surely we can complain of no "ingratitude" on the part of the press; its treatment has been almost uniformly generous and appreciative; witness the "obituaries" we have copied, not omitting frank and honest strictures on our course. We have long realized that we were not made for the competitive, sharp enterprise of modern journalism. That turn of mind which looks at the ideal rather than the practicable, and the native indolence of temperament which sometimes goes with it, have made our movements slow. Hurry who will, we rather wait and take our chance. The work which could not be done at leisure, and in disregard of all immediate effect, we have been too apt to feel was hardly worth the doing. To be first in the field with an announcement, or a criticism, or an idea, was no part of our ambition; how can one recognize competitors, or enter into competition, and at the same time keep his eye upon the truth? If one have anything worth saying, will it not be as good to-morrow as to-day? A poor qualification for the journalistic scramble of this year 1881! Indeed we cannot scramble. And, far from making any boast of it, we must accuse ourself of great omissions and procrastinations not in accordance with the modern idea of an editor, even in the quiet field of Art. Yet somehow we feel that we have performed a considerable amount of labor, such as it was, in our day.

One of our frank contemporaries, whom we copy elsewhere, says that this has never been a "peoples'" paper. Yes, you have us there. To be a tribune of the people, in your sense, we never felt to be our mission. *Non omnia possumus omnes.* We do not believe in writing down to people. We have been perhaps too sensitively unwilling to insult the popular intelligence by thinking anything too good—any thought, or view of Art, or any music—for the average listener or reader. "State the best that there is in you and the great world will come round to you;" that, in effect, is the Emersonian maxim which has saved many an ingenuous young mind from renouncing its birthright. The few, the most appreciative (and they are not always the most technically prepared ones) must be reached first; what these see, feel and approve, will surely make its way to wider and wider acceptance. This at least has been the lesson of our life. Now if you begin with trying to ingratiate the general mass, "the people," you are in danger either of talking baby talk to them, or of turning your art journal into a musical primer and A B C book, or of chopping everything up into that poor mincemeat (too often dogs' meat) of small paragraphs and items, which so abound in many musical papers, and which catch the idle eye, but do not inform the mind; or of running into petty personalities, which may "spice" a paper, while they sink its dignity; or finally, you fall into the temptation of always striving after and proclaiming the *exceptional,* when wholesome daily bread is the thing most wanted. On this point we make our own confession without shame. In the lower stages of culture, the people, especially we Americans, are easily stirred up to "seek a sign," to be on the *qui vive* for every so-called "big thing." World's fairs are on the brain, and threaten us so frequently that the exceptional spreads over all, and there is no room, time or thought left for the common. It tends to be all mountain with no valleys; all excitement, no repose; all exception and no rule. In music, too, we have our monster festivals and Peace Jubilees, each seeking to surpass the other by its unprecedented scale of magnitude, as if the measure of value were mere size. We have borne our share of satire and rebuke in times past for our cold response to such appeals. We think the world shows signs of coming round to our unpopular way of thinking. And we congratulate our Boston, at least, that she has outgrown such childish ambitions, and has settled down upon regular triennial oratorio festivals (like those of Birmingham and the Rhine cities), within the limits of artistic taste and common-sense.

It only remains for us to return our heartfelt thanks to our faithful and able contributors and correspondents, with all of whom it has been a labor of love, a service of sincere devotion to the good cause in music, to help us make the *Journal* useful and attractive. Some of these have stood by us from the first and proved themselves true friends. The same may be said of many of our subscribers. On their account especially it makes us sad to feel that the little bark, which they have helped so long to keep afloat, cheering our loneliness in the long work, must now go down before reaching the end of its thirtieth annual voyage. They have not the comfort, which we shall have, of a great sense of rest and freedom when the burden is rolled off from our shoulders.

But we do not despair of musical journalism. If it is impracticable within the narrow limits of a little one-man organ like our own, without capital, without the means of enlargement, and unwilling to avail itself of questionable and distasteful ways for gaining circulation, it is still possible that some day somebody will furnish the means for building up a journal upon a much broader foundation, with capital, with room for greater variety of matter in its columns, with means of commanding first-class *paid* contributors, and with not merely one to do all the editorial work, but with a corps of editors, each responsible in his department, and representing, it may be, various sides in some of the great questions, as of old and new school. Such a journal would absorb any rivals worth absorbing; it would have *news* enough, well-sifted news, in spite of the newspapers, while it could afford to treat at length, without fear or favor, questions of principle and taste in Art. All this combined under one experienced, catholic and comprehensive head, who need not feel always bound to write himself on every topic, would be a musical journal worth the while. It is essentially the plan suggested by our unknown warm sympathizer in the *Springfield Republican.* We doubt not it will come. Some music-loving millionaire, not content with guarantying orchestras and building splendid music-halls, will some day feel the need of a great, many-sided, high-toned musical journal. We may live to see it after the springs of active energy are dried up in ourselves. But Art is long, though life is short. And so we humbly take our leave.

JOHN S. DWIGHT.

Music as a Means of Culture

We as a democratic people, a great mixed people of all races, overrunning a vast continent, need music even more than others. We need some ever-present, ever-welcome influence that shall insensibly tone down our self-asserting and aggressive manners, round off the sharp, offensive angularity of character, subdue and harmonize the free and ceaseless conflict of opinions, warm out the genial individual humanity of each and every unit of society, lest he become a mere member of a party, or a sharer of business or fashion. This rampant liberty will rush to its own ruin, unless there shall be found some gentler, harmonizing, humanizing culture, such as may pervade whole masses with a fine enthusiasm, a sweet sense of reverence for something far above us, beautiful and pure; awakening some ideality in every soul, and often lifting us out of the hard hopeless prose of daily life. We need this beautiful corrective of our crudities. Our radicalism will pull itself up by the roots, if it do not cultivate the instinct of reverence. The first impulse of freedom is centrifugal,— to fly off the handle,—unless it be restrained by a no less free impassioned love of order. We need to be so enamored of the divine idea of unity, that that alone—the enriching of that—shall be the real motive for assertion of our individuality. What shall so temper and tone down our "fierce democracy"? It must be something better, lovelier, more congenial to human nature than mere stern prohibition, cold Puritanic "Thou shalt *not!*" What can so quickly magnetize a people into this harmonic mood as music? Have we not seen it, felt it?

The hard-working, jaded millions need expansion, need the rejuvenating, the ennobling experience of joy. Their toil, their church, their creed perhaps, their party livery, and very vote, are narrowing; they need to taste, to breathe a larger, freer life. Has it not come to thousands, while they have listened to or joined their voices in some thrilling chorus that made the heavens seem to open and come down? The governments of the Old World do much to make the people cheerful and contented; here it is all *laissez-faire,* each for himself, in an ever keener strife of competition. We must look very much to music to do this good work for us; we are open to that appeal; we can forget ourselves in that; we blend in joyous fellowship when we can sing together; perhaps quite as much so when we can listen together to a noble orchestra of instruments interpreting the highest inspirations of a master. The higher and purer the character and kind of music, the more of real genius there is in it, the deeper will this influence be.

Judge of what can be done, by what already, within our own experience, has been done and daily is done. Think what the children in our schools are getting, through the little that they learn of vocal music,—elasticity of spirit, joy in harmonious co-operation, in the blending of each happy life in others; a rhythmical instinct of order and of measure in all movement; a quickening of ear and sense, whereby they will grow up susceptible to music, as well as with some use of their own voices, so that they may take part in it; for from these spacious nurseries (loveliest flower gardens, apple orchards in full bloom, say, on their annual *fête* days) shall our future choirs and oratorio choruses be replenished with good sound material. . . .

We esteem ourselves the freest people on this planet; yet perhaps we have as little real freedom as any other, for we are the slaves of our own feverish enterprise, and of a barren theory of discipline, which would fain make us virtuous to a fault through abstinence from very life. We are afraid to give ourselves up to the free and happy instincts of our nature. All that is not pursuit of advancement in some good, conventional, approved way of business, or politics, or fashion, or intellectual reputation, or professed religion, we count waste. We lack *geniality;* nor do we as a people understand the meaning of the word. We ought to learn it practically of our Germans. It comes of the same root with the word *genius.* Genius is the spontaneous principle; it is free and happy in its work; it is artist and not drudge;

its whole activity is reconciliation of the heartiest pleasure with the purest loyalty to conscience, with the most holy, universal, and disinterested ends. Genius, as Beethoven gloriously illustrates in his Choral Symphony (indeed, in all his symphonies), finds the keynote and solution of the problem of the highest state in "Joy," taking his text from Schiller's Hymn. Now, all may not be geniuses in the sense that we call Shakespeare, Mozart, Raphael, men of genius. But all should be partakers of this spontaneous, free, and happy method of genius; all should live childlike, genial lives, and not wear all the time the consequential livery of their unrelaxing business, nor the badge of party and profession, in every line and feature of their faces. This genial, childlike faculty of social enjoyment, this happy art of life, is just what our countrymen may learn from the social "Liedertafel" and the summer singing-festivals of which the Germans are so fond. There is no element of national character which we so much need; and there is no class of citizens whom we should be more glad to adopt and own than those who set us such examples. So far as it is a matter of culture, it is through art chiefly that the desiderated genial era must be ushered in. The Germans have the sentiment of art, the feeling of the beautiful in art, and consequently in nature, more developed than we have. Above all, music offers itself as the most available, most popular, most influential of the fine arts,—music, which is the art and language of the feelings, the sentiments, the spiritual instincts of the soul; and so becomes a universal language, tending to unite and blend and harmonize all who may come within its sphere.

Such civilizing, educating power has music for society at large. Now, in the finer sense of culture, such as we look for in more private and select "society," as it is called, music in the salon, in the small chamber concert, where congenial spirits are assembled in its name—good music of course—does it not create a finer sphere of social sympathy and courtesy? Does it not better mold the tone and manners from within than any imitative "fashion" from without? What society, upon the whole, is quite so sweet, so satisfactory, so refined, as the best musical society, if only Mozart, Mendelssohn, Franz, Chopin, set the tone! The finer the kind of music heard or made together, the better the society. This bond of union only reaches the few; coarser, meaner, more prosaic natures are not drawn to it. Wealth and fashion may not dictate who shall be of it. Here congenial spirits meet in a way at once free, happy, and instructive, meet with an object which insures "society"; whereas so-called society, as such, is often aimless, vague, modifying and fatiguing, for the want of any subject-matter. Here one gets ideas of beauty which are not mere arbitrary fashions, ugly often to the eye of taste. Here you may escape vulgarity by a way not vulgar in itself, like that of fashion, which makes wealth and family and means of dress its passports. Here you can be as exclusive as you please, by the soul's light, not wronging any one; here learn gentle manners, and the quiet ease and courtesy with which cultivated people move, without in the same process learning insincerity.

Of course the same remarks apply to similar sincere reunions in the name of any other art, or of poetry. But music is the most social of them all, even if each listener find nothing set down to his part (or even hers!) but *tacet*.

We have fancied ourselves entertaining a musical house together, but we must leave it with no time to make report or picture out the scene. Now, could we only enter the chamber, the inner sanctum, the private inner life of a thoroughly musical person, one who is wont to *live* in music! Could we know him in his solitude! (You can only know him in yourself, unless he be a poet and creator in his art, and bequeath himself in that form in his works for any who know how to read.) If the best of all society is musical society, we go further and say: The sweetest of all solitude is when one is alone with music. One gets the best of music, the sincerest part, when he is alone. Our poet-philosopher has told us to secure solitude at any cost; there's nothing which we can so ill afford to do without. It is a great vice of our society, that it provides for and disposes to so little solitude, ignoring the fact that there is more loneliness in company than out of it. Now, to a musical person, in the mood of it, in the sweet hours by himself, comes music as the nearest friend, nearer and dearer than ever before; and he soon finds that he never was in such good company. I doubt if symphony of Beethoven, opera of Mozart, Passion Music of Bach, was ever so enjoyed or felt in grandest public rendering, as one may feel it while he recalls its outline by himself at his piano (even if he be a slow and bungling reader and may get it out by piecemeal). I doubt if such an one can carry home from the performance, in presence of the applauding crowd, nearly so much as he may take to it from such inward, private preparation.

Are you alone? What spirits can you summon up to fill the vacancy, and people it with life and love and beauty! Take down the volume of sonatas, the arrangement of the great Symphony, the recorded reveries of Chopin, the songs of Schubert, Schumann, Franz, or even the chorals, with the harmony of Bach, in which the four parts blend their several individual melodies together in such loving service of the whole, that the plain people's tune becomes a germ unfolding into endless wealth and beauty of

meaning; and you have the very essence of all prayer, and praise, and gratitude, as if you were a worshiper in the ideal church. Nothing like music, then, to banish the benumbing ghost of ennui. It lends secret sympathy, relief, expression, to all one's moods, loves, longings, sorrows; comes nearer to the soul or to the secret wound than any friend or healing sunshine from without. It nourishes and feeds the hidden springs of hope and love and faith; renews the old conviction of life's springtime,— that the world is ruled by love, that God is good, that beauty is a divine end of life, and not a snare and an illusion. It floods out of sight the unsightly, muddy grounds of life's petty, anxious, doubting moments, and makes immortality a present fact, lived in and realized. It locks the door against the outer world of discords, contradictions, importunities, beneath the notice of a soul so richly occupied: lets "Fate knock at the door" (as Beethoven said in explanation of his symphony),—Fate and the pursuing Furies,—and even welcomes them, and turns them into gracious goddesses,—Eumenides! Music, in this way, is a marvelous elixir to keep off old age. Youth returns in solitary hours with Beethoven and Mozart. Touching the chords of the 'Moonlight Sonata,' the old man is once more a lover; with the *andante* of the 'Pastoral Symphony' he loiters by the shady brookside, hand in hand with his fresh heart's first angel. You are past the sentimental age, yet you can weep alone in music,—not weep exactly, but find outlet more expressive and more worthy of your manly faith.

A great grief comes, an inconsolable bereavement, a humiliating, paralyzing reverse, a blow of Fate, giving the lie to your best plans and bringing your best powers into discredit with yourself; then you are best prepared and best entitled to receive the secret visitations of these tuneful goddesses and muses.

> "Who never ate his bread in tears,
>   He knows you not, ye heavenly powers!"

So sings the German poet. It is the want of inward, deep experience, it is innocence of sorrow and of trial, more than the lack of any special cultivation of musical taste and knowledge, that debars many people—naturally most young people, and all who are what we call shallow natures—from the feeling and enjoyment of many of the truest, deepest, and most heavenly of all the works of music. Take the Passion Music of Bach, for instance; if you can sit down alone at your piano and decipher strains and pieces of it when you *need* such music, you shall find that in its quiet quaintness, its sincerity and tenderness, its abstinence from all striving for effect, it speaks to you and entwines itself about your heart, like the sweetest, deepest verses in the Bible; when "the soul muses till the fire burns."

Such a panacea is this art for loneliness. But sometimes too it may intensify the sense of loneliness, only for more heavenly relief at last. Think of the deep composer, of lonely, sad Beethoven, wreaking his pain upon expression in those impatient chords and modulations, putting his sorrows into sonatas, and wringing triumph always out of all! Look at him as he was then,—morose, they say, and lonely and tormented; look where he is now, as the whole world knows him, feels him, seeks him for its joy and inspiration—and who can doubt of immortality?

Now, in such private solace, in such solitary joys, is there not culture? Can one rise from such communings with the good spirits of the tone-world and go out, without new peace, new faith, new hope, and good-will in his soul? He goes forth in the spirit of reconciliation and of patience, however much he may hate the wrong he sees about him, or however little he accept authorities and creeds that make war on his freedom. The man who has tasted such life, and courted it till he has become acclimated in it, whether he be of this party or that, or none at all; whether he be believer or "heretic," conservative or radical, follower of Christ by name or "Free Religionist,"—belongs to the harmonic and anointed body-guard of peace, fraternity, good-will; his instincts have all caught the rhythm of that holy march; the good genius leads, he has but to follow cheerfully and humbly. For somehow the minutest fibres, the infinitesimal atoms of his being, have got magnetized as it were into a loyal, positive direction towards the pole-star of unity; he has grown attuned to a believing, loving mood, just as the body of a violin, the walls of a music hall, by much music-making become gradually seasoned into smooth vibration.

IX

George F. Root
The Story of a Musical Life
(Cincinnati, 1891)

[George Frederick Root (1820-1895) was born in Sheffield, Massachusetts, raised from the age of six in North Reading, and was given his professional start as a musician in Boston. He was a very talented young man, and he began teaching music not long after he had formally begun learning it. He sang, taught singing schools, and eventually made his mark as a pioneering vocal teacher while assistant to Lowell Mason (*q.v.*) in Boston and then in New York. Although Root attained national significance as an educator and publisher in Chicago, his claim to lasting fame is based upon his activities as a composer. His many sentimental ballads, such as "Rosalie, the Prairie Flower" ("Far away she's blooming in a fadeless bower, sweet Rosalie the prairie flower"), and hymns, such as "The Shining Shore" ("My days are gliding swiftly by"), were very popular. Root is best known, however, for his stirring Civil War songs, particularly the "Battle Cry of Freedom" ("Yes, we'll rally round the flag, boys") and "Tramp! Tramp! Tramp!" (". . . the boys are marching"). The Singing Hutchinsons, the most popular of the "singing families" who captured the fancy of mid-century America, sang the "Battle Cry of Freedom" all over the country as part of their abolitionist crusade. The Rainers, a Swiss "singing family" mentioned in the following excerpt, started the vogue of such families when they first toured America.

The Story of a Musical Life is Root's autobiography. It gives an interesting and detailed account of the life and musical times of a popular musician and educator during a period of great stress and change in our country. Much of the book is devoted to his career as a teacher of teachers, as he, Lowell Mason and other leaders held "Normals," or music conventions, throughout the country, but the opening chapters deal with Root's early life, much of which was spent in Boston. The following pages take up the account in 1838 on the day after the young man arrived in Boston from North Reading in order to study music with a prominent local teacher, A. N. Johnson.]

THE STORY OF A MUSICAL LIFE

The next morning I commenced the duties and pleasures of my new vocation in Harmony Hall, as Mr. Johnson's music-room was called. This place was leased by the Musical Education Society, but Mr. Johnson had the use of it for conducting the society once a week. It was a light, cheerful room, up one flight of stairs; a platform, with a piano on it at one end, and a little curtained office, with a desk, at the other. After being told what my duties in regard to fires and care of room would be, I went with eagerness to the piano for my first lesson. The idea of calling it drudgery—this making musical sounds upon a pianoforte—nothing could be more absurd, as it seemed to me. It was a delight, even though my large, clumsy fingers would go right in the simplest exercises of Hunten's Instruction book only by the most laborious practice. But that was cheerfully given. Every minute when Mr. Johnson was out, or when I was not answering a call at the door, I was at work, and during Mr. Johnson's lessons in the room, while I was out of sight at the curtained desk, I was trying to get some flexibility into my stubborn fingers, while looking over some music-book. I had learned to read the notes of simple music both on treble and base staffs by the various instruments I had played.

When I say I had never sung, I do not mean that I had never used my voice at all in that way. I had occasionally joined in the base of simple church tunes, but was never encouraged by listeners to continue my performances long, or to make them prominent. It was always:—"George, you'd better take your flute." But Mr. Johnson said that if I was going to teach I ought to be able to use my voice correctly, and sing at least enough to give examples of tone and pitch. I dare say he saw then, what I realized after awhile, that I had begun too late to make much of a player upon piano or organ, and that if I developed any gift for teaching, my success must be in singing-classes and other vocal work. So I went at it. I sang in the Musical Education Society and in Mr. Johnson's choir at the Odeon, and often growled a base to my five-finger exercises while practicing.

But here I ought to say something about the condition of music in our part of the country in those days. Not many years before, a singing-school had been held in the old red school-house, where "faw, sol, law, faw, sol, law, me, faw," were the syllables for the scale—where one must find the "*me* note" (seven) to ascertain what key he was singing in, and where some of the old "fuguing tunes," as they were called, were still sung. I well remember how, shortly after, we heard that a new system of teaching music had been introduced into Boston, in which they used a blackboard and sang "do, re, mi," etc., to the scale. But how silly "do" sounded. We thought it smart to say that the man who invented that was a *dough*-head, and how flat were *fa* and *la*, in comparison with the dignified "faw" and "law." Later, however, when some tunes connected with the new movement came, we changed our minds about the man who was at the head of it. Nothing before, so heavenly, had been heard as the melody to "Thus far the Lord hath led me on" (Hebron); and one of the great things in going to Boston was that I should probably see LOWELL MASON.

It is an interesting fact that some music, at every grade, from lowest to highest, has in it that mysterious quality which makes it live, while all the rest fades away and is forgotten. Sometimes I think the more we know the less keen are our perceptions in regard to that divine afflatus. We understand better the construction of the music we hear, but do not feel, as in more unsophisticated states, the thrill of that mysterious life—at least I do not, and I put it forth as a possibly true theory in general, because every tune that produced that enchanting effect upon me then, lives in the hearts of the people now, while those that did not have dropped out of use.

Certain it is, if music writers and publishers could know of every composition whether it had in it that mysterious vitality or not, there would be far less music issued, for but few musical compositions in proportion to the number printed have in them the elements even of a short life.

I worked steadily at my piano lessons, and got on well, considering the obstacles I had to overcome in my grown-up hands. But piano playing was not then what it is now, by a difference that it would be hard to describe. A piano in a country town was a rarity, and a person even in Boston who could play as well as hundreds of young people all over the country now play, would have attracted universal attention.

I think I could not have been practicing more than two weeks before Mr. Johnson started me in the playing of chords by the method that has since been so well known under the name of Johnson's Thorough Base. By this means I was to learn to play Hebron and Ward and Hamburg and Boylston, and all those tunes that had moved me as no music had ever done before. I need not say that I worked with a will, but I remember well that I was in a chronic state of astonishment that my hands would *not* do what I saw so clearly should be done, and that I must play a succession of chords over so many, many times before they would go without a hitch.

It was not long after this that Mr. Johnson said to me one day; "I wish you would learn two of those tunes to play at the Wednesday night prayer-meeting." "What! play for the people to sing?" "Yes; you can do it; you need not play the tune through first; just play the first chord, and then start, and they'll all go with you. It will be all the more sure if you sing the first word or two." "But I shall make some mistakes, I'm afraid." "Well, if you do they won't be noticed." "But I may run against a stump and stop." "Well, they'll go on, and you can catch up at your leisure." Talk about courage! I mean on Mr. Johnson's part. He would take more and greater risks of that sort than any man I ever knew. But he knew I would strain every nerve to accomplish what he wished, and he always said he could rely on my—I think "self-confidence" was the term he used, but there is a much shorter word now coming into our vocabulary which would perhaps have expressed his meaning more forcibly. However, I went through it, and after that, for some months, prepared my two tunes every week for the prayer-meeting.

This church arrangement was peculiar. It was a Congregational church, under the pastoral care of Rev. Wm. M. Rogers, then one of the most popular clergymen of Boston. Its services were held in what had been the Federal St. Theater (corner of Federal and Franklin Streets), but was now called the "Odeon." It was owned or leased by a new organization called the "Boston Academy of Music," and used exclusively by that association and this Congregational church. It had been somewhat remodeled, though it had still the theater look. The stage was fitted with raised seats for a large chorus. There was a large organ at the back, and a conductor's platform in front, occupied on Sundays by the minister's pulpit. Lowell Mason was at the head of the Boston Academy of Music, and the conductor of its large chorus, and George James Webb was the organist, but on Sundays Mr. Johnson was the organist, and his choir the performers. The prayer-meetings were held in a long room over the front entrance, called "The Saloon." I don't think that word was then used at all as the name of a drinking place. It had more the signification of drawing-room or parlor. I don't know how it came to be applied to that little hall, but as I remember the notices, they would sound strangely now:—"The Sunday-school after service in the *saloon*," "The ladies' meeting Tuesday afternoon in the *saloon*," "The prayer-meeting Wednesday evening in the *saloon*," and there we had our choir rehearsals, and later, singing classes, so that in those days that word became connected in my mind with all that was "pure and lovely and of good report," instead of bearing the bad signification which attaches to it now.

. . . . .

I do not think it could have been more than six weeks from my beginning with Mr. Johnson that I had another surprise. One day a young man called to inquire about taking lessons upon the piano. He was a mechanic—an apprentice to a jeweler I think. Mr. Johnson asked him if he could play at all. No, he knew nothing about music whatever. Mr. Johnson reflected a moment and then said, as if it were the result of very serious and important deliberation: "I think my assistant here, Mr. Root, would be best adapted to your case." My astonishment was unbounded, but if this young man knew nothing I was a little ahead of him, and it would be a delight to help him over the road I had just traveled. That was my first pupil, and what I lacked in experience I made up in good will and attention. At any rate he was well satisfied, as I had good reason to know afterward. It was not long before others came and inquired for me instead of Mr. Johnson, on account of young Slade's recommendation.

About this time, certainly not more than seven weeks from the beginning of my connection with Mr. Johnson, he proposed a new bargain. The first had not been for any definite time—we were "to see how we liked," as he said, but of course the seeing was wholly on his side. He had now evidently made up his mind, and an agreement was made for a year at a very considerable increase in pay. That I was glad and thankful goes without saying. The news flew to the old farm as fast as Uncle Sam's machinery in those days could take it (there was no dream yet for years of telegraph), and at "Thanksgiving," toward the end of November, when I made my first

visit home, we had a happy time, as you may imagine.

About this time Mr. Mason advertised that new members would be admitted to the Boston Academy's Chorus. Those who wished to join must be at a certain place at a certain time, and have their voices and reading ability tested. Mr. Johnson said I had better go; that the Academy's work was more difficult than that of the Musical Education Society, and that the practice would be good for me in every way. I shook in my shoes at the suggestion, but Mr. Johnson's courage was equal to the occasion, and I went. That was my first sight of Lowell Mason, and also of Geo. Jas. Webb, who did the trying of the voices, while Mr. Mason looked on. I passed, and was much surprised when Mr. Mason came to where I was sitting and asked me to join his choir—that famous Bowdoin Street Choir, the like of which has rarely been equaled, in my opinion, in this or any other country. I told him why I could not—that I was with Mr. Johnson, etc., but that invitation settled the voice question in my mind. I was going to sing. Lowell Mason had wanted me in his choir, and that was as good as a warranty that I could succeed.

Meanwhile I did not neglect my flute. I was so well along on that that Mr. Johnson thought something might come of it. So I took some lessons and gave some lessons on that instrument, and some time in the following year I organized a flute club of my pupils and others. There were some pretty good singers in it, and we called it the "Nicholson Flute and Glee Club." "Nicholson's Flute Instructor" was my delight, both for method and music, hence the name. We had music arranged in six parts for our ten flutes. Simon Knaebel, a good orchestra and band musician, I remember, did the arranging. We had marches, quicksteps, waltzes, etc., all simple but popular then. We gave some concerts in the neighboring towns, and on one grand occasion played at some performance in the Odeon, and, what is better, were encored. It was rather absurd to have harmony, the base of which could go no lower than middle C; but it was a novelty, and to us a source of great enjoyment.

One important day, soon after my admission to the Boston Academy's Chorus, Mr. Johnson said I had better take some voice lessons of Mr. Webb; that private voice teaching was very profitable, and he thought I could fit myself to do that work. Mr. Johnson never flinched from what he thought I ought to do. I was glad enough, however, to take lessons of Geo. Jas. Webb, the best vocal teacher in Boston, an elegant organist, an accomplished musician, and a model Christian gentleman. He received me with great kindness, and after trying my voice in various ways, gave me some exercises to work upon. At my next lesson, after I had sung what he had before given me to practice, he looked up with an expression of pleased surprise and said: "Well, Mr. Root, I believe you *will* learn to sing." I replied, "Of course; that is what I fully intend to do." "Ah, but," he responded, "at your first lesson I thought it extremely doubtful whether it would be worth your while to try." Of course he had reference to solo singing, and not to joining with the bases in a chorus, which I could then do fairly well.

My lessons went on with him for months—a year, perhaps, and I came not only to delight in them, but in the friendly atmosphere of his pleasant home. I used always to be glad when I could see his little Mary—four or five years old perhaps; she was so bright and so full of music. Once I remember she came into the teaching room, where I was waiting for my lesson, and said: "Papa will come pretty soon, but I've been to the 'Rainers.'" The Rainers were a family of Swiss Yodlers, the first, I think, to come to this country, and were singing in costume and in their native language their pretty Swiss songs. Everybody went to hear them. "I've been to the Rainers," she went on, as she climbed upon the piano stool, "and wasn't it funny what they said?" Here she piped up with a comical motion of her head, but with accordant tones on the piano:—

Take a piece a yarn, Take a piece a yarn.

Mr. Webb, coming in at that moment, laughed and explained that Mary was very fond of giving her imitation of Simon Rainer's manner and her translation of his German. I thought often of this little incident in after years, while listening to her splendid rendering of "I know that my Redeemer liveth," or some other oratorio classic, and later, while enjoying her gracious hospitality as the wife of Dr. William Mason, in their lovely home in Orange, New Jersey.

Speaking of foreign performers, it was about this time that we heard Herwig, who was, I think, the first really great violinist to come to this country. His harmonic playing—making his violin sound like a fine high wind instrument, caused great astonishment, and filled his houses to overflowing. It was some years afterward that we heard Vieuxtemps, Sivori, and Ole Bull on his first visit, but Artot came soon after Herwig. About that time also came the first pianists that much excelled the best we had heard. Jane Sloman was first, and in a few months Rakemann. They had great success then, but such playing now would be considered only mediocre—I

mean as concert playing. Every large city in the country has better players.

But a matter of greater interest to me was the advent in those days of Braham, who had been for a generation the greatest English tenor. He was an old man, and it was said his voice was not what it had been, but no one who then heard him sing "Thou shalt dash them in pieces like a potter's vessel" probably ever heard anything before or since to compare with his tone upon the word "dash"—so large and at the same time so terrifically intense. Marcus Colburn, one of our resident tenors, came the nearest to him in power, and would have made as great a singer probably, if he had had the opportunity, for his voice excelled Braham's in a certain sweet and ringing quality.

That brings to my mind a rather ludicrous scene in which Mr. Colburn and I were chief actors. Mr. Colburn was a giant in size, over six feet in height, and very portly—weighing probably near to three hundred pounds. After I came to be regarded as a promising base singer it came about—I don't remember whether through Mr. Johnson's courage or that of some one else—that I was appointed to sing with Mr. Colburn from Neukomm's Oratorio of "David" the duet between David and Goliath, at a concert at the Odeon. It was absurd enough when we went forward together to begin, for this giant was David, and I, a stripling in comparison to him, was Goliath; but when I had to sing, in the most ponderous tones I could assume, "I can not war with boys," the audience broke out into irrepressible laughter, in which Colburn, who had the most contagious laugh in the world, joined, and that "broke me all up," as they say now-a-days. We went through our performance, however, though we did not consider it an unqualified success.

But the most important event to me, in the way of public performances, in those days (1839), was the singing of Henry Russell, [*] an English Jew, who composed and sang "The Ivy Green," "Our Native Song," "A Life on the Ocean Wave," "The Old Sexton," "Wind of the Winter Night," and many other songs of that grade. He had a beautiful baritone voice and great command of the keyboard—played his own accompaniments, gave his concerts entirely alone, and in a year in this country made a fortune. Songs of his, like "The Maniac" and "The Gambler's Wife," were exceedingly pathetic, and always made people cry when he sang them. He looked so pitiful and so sympathetic—"he felt every word," as his listeners would think and say—and yet, when he retired to his dressing room, he was said to have been much amused at the grief of his

[*See Dwight's *Dial* essay for a "high culture" view of Russell.]

69

weeping constituents, showing that he had not really the heart in his song that he appeared to have.

Of course it is a part of the singer's art to assume emotions that he does not really feel, and that is all right if the emotions he assumes are healthful and good. For instance, a man may sing of the delights of a farmer's or a sailor's life in such a way as to make his hearers think he likes that life best, when, in point of fact, he may much prefer some other. But good taste requires that the singer should treat respectfully the emotion he excites.

I was so taken with Russell's songs that I worked harder than ever before to be able to play and sing them as he did. When the accompaniments were too much for me, or the pitch too high, I modified and simplified and transposed, and in a few months had them at my tongue's and fingers' ends, and I have sung certain of them ever since—more than fifty years. While Russell was in this country, Joseph Philip Knight came over and gave us "Rocked in the Cradle of the Deep," which Russell added to his repertoire, and I, with certain modifications, to mine.

This is a good place to speak of the absurdity of saying that simple music keeps the tastes and musical culture of the people down. You might as well say that a person is kept in addition, subtraction, multiplication and division by having around him more examples in elementary arithmetic than he needs. If he is interested in the subject, he'll go on after he has mastered the simpler to that which is more difficult, if the examples or books that he needs are within his reach. You can not keep him in the lower grade by multiplying elementary books. If he is not interested, or is more occupied with other things, he may never go beyond those elementary mathematics which are needed for the common duties of life; but since he can not get higher *without going through them,* it is useless to put that which is higher before him *until they are mastered.*

For a few months Russell's songs filled me with delight. They were just what I needed to help me out of my elementary condition. Before a year was over they had done their work, and I craved something higher. Schubert's songs came next. Is it supposed for an instant that songs of the Russell grade, had they been multiplied a hundred-fold, would have had any effect in keeping me back, if I could get what I wanted? Certainly not; and Schubert's songs, and others of that grade, were, and are, plenty, and more easily obtained, because, being non-copyright, they are free to all publishers. Those not in music, or not so musical naturally, do not get through the elementary state so soon; in fact, many business and professional people, giving very little time or thought to the subject, never get through; they prefer the simpler music to the end of their days. But there is no royal road for such. They must get their fill of the simple—must hear it until they crave something higher—before that which is higher can be of any use to them. It is an axiom that emotional or aesthetic benefit by music can come to a person only through music that he likes. By that alone can he grow musically.

Just as the elementary departments of mathematics are the foundations of that great subject, so tonic, dominant and sub-dominant (the simplest harmonies) are foundations in all music—the highest as well as the lowest. No one derides or looks with contempt upon the elements of mathematics, or upon the thousand ways by which those simpler things are made interesting to the learner. On the contrary, the most learned mathematicians appreciate their importance and delight in their success. So it should be in our science and art; and, without apologizing for what is incorrect or untasteful in the simple music of the day, I say, unhesitatingly, that all correct musical forms, however elementary, find some one to whom they are just what is needed, either for practical or aesthetic benefit, or both. Since, therefore, there are always so many grown-up men and women, learned and strong in other things, who are still in elementary musical states, I keep, ready for use, the simple songs that helped me, and am always glad to sing them where they will do any good.

I do not quite remember where my first "singing-school" was taught, but I think an experimental class was held in Harmony Hall during my first winter (1838-9), under the guise of helping some young ladies and gentlemen to "read notes," who were desirous of joining the Musical Education Society. I had seen Mr. Johnson teach a few times, but I had no orderly method, and my work must have been exceedingly desultory and crude. Something carried me through, however, and the next autumn I had a large class at the North End, which lasted nearly through the winter, and which, on the closing night, made me very proud and happy by the gift of a silver goblet, suitably engraved, and which now occupies a place among my treasures.

About this time I became acquainted with I. B. Woodbury. He was two or three years older than myself, and had commenced his musical work a year or two before me. He had a small room, also, in Tremont Row. He was a most indefatigable student and worker. I think it was during my first winter in Boston that he taught a singing-school in Beverly, and often walked back to Boston, fifteen miles, after nine o'clock at night, to be ready for his lessons in the morning. We who were inured to the hardships of New England country life in those days did not think of such things as they would be thought of now. Mr. Woodbury was very economical, and in a year or two had saved enough money to go to London and take lessons for a few months. Soon after he came home he began to write, and it was not long before he published his first book of church music. He was prosperous and very ambitious. He said to me once, "When I die I shall surprise the world," and he did. He was not strong constitutionally, and the flame burned so fiercely that the end for him came early. It was then found that he had left almost his entire estate to found a Musical Institution —the money to be used for that purpose after it had been invested long enough to produce a certain sum. But the law stepped in and changed this disposition of his fortune in favor of his wife and children. Mr. Woodbury was a genial, pleasant gentleman, and because he wrote only simple music, never was credited (by those who did not know him) with the musical ability and culture that he really possessed.

Speaking of Mr. Woodbury's long walk, and the hardihood of New England country boys, reminds me of what I used sometimes to do to be home on Thanksgiving Day. That was then by far the greatest day of the year in New England, viewed in a social or religious way. Christmas was hardly noticed. Everybody would be at the father's or grandfather's home for "Thanksgiving," if within the bounds of possibility. If I had a singing-school the night before, I would start, after a short sleep, perhaps at two or three o'clock in the morning, and walk homeward, somebody starting from there at the same time in a wagon to meet me, so that I might be at home for breakfast. Once, after my father returned from South America, a young man from North Reading, who was learning a trade in Boston, took this walk with me. We were in the highest state of boyish exhilaration, and when my companion suggested that it would be a good scheme to be on the lookout for the wagon, and, when we heard it, to conceal ourselves and surprise horse and rider in highwayman fashion, I agreed. It was my father whom we met, and it was a lonely part of the road. We sprang out at the horse, and he said: "Hullo! what are ye about?" and immediately added when he saw who we were: "Boys, this would have been anything but a Thanksgiving Day for us if I had been armed as I was in South America." We saw at once how foolish we had been, although, as no one carried arms in those days, no idea of risk came to our minds. We did not tell of our exploit at home, but I have often thought how my father "stood fire," and what crestfallen highwaymen we were for the rest of the journey.

I must not omit to speak of one most interesting pupil that I had during my second year in Harmony Hall. One day I answered a gentle rap at the door,

and a large, fine-looking old gentleman entered. He said: "I suppose you will think it strange that an old man like me should wish to learn to play upon the organ, but I have a small one in my house (there were no reed organs then), and if I could learn to play a few of my favorite tunes upon it I should be very glad. I live in Farmington, Maine, but am spending a few days with my son in the city here." I told him that he could not do much in a few days, but that I would do my best for him if he decided to try. He did so decide, and seemed to enjoy the lessons, as I certainly did his acquaintance, although he did not accomplish all he had hoped in the way of learning his favorite tunes. He was a typical New Englander, of the best kind of those days—one who had lived a long, blameless life, practicing all the virtues of the Puritans without their hardness. His quaint, shrewd remarks were a constant source of pleasure and benefit, for they were from the "innocence of wisdom."

I mention this circumstance, first, because this lovely old gentleman was the father of the brothers Abbott, the oldest of whom was Jacob Abbott, the author of "The Young Christian" and "The Corner Stone," and later of the "Rollo" books, and grandfather of Dr. Lyman Abbott, the present pastor of Plymouth Church, Brooklyn, and editor of the *Christian Union,* and of Benjamin V. and Austin Abbott, distinguished lawyers and legal authors in New York City. I also mention this circumstance because it led to an important change in my life and prospects four years later.

I must not omit to speak of the "Old Corner Bookstore," which still stands at the corner of School and Washington Streets. It was a bookstore then as now, only at that time, on one side, with one counter, was the sheet-music and music-book establishment of "Parker & Ditson." I went there often for music, and was often waited upon by the handsome, dark-eyed junior partner of the concern—the man who then was making the beginning of what is now one of the largest music houses in the world. [*]

[*Oliver Ditson (1811-1888)]

X

William Foster Apthorp
"Musical Reminiscences of Boston Thirty Years Ago" from *By the Way,* Vol. II: *About Musicians* (Boston 1898)

[William Foster Apthorp (1848-1913) was born in Boston, grew up in a musical atmosphere presided over by Dwight and his fellow pioneers, and graduated from Harvard in 1869, having studied music there with B. J. Lang and John Knowles Paine. Apthorp was an excellent musician and a perceptive critic and soon made his influence felt in articles for *Dwight's Journal of Music,* the *Atlantic Monthly* and elsewhere. He also edited a very important early collection of the essays and letters of Hector Berlioz, and he was active as editor and translator of the songs of Robert Franz and others. As a teacher, Apthorp was highly distinguished in the areas of music theory and history; he taught at Boston University and the New England Conservatory, and he gave widely acclaimed lecture series at the Lowell Institute and the Peabody Institute in Baltimore. As a journalist, he was the music critic for the *Boston Evening Transcript* for twenty years after 1881—the post later occupied by Henry Taylor Parker (*q.v.*). Some of his newspaper pieces, *Atlantic* articles, and Lowell lectures were collected in *Musicians and Music-Lovers* (New York, 1894). From 1892 to 1901 he edited and wrote for the program books of the Boston Symphony Orchestra, and in 1898 he published a selection of the "Entr'actes" from these programs in two small volumes, *By the Way about Music* and *By the Way about Musicians.* The following "Musical Reminiscences of Boston Thirty Years Ago" is a chapter from the second of these volumes. It is a perceptive, extremely intelligent—and often very amusing—overview of an important patch of Boston's musical history from the pen of one of this country's finest writers on music.]

Musical Reminiscences of Boston Thirty Years Ago

These are, in the strictest sense of the term, what they purport to be: *Reminiscences.* I have consulted nothing but my own memory.

It is hard for us older ones to realize that a whole generation of concert-goers has sprung up, who do not remember the old symphony concerts of the Harvard Musical Association—let alone those of the older Orchestral Union and the still older Germania. I can still remember the Germania concerts under Karl Bergmann's régime, just before he went to New York and was succeeded by Mr. Zerrahn. I can not, to be sure, remember much about them, only one or two incidents being firmly engraved on my memory. At one of the public afternoon rehearsals,—for we had afternoon rehearsals then, as now,—all the seats on the floor of the Music Hall had been taken up, and the small audience occupied the galleries. There used to be no printed programs at these rehearsals, but Bergmann would announce the several numbers *viva voce*—often in the most remarkable English. One of the numbers on the occasion I now speak of was the *Railway Galop,*—composer forgotten,—during the playing of which a little mock steam-engine kept scooting about (by clock-work?) on the floor of the hall, with black cotton-wool smoke coming out of its funnel. I have a vague recollection, too, of another rehearsal, just before which something nefarious had happened to the heating apparatus, so that the temperature was down in the forties. Dresel played a pianoforte concerto with his overcoat on, the sleeves partly rolled up, and the bright red satin lining flashing in the faces of the audience. Brignoli sang something, too; in a black cape that made him look like Don Ottavio—and persisted in singing with his back to the audience.

With Mr. Zerrahn's accession to the conductorship comes an hiatus in my memory; I was in Europe, and my reminiscences knot on again with the year 1860. Boston then had the Orchestral Union, the Handel & Haydn Society, the Mendelssohn Quintet

Club, and, for pianoforte-playing, what was sometimes jokingly called the Ottoman Quartet. The four leading resident pianists—Otto Dresel, B. J. Lang, Hugo Leonhard, and J. C. D. Parker—were fond of playing pieces for two pianofortes, eight hands (*a otto mani*), in public now and then; hence the nickname, with which Dresel's Christian name may also have had something to do. The Mendelssohn Quintet Club, the only organization which gave instrumental chamber-music in those days, consisted of Wilhelm Schulze (*first violin*), Carl Meisel (*second violin*), Thomas Ryan [*] (*first viola* and *clarinet*), Göring (*second viola* and *flute*), and Wulf Fries (*'cello*). Only two of these artists were original members of the Club: Ryan and Fries. August Fries, the original first violin, had gone back to Norway (or was it to Sweden or Denmark?), and the Hungarian, Riha—so spelled out of compassion for Anglo-Saxon inability to wrestle successfully with his real name, Drzjr—was dead. I think he was one of the original violas; perhaps second violin. Schulze was also leading first violin in the orchestra, as Ryan and Wulf Fries were leading viola and 'cello.

What a time of it that old Orchestral Union had! Their concerts came on Wednesday afternoons, and were well attended at first. But, with the war, the audiences began to drop off, as times grew harder. The orchestra was an exceedingly variable quantity: there were only two horns, and a second bassoon was not to be thought of. The second bassoon-part had to be played on a 'cello; and uninitiated visitors used sometimes to wonder what that solitary 'cello was doing in the midst of the wood-wind. Hamann, the first horn, had little technique, but a good tone, and was moreover an excellent musician; he had a fad of playing the easier Mozart, Haydn, and Beethoven horn-parts on a real plain horn, which he had had made to order, and regarded with unconcealed affection. I think there were hardly ever more than six first violins: I certainly remember one performance of Beethoven's A major symphony with only three first violins and two second. The solitary bassoonist was conspicuous by his singularity, not by his virtuosity. At a benefit concert tendered to Mr. Zerrahn, at which a small picked "chorus of young ladies" sang the "Lift thine eyes" terzet from *Elijah*, the few measures of introductory tenor recitative were played as a bassoon solo. The hapless bassoonist got most of the notes wrong; I do not think I ever heard such a tremulous tone issue from any other wind instrument.

But nothing could fluster Mr. Zerrahn; I never saw him lose his head, nor any performance come to grief under his bâton. And, with the orchestral material and few rehearsals of those days, things were on the verge of coming to grief pretty often. At one of the Handel & Haydn festivals—I think, the first one, the demi-centennial—the then famous boy-soprano, Richard Coker, sang Meyerbeer's *"Robert, toi que j'aime"* at an afternoon concert. He was accompanied on the pianoforte by his father. When about halfway through the air, Coker, Sr., discovered to his dismay that the remaining sheets of the music were missing; Mr. Zerrahn immediately sprang to the conductor's desk, waved his bâton, and the rest of the air was accompanied by the orchestra from memory.

I remember another instance of Mr. Zerrahn's presence of mind. It was at a performance of Mendelssohn's *Hymn of Praise* by the Handel & Haydn. The tenor had just finished that air with the incomprehensible words, closing with the oft-repeated question, "Watchman, will the night soon pass?" In reply to this, the soprano should strike in unaccompanied, in D major, with "The night is departing!" twice repeated; the wood-wind coming in *piano* on the second "departing," and the whole orchestra *fortissimo* on the final syllable. Well, on this occasion, the soprano was standing a little farther forward on the stage than Mr. Zerrahn; so she could not see his beat without turning her head. She struck in bravely with her "The night is departing;" but unfortunately not in D major—it was fairly and squarely C major: a whole tone flat! A shudder ran through the orchestra and a good part of the audience: what was Mr. Zerrahn to do with the ensuing chorus in D major? His mind was made up in a second; he motioned to the wood-wind not to come in with their chords, and stood there, waiting patiently for the hapless soprano to finish her phrase, and let the orchestra come in with its D major *fortissimo* afterwards, instead of on the last syllable. And now came one of the most comical tugs of war I have ever witnessed between singer and conductor. Of course the soprano was wholly unaware of having made a mistake; so, not hearing the usual 6-4 chord on her second "departing," she thought the wind-players must have counted their rests wrong, and held her high G—which ought to have been an A—with a persistency worthy of a better cause, to let them catch up with her. She held that G on and on, looking as if she would burst; but still no 6-4 chord! At last—it seemed like hours—human lungs could hold out no longer, and the breathless soprano landed panting with her final "ting" on C-natural, amid a death-like silence of the orchestra. You could have heard a pin drop. Just as she was turning round to see why she had thus been left in the lurch by the accompaniment, Mr. Zerrahn's bâton came down with a swish, and the orchestra thundered out its

[*See Ryan's own *Recollections* selected in the following chapter.]

D major; this unlooked for tonality evidently gave the poor soprano a shock, as if a glass of ice-water had suddenly been thrown in her face. At last she realized what she had been doing.

We had opera in those days, too. Max Maretzek was the great operatic gun then, both as impresario and conductor; I think his company still kept up the old title of "Havana Troupe." The Boston Theatre was its battle-field; the dress-circle—that is, all of the first balcony behind the first two rows of seats—was cut up into open boxes, the partitions coming up no higher than the arms of the seats. But I never could discover that people "took a box;" the seats were sold separately, just as if the partitions did not exist. The entrance to the top gallery was fifty cents, though it was afterwards raised to a dollar. The opera orchestras were pretty small, and not of the best quality; but, as the huge modern opera scores had not come in, the parts were generally well enough filled. There was a bass-tuba for *Robert le Diable*, and there were generally four horns.

The mise en scene was, for the most part, primitive enough. The scenery generally belonged to the theatre, and in those days the Boston Theatre had not launched out upon its gorgeous stage settings—except for things like the *Black Crook* or *White Fawn*. The *"bujo loco"* of the septet in *Don Giovanni* was always represented by a blue-and-gold baronial hall; and who that ever saw it can forget that street-scene, with the red brick wall, which figured in almost every opera, no matter in what part of the world nor in what age the scene was laid?

The costumes belonged either to the principal artists or to the company, and were of varying degrees of splendour. There was one fixed rule: the soprano heroine invariably wore a décolleté ball-dress—white, if Fortune smiled; black, if down on her luck. Epoch, country, in-doors or out-of-doors, rain or shine, made no difference; the heroine—unless she was a peasant—stuck to that ball-dress as for dear life.

But the performances were often capital, and there was much good singing. I can just remember Medori, an heroic soprano of equally heroic proportions, generally reputed to be second only to Adelina Patti. She had a bad *tremolo* in her otherwise fine voice, when I heard her; but was unmistakably an artist. Her successor in the grand soprano parts was Carrozzi-Zucchi, a fiery, beetle-browed Italian, with apparently unlimited vocal power, and flamboyantly dramatic in her singing. If I remember aright, she had the failing of being unable to pronounce the consonant *R*. I am pretty sure it was she, for one incident I remember tallies exactly with her style. It was in Verdi's *Ernani*: Elvira had just finished the slow *cantilena*—"Ernani, involami"—of her grand

aria, and was about to launch forth upon the *cabaletta,* which begins *"Tutto sprezzo che d' Ernani non favella a questo cuore* (I despise all that does not speak of Ernani to this heart)." Here Carrozzi-Zucchi's defective *R* played her a trick. In her most furiously dramatic manner, with a fine scowl darkening her expressive face, she rushed up to the footlights and thundered forth *"Tutto sp'ezzo che d'E'nani, &c.* (I *smash* all that, &c.)," to the blank astonishment of a little Italian who happened to be in the seat next mine; I overheard him exclaim under his breath, *"Davvero spezzarebbe tutto!* (Indeed she would smash everything!)."

The first cast of Gounod's *Faust* in Boston was memorable. It has seldom been equalled in our city.

Faust	MAZZOLENI
Mefistofele	BIACHI
Valentino	BELLINI
Margherita	KELLOGG
Siebel	SULZER

It was announced on the play-bills that "In order to give éclat to the performance, Signor Bellini has consented to accept the comparatively small part of Valentine." Mazzoleni was no longer in his first youth; he was a robust tenor, with a rather too metallic voice of very peculiar quality, and sang uncommonly well; he was a good actor, and his love-making was superb—indeed he had been a lawyer by profession, before taking to the boards, and was an adept at pleading. Until Capoul came, years after, no other such stage lover was to be seen here in opera. Biachi was a rich-voiced *basso cantante* and also an excellent actor; I doubt if his Mefistofele has been surpassed here since; he gave the part its full caustic humour, but without a suspicion of buffoonery. Bellini was a conventional actor, though he had a grand stage-presence and manner; but he had the most glorious baritone voice I ever heard in my life, and was a capital singer. And how charming Kellogg was in those, her younger, days! when she sang Margherita in *Faust,* Zerlina in *Don Giovanni* and *Fra Diavolo,* Amina in *la Sonnambula,* Elvira in *i Puritani,* and had not yet aspired to the heavy dramatic business! Her light soprano voice was purity itself, and she sang to perfection. Her Margherita stands unapproached in my memory—that is, unapproached from a Barbier-Carré-Gounod point of view; for there was nothing of Goethe's Gretchen in it. Enrichetta Sulzer—Mrs. Annibale Biachi in private life—was in no wise remarkable, though she sang Siebel well enough. But the whole cast worked together like a charm; the ensemble was admirable.

74

The success of *Faust* was immediate and overwhelming; probably Goethe's poem was largely answerable for it, for Gounod's music was in a then new and unfamiliar style, and old opera-goers used to complain that "there was only one tune"—Siebel's flower-song—"in the whole work." The soldiers' chorus was regularly encored.

Singers like Mazzoleni, Bellini, Biachi, Medori, Carrozzi-Zucchi, and others—I wonder, by the way, if any one still remembers the stentor-voiced Maccaferi, who used to make the rafters tremble in Petrella's *Ione*—were of the bird-of-passage sort; they seldom appeared for more than two or three seasons. But Brignoli we had nearly always with us—that is, when the opera came. His was a phenomenal voice; of the pure lyric tenor quality, but of robust calibre and power. His singing was the perfection of vocal art; he could sing anything, from Elvino to Manrico, from Don Ottavio to Ernani. He had little sensibility and no dramatic power; he seldom, if ever, sang with what is commonly called "expression;" but the silvery beauty of his voice and the perfection of his vocal art and phrasing made up for it. He could probably have shared with Rubini the well-earned reputation of being the worst actor that ever walked the boards. He did not even try to act; now and then, in love-scenes, he would take the soprano's hand and clasp it to his expansive chest—at times to the soprano's conspicuous discomfiture; for, when Brignoli had once got hold of it, it was no easy matter to get it away again—but this was about all he ever did. His stage walk was notorious; one would have thought that gait acquired in following the plough. He was the idol of the public. Curiously enough, with all his consciousness of artistic mastery and popularity, he never could get over his stage fright; he was the most impudent-looking man in the world, but really one of the most timid. Adelaide Phillipps once told me that she often had actually to push him out from the side-scenes, or he would never have screwed up the courage to go on.

Morensi, the mezzo-soprano, was also an excellent singer. I heard her years after she left this country, with Adelina Patti, Fraschini, and Delle Sedie, in *Rigoletto* at the Italiens in Paris. She was a great Donna Elvira in *Don Giovanni,* although she conscientiously left out every high B-flat in her part, and put a rest in its place. Her voice only went up to A. Susini, the old basso of the Havana Troupe, was rather in the sear and yellow leaf then; I only heard him once or twice in *buffo* parts. He married Miss Hinkley, whose untimely death cut short a brilliantly promising career.

Adelaide Phillipps was as much a regular operatic stand-by in those days as Brignoli himself. She be-

gan as a dancer at the Boston Museum, but soon developed a rich, luscious contralto voice, which she had admirably trained. It was probably to her early ballet training that she owed her conspicuously commanding bearing and grace of movement on the stage. She was a grand singer and one of the best actresses of the day on the lyric boards. Her Maffeo Orsini, in *Lucrezia Borgia,* will never be forgotten by any who saw it. Probably no one since Alboni ever sang *"Il segreto per esser felici"* with such rollicking dash and cavalier elegance as she. Trebelli was not in it with her!

The operatic repertory was not very varied. Bellini, Donizetti, and Verdi were the chief stand-bys then. Gounod's *Faust* was the most successful, if not the only successful, novelty; Meyerbeer's *Dinorah* did not take well with the public, and Petrella's *Ione* was but a flash in the pan. Two standard operas, very popular then, seem quite lost to the present repertory; a loss much to be regretted, for they are truly great works. These were Donizetti's *Lucrezia Borgia* and Verdi's *Ernani.* The prologue to *Lucrezia* is an unsurpassed gem in its way; and the third and fourth acts of *Ernani* contain some of the greatest music Verdi ever wrote. Donizetti's *Poliuto* and *Dom Sebastiano* seemed for a moment on the brink of success; but they soon ceased to draw well. The surest cards, after all, were Mozart's *Don Giovanni* and Verdi's *il Trovatore.* The trouble with *Don Giovanni* was its enormous cast: *"lauter premiers sujets!* (nothing but leading artists!)," as the good Maretzek would sadly exclaim. I remember, however, one admirable performance of it under Maretzek, with a cast that has seldom been beaten here.

Don Giovanni........	BELLINI
Il Commendatore....	WEINLIG (I think)
Donna Anna.........	MEDORI
Don Ottavio.........	LOTTI
Donna Elvira........	STOCKTON
Leporello............	BIACHI
Zerlina.............	KELLOGG

Henrietta Stockton was the one weak spot in the cast; Lotti was fairly adequate, and the others were superb. Bellini, to be sure, would insist upon rattling off *"Finch' han dal vino"* at lightning speed, and giving out a stentorian F-sharp in the closing cadence of the serenade. Medori's *"Or sai chi l'onore"* fairly took your breath away with its dramatic fire. But we had no good Donna Elvira till Morensi came, a year or two later.

Bellini's *Sonnambula, Norma,* and *i Puritani* held their own well and were very popular. Rossini's *Barbiere* drew splendidly, but was seldom given—for lack of good florid tenors; *"Ecco ridente"* was a stumbling-block hard to get over! Ah! I had almost forgotten another successful and delightful novelty: the Riccis' *Crispino e la Comare*. This charming little *opera buffa* had a great run; Clara Louise Kellogg was a simply bewitching Annetta.

Evening dress was rather the exception than the rule at the opera in those days, although the gas was not turned down during the acts; and gay opera-cloaks would alternate with waterproofs—those waterproofs for which the Boston female has become so justly famous.

German opera was represented by the Annschütz company, with Bertha Johannsen, Marie Frederici —her maiden name was Friedrichs, and she was Mrs. Himmer in private life,—Pauline Canissa, Franz Himmer, Theodor Habelmann, and Joseph Hermanns. Johannsen was a really great artist, and sang Donna Anna, Beethoven's Leonore, and other grand soprano parts superbly; she was a mighty actress, too. Frederici made an enormous hit as Agathe, in *der Freischütz,* and was much admired in Gounod's Margarethe; she had a wondrously rich mezzo-soprano, running up to high B-flat and with contralto fullness of tone down to G; but she was, on the whole, little of an artist, and only did what she was told, with poll-parrot fidelity. Hermanns—who had been picked out of the Covent Garden chorus on account of his grand bass voice and imposing stature—made a tremendous hit as Mephistopheles. His voice had a peculiar resonant quality— very much for a bass what Mazzoleni's was for a tenor—and people used to take out their watches to time his trill in the serenade. He was next to nothing of an artist; but I fancy I was alone in finding his Mephistopheles execrable. The only part he did really well was Rocco, in *Fidelio*.

Faust—the Walpurgisnight-scene in which was persistently advertised as a special feature, and never once given,—*Fidelio*, the *Freischütz*, Boieldieu's *Weisse Dame,* Nicolai's *Lustigen Weiber von Windsor,* and Mozart's *Don Juan* were the favourite operas. When Carl Formes was added to the troupe, a year or two later, Meyerbeer's *Robert der Teufel* was revived for him; his Bertrand was a wonder of singing and acting. And to hear him rattle off *"Schaudernd zittern meine Glieder, Angst schlägt meinen Muth darnieder"* in the septet in *Don Juan*— in steady *crescendo* up to *fortissimo,* and with every syllable distinct—was a caution! He was a great artist, although on the downward path when I heard him. Advancing age had a peculiar effect upon him: it did not diminish the beauty nor volume of his voice in the least, but it gradually robbed him of the power of singing in tune.

One of the great events of the period about which I am now writing—1860-70 in round numbers—was the demi-centennial festival of the Handel & Haydn Society in 1865. What I especially remember about this particular festival was the orchestra. The orchestral resources of Boston had never been conspicuous, either for quality or numbers; since the beginning of the war, the orchestra of the Orchestral Union and those which made us yearly visits with opera companies had been miserably small. I doubt if any of my generation, certainly of those whose experience did not extend to New York or the other side of the Atlantic, had ever heard a well-balanced orchestra. Our notions of orchestral effect were derived from what we heard. I remember distinctly how impossible it was for me, at the time I speak of, to understand what older musicians meant by calling the strings the "main power" in an orchestra. In all orchestras I had heard, the wood-wind—let alone the brass and percussion—was more powerful dynamically than the often ridiculously small mass of strings; especially as the then wind-players seldom cultivated the art of playing *piano*. But, for this demi-centennial of the Handel & Haydn, our local orchestra was increased to nearly a hundred by the addition of players engaged from New York and elsewhere. I shall never forget the overwhelming effect of the third and fourth measures of the symphony to Mendelssohn's *Hymn of Praise*—where the unison trombone-phrase of the first two measures is answered *fortissimo* in full harmony by the entire orchestra. Nothing I have heard since, in Berlioz's or Wagner's most resounding instrumentation, has sounded so positively tremendous to me as this first onslaught of an orchestra with a large mass of strings! This was the beginning, not of large, but of what might be called normal orchestras in Boston. At the symphony concerts of the Harvard Musical Association, founded not long afterward, the orchestra ranged from fifty to sixty players (for full modern scores); before the Handel & Haydn demi-centennial, our orchestra had run as low as twenty-four, and seldom exceeded thirty-five. When we had eight first and eight second violins, we thought no small beer of ourselves! The advance in quality was, however, by no means commensurate with the increase in numbers; for years our orchestra remained a good deal of a "scratch team"—what a distinguished visiting violinist once called *"une agrégation fortuite d'éléments hétérogènes* (a fortuitous aggregation of heterogeneous elements)."

About this time, and earlier, star-concerts were all the rage; and I must say—due allowance being made for the inveterately inartistic plan—we had some pretty good ones. As opera managers did not quite dare to engage stars of the very first magnitude for their troupes,—not caring to compete with London, Madrid, and St. Petersburg in the matter of salaries,—it was at these star-concerts that we first heard some of the greatest singers of the day. If their success in concert was unquestionable, the opera people would then screw up courage to engage them next season. One of the best and most successful of these concert combinations was the Bateman troupe —as it was also one of the most ill-assorted from an artistic point of view. It brought us Euphrosyne Parepa, then at the apex of her glory; Carl Rosa, the violinist, then at the beginning of his career; Eduard Dannreuther, the pianist; Lévy, the eighth world-wonder of the cornet-à-pistons. Rosa was decidedly more of an artist than he was a violin virtuoso; but we thought a good deal of his playing then, and he certainly played a deal of good music. He was engaged as solo violinist at one of the first Harvard Musical concerts; and the applause knew no bounds when, after playing his last solo, he, in the fullness of his artistic heart, took a seat beside Wilhelm Schulze at the head of the first violins, to play the third *Leonore* overture—the last number on the program—with the orchestra. Dannreuther was a classical pianist, though by no means a virtuoso; he soon left the company in disgust with his surroundings, and went back to England. Parepa and Lévy were the great guns of the troupe. Parepa's wonderful voice,—her G *in alt* figured on all the posters,— perfect method, and grand, if rather cold, style carried everything before them; and Lévy's double-tonguing in triplets turned the popular head as nothing else could. Encores were Article XL. in the creed of audiences then, and I doubt if Parepa made as many conquests with "Ocean, thou mighty monster!" as with "Five o'clock in the Morning." John L. Hatton was the accompanist of the troupe. I remember one concert at which Bateman, in his most First-Gentleman-in-Europe manner, stepped forward on the platform, medical certificate in hand, deploring in tragic accents worthy of his daughter the sudden indisposition of an important member of the company, and winding up with the announcement: "Madame Parepa, with her usual nobility of nature, has kindly consented to stand in the gap; and my old friend, *your* old friend, EVERYBODY's old friend, John Hatton, will sing his inimitable 'Little Man dressed all in Grey.'" And he did sing it, too, to every one's delight, accompanying himself, and preluding it with the first few measures of Bach's G minor fugue!

The Great Organ seldom figured at variety concerts. I believe an extra charge was made for the use of it, and managers thought they could do quite as well without it. But organ concerts came thick and fast; almost every organist in the city and suburbs had his turn at the big (and unwieldy) instrument. After a while, it began to form part of the most adventurous combinations; I remember one evening when a fantasia on themes from Wallace's *Maritana* was played as a duet for mouth-harmonica and the Great Organ; a combination, as the program informed us, "never before attempted in the history of Music!"

The Handel & Haydn demi-centennial came in the spring of 1865; before the year was out, the Harvard Musical Association began its symphony concerts— or did these concerts begin after New Year? I forget; at any rate, they began either in December, 1865, or in January, 1866. But, before speaking of these concerts, I must mention another institution which passed away a year or two before, and had done a great deal of good amid hard struggles and difficulties. This was the old Philharmonic. I can not remember exactly on what basis the old Philharmonic concerts —not to be confounded with those of the Boston Philharmonic Society, founded much later—existed; I am under the impression that they were mainly, if not wholly, a private enterprise of Mr. Zerrahn's. They were subscription concerts, given in the evening, with (I think) a preliminary public rehearsal in the afternoon. They were given in the Music Hall, for the most part, though at times in the Boston Theatre, and were for years the principal orchestral concerts in the city. The orchestra was somewhat larger than that of the Orchestral Union. The concerts foundered during the hardest years of the war, a little after the Wednesday afternoon concerts of the Orchestral Union had struck colours; when they stopped, I think the Orchestral Union plucked up courage again, and continued giving concerts until the H. M. A. began.

The symphony concerts of the Harvard Musical Association began flourishingly, and their success went on increasing for some years. Crowded houses were the rule. This success did not, however, continue far into the seventies; the audiences began to drop off, subscriptions to decrease, and little by little the stigmata of unpopularity began to show themselves on the institution. There were several reasons for this, most, if not all, of which may be summed up in the one fact that the H. M. A. concerts were the connecting link between the old and the new musical Boston. They represented our transition period.

The Association started out on pretty severe classical and conservative principles; and, when the time came for going with the general current of musical thought and feeling, they continued to be strongly conservative and even reactionary. The Head-Centre —if not the heart and soul—of the Association was the late John S. Dwight; and his musical principles are still too well known to need dilating upon here. Many influential members of the Association were eager to have it join hands with what was then generally called the party of progress; but Dwight was inexorable, and would not yield an inch. No committee-man could, in the end, make headway against his triumphant "system of inertia;" the spirit of the concerts remained conservative to the end.

Another reason for the growing unpopularity of the concerts was still less in the Association's power to overcome. In 1869 Theodore Thomas began making our city flying visits with his New York orchestra, then unquestionably one of the finest in the world; and his concerts gave us Bostonians some rather humiliating lessons in the matter of orchestral technique. The H. M. A. was naturally slow in taking these lessons to heart; indeed it only did take them to heart when it was already too late to profit by them, after the yearly income from the concerts had so dwindled away that it was well-nigh hopeless to think of affording the needful money for engaging better orchestral material and having more rehearsals. In fact, the only practical influence I can remember the Thomas concerts having upon the H. M. A. was that, for some years, both conductor and a large part of the orchestra seemed bitten with the extreme-*pianissimo* mania; we had a series of the most astounding half-audible *pianissimo* string-effects, even in Beethoven symphonies. That silly little muted-string transcription of Schumann's *Träumerei,* which Thomas played again and again, had turned all heads! Still the public could not but draw its own comparisons between the playing of the Thomas Orchestra and that of our own; and such comparisons only added to the already serious unpopularity of the H. M. A. "Dull as a symphony concert" almost passed into a proverb.

Of course the opposition somewhat overdid the business. The H. M. A. orchestra did not play by any means so badly as some people would have had you believe; neither were the programs so dull and "ultra-classical" as they were commonly reputed to be. Not a little of the "New Music" was played; and, curiously enough,—considering the loud and repeated demands for it,—generally very coldly received by the audience. There was really a good deal of variety in the H. M. A. programs. When Wilhelm Gericke first came here and looked over the programs of the H. M. A. for the seventeen years of their existence, his astonishment at the vast field covered by them was unbounded. "I don't see what is left for me to do!" he exclaimed, "you seem to have had everything here already, much more than we ever had in Vienna!" But the public was disgruntled, the Association had got a bad name, and people in general noticed the old things on the programs much more than they did the new ones. The rats were leaving the sinking ship, and fewer and fewer music-lovers cared to book for a passage. Yet, in face of all this, one curious fact remains: through the whole

seventeen years of its symphony concerts, the Harvard Musical Association came out ahead pecuniarily; with all the miserably small audiences of the later years, it never lost a cent on its concerts! The success of the first few years was enough to carry the concerts through, besides allowing the Association to spend a tidy sum every year on increasing its library.

I like now to look back upon some of the enthusiasms of those earlier years of the H. M. A. concerts; for we had our enthusiasms then, as now. Few musical events in this city have surpassed—in the *furor* of enthusiasm it called forth—the first performance of Niels Gade's C minor symphony. The scherzo, with its ever-recurring joyous refrain, carried everything before it! Schumann's *Genoveva* overture made almost as strong and unexpected an impression, if in a more restricted circle; I think the *Genoveva* marked the turning-point in the public's attitude toward Schumann here. Before it, the general run of music-lovers inclined to look upon Schumann as incomprehensibly new-fangled; after it, people began to prick up their ears and listen to him with more and more sympathy and comprehension. The *Genoveva* was even enough to induce them to listen respectfully to his C major symphony, which was brought out here at the same concert—and, by the way, how like Pandemonium-let-loose the first movement sounded, with the then playing! Like the very rags and tatters of music! Goldmark's *Sakuntala* turned nearly all heads; Mr. Zerrahn and the orchestra were particularly wild over it, and I think it was given three times in half a season. Saint-Saëns's *Phaèton* had an almost equal success, and notably with the players. I remember Schulze saying, one day after a rehearsal, "It may not be of any very solid value; but it is tremendous fun. I tell you, when those trills come our way, in the violins, they make us *feel like kings!*" Brahms's C minor symphony made us stare, though! I doubt if anything in all music ever sounded more positively terrific than that slow introduction to the first movement did to us then. Some twenty or thirty years before, Schumann's B-flat major variations had seemed about the *ne plus ultra* of "cats'-music;" but they were nothing to the Brahms C minor. Naturally the imperfect performance had much to do with the fearful impression the work made upon us at the time; but the novelty of the style was for a great deal in it, too. I think the only Boston musician who was really enthusiastic over the Brahms C minor from the beginning was B. J. Lang. But the rest of us followed him soon enough; I myself bringing up in the rear, after six years or so. It took considerably longer than that, though, for Brahms to win anything like a firm foothold in Boston. It was the old story over again. Schumann had to fight long for recognition from the public; Wagner did anything but come, see, and conquer. Liszt and Berlioz frightened almost all listeners at first. And, when Brahms came, he seemed the hardest nut to crack of all! Tchaikovsky took us by storm, when von Bülow first played his B-flat minor concerto here, and the *Andante* of his D major quartet soon became the *"Stella confidente* of quartet-players."* But Tchaikovsky stock was not long in falling a goodish way below par; and it took it some time to rise again. If the Harvard Musical Association's concerts stuck pretty fast to the classics, they had at least an excuse in the coldness with which almost all the new things were received —no matter how loudly press and public might have clamoured for them. The public persistently cried for the new things, and turned up its nose when it got them.

XI

Thomas Ryan
Recollections of an Old Musician
(New York, 1899)

[Thomas Ryan arrived in Boston as a seventeen-year-old boy from Dublin in May of 1845. Within three days he was earning seven dollars a week playing the flute in the orchestra of the Washington Street Theatre, and for some six decades thereafter he was one of Boston's most active and valuable musicians. As a violist, clarinetist, flautist and/or violinist, he played in most of the important theaters, including the Howard Athenaeum and the old Tremont Temple (in which he played at Jenny Lind's Boston debut); he also played in most of Boston's pioneering symphonic organizations, as well as in Patrick Gilmore's Peace Jubilees. Most significantly, he was a member of the Mendelssohn Quintette Club, a group of musicians who, more than anyone else, were responsible for introducing good chamber music to this country. Their colorful concert career involved confronting the literal as well as cultural frontier: the Quintette Club was the first serious musical organization to tour the West—as far west, in fact, as Australia and Tasmania!

Near the end of his long career, Ryan wrote his *Recollections of an Old Musician,* as vivid and engaging a musical autobiography as has ever appeared in this country. The book is a mine of information about the theatrical and musical personalities and events of Ryan's experience. He is not always entirely accurate, but even his errors can be interesting —such as the revealing slip, "John Sebastian Dwight" —and the overall picture has indeed the look of real life to it. The fifth chapter offers a glimpse of the orchestra of the Boston Academy of Music and an anecdote that reveals much about a musical, specifically symphonic, organization in its cultural infancy. The twenty-second and twenty-third chapters present a participant's account of two of the most famous events in Boston's musical history, the Peace Jubilees of 1869 and 1872. These gigantic affairs are utterly neglected in Dwight's "History" (he had opposed them vigorously during their inceptions, although he did attend and write perceptively and appreciatively of the first festival); that omission is corrected in Ryan's accurate but nonetheless incredible tale of these great gatherings and of the man who was responsible for them, the extraordinary bandleader and entrepreneur (and composer of "When Johnny Comes Marching Home") Patrick S. Gilmore. Ryan is understandably very positive and enthusiastic about Gilmore's accomplishment, but this does not prevent him from displaying a certain clear-eyed humorousness about the goings-on. Gilmore himself wrote a long account of the 1869 festival (which included the names of every one of the "immortal ten thousand" of the chorus, as well as everyone else who participated or was officially invited to the event), but Ryan's version is more concise and delightfully free of the self-importance that mars Gilmore's history.]

Recollections of an Old Musician

CHAPTER V

In my early days in Boston, series of concerts were given in the Federal Street Theatre, on the corner of Franklin Street, by the so-called Boston Academy of Music. There was always a goodly number of music-lovers in Boston,—and we cannot give too much credit to the pioneers who did the ploughing and seeding of musical taste. "The Boston Academy of Music" was formed and named in 1833, by Messrs. William C. Woodbridge, Lowell Mason, and a few kindred souls, who laid out this ambitious but beneficent programme:

1. To establish schools of vocal music and juvenile classes.
2. To establish similar classes for adults.
3. To form a class for instruction in the methods of teaching music.

4. To form an association of choristers and leading members of choirs for the purpose of improvement in church music.

5. To establish a course of popular lectures on the nature and object of church music.

6. To have scientific lectures.

7. To give exhibition concerts.

8. To introduce vocal music into schools.

9. To publish circulars and essays.

The Academy, after a few years of action on this basis, resolved itself into an organization of music-lovers and amateur instrumentalists, assisted by professionals, making an orchestra of perhaps forty, and gave concerts.

The programmes were of very mixed music, but aspiring to the best. Beethoven's *Fifth Symphony* was brought out by them for the first time in Boston. Each programme was generally made up of a French opera overture, one or two instrumental solos by members of the orchestra or strangers, a movement from an easy symphony, a potpourri, and a few vocal pieces.

The President of the Society, at the time of which I am writing, was Gen. B. F. Edmands, a most amiable man and an efficient worker. I was engaged by him as one of the second violins. He saw that I was an ambitious boy, and took a fancy to me. That ambition got me into a little trouble later on, and was the cause of a bit of musical history of the times worth recording.

Before coming to Boston I had played second clarinet in the Dublin (Ireland) Philharmonic Society. In the season of 1844-45, that Society brought out the *Scotch Symphony* and the *Midsummer Night's Dream* overture, by Mendelssohn. When I made the acquaintance of General Edmands, I took the liberty of telling him that Mendelssohn's music was in great favor in Europe, and urged him to get the above works. They were sent for. When received, it was discovered that no score had come.

We must remember that fifty years ago there were not many professional musicians of sufficient technical ability to cope with Mendelssohn's music, which even to-day is classified as difficult. Our orchestra was made up half of amateurs and half of professionals. We could have no lightning-express trains in *tempo;* most music was played *tempo commodo.* All trains were accommodation trains. "Music was made for man, and not man for music." Those were the governing principles, and in general furnished the motive power.

One other point to remember is the fact that in old days an overture generally meant a big, noisy, pompous, slam-bang affair, intended for a curtain-raiser to an opera,—a certain festive noise to be made while people were tumbling into their seats, or looking around to see who had come, etc. This type of overture was the only one the average player had any acquaintance with; indeed, in point of history, we must not overlook the fact that Mendelssohn was the creator of the so-called romantic overture, under which head come *Fingal's Cave, Calm Sea, Ruy Blas,* etc. Therefore, when I say that the *Midsummer Night's Dream* was taken up for the first time by our orchestra, all cultured persons who are familiar with that delicate, fairy-like composition may well smile to think that any but experts should attempt the difficult feat of playing it.

Well, we tried it. Our conductor was Mr. Geo. J. Webb,—an excellent general musician, but who had never heard the overture. He began by telling us that he had no score; so he stood up alongside of the first-violin desk and prepared to conduct. Rapping on the desk, he gave the signal to begin; out piped two flutes,—nothing else. He rapped again, implying that the players had not been ready to begin; then he said, "We will try again." He gave the signal—and out piped the two flutes. That caused a little titter of surprise, and we all looked quizzically at each other. Mr. Webb, however, dutifully gave the signal for the next "hold" or chord, when two clarinets joined the two flutes! More surprise. At the third hold (chord) the fagotti and horns were added, and at the fourth hold (chord) the entire wood and wind instruments, all sounding most distressingly out of tune. This dissonant and unlooked-for result was followed by a dead pause; then every one of the players broke out with a hearty laugh of derision.

I was on pins and needles and muttered, "Go on, go on!" After a while the people sobered down, and we tried to commence with the string part. The first and second violins (each relative part divided into two parts) began at an "accommodation-train" *tempo.* At the end of the violin passage, the wood and wind again held a very dissonant chord for two measures, which this time sounded so abominably out of tune that it really was as bad as if each man played any note he pleased; and it was so irresistibly funny that again everybody burst out laughing. But I buried my head under the music desk and cried; my idol was derided, every one poked fun at me.

That last dissonant chord ended the first rehearsal of the *Midsummer Night's Dream* overture. We never tried it again.

Time, however, set me right. A few years later, the Germania Musical Society visited Boston. The Germania was a fine orchestra of about thirty artists, and every one could play well his part. Their first concert was given on April 14th. Their *pièce de résistance* was the overture to *Midsummer Night's Dream,* and it was beautifully played. So I had my revenge and could poke fun at my fellow-players by saying, "Now you can hear what Mendelssohn is as a composer." (The overture was written in 1826, when he was only seventeen years old, as everybody should know.)

This is the programme of the Germania concert:

1. OVERTURE TO "ZAMPA" . . . .   *Hèrold.*
2. WALTZ, "The Pesther" . . . .   *Lanner.*
3. FANTAISIE FOR VIOLIN . . . .   *Ernst.*
       MR. WM. SCHULTZE.
4. BETTY POLKA . . . .   *Lenschow.*
5. OVERTURE, "Midsummer Night's Dream,"
       Mendelssohn.
6. VARIATIONS ON SWISS AIR FOR THE FLUTE,
       Boehm.

    MR. PFEIFFER.

7. FINALE, "Siege of Corinth" . . . . . .   *Rossini.*
8. FESTIVAL OVERTURE, Dedicated to the President of the United States, General Taylor,
       Lenschow.
9. WALTZ, "Sounds from the Heart" . .   *Strauss.*
10. PANORAMA OF BROADWAY, NEW YORK. "A descriptive potpourri, received with the greatest applause by large and fashionable audiences," arranged by . . . .   *Lenschow.*

    . . . . .

CHAPTER XXII

It may be well to say that I am not undertaking to write the musical history of the United States, nor even of Boston; but I believe the Jubilees are as worthy of being put on record as would be a first performance in America of the *Parsifal* by Richard Wagner; though in comparison with the latter, the Jubilee music is like a boy compared with a man. But without the first, the other could not be. *Parsifal* is the man fully grown (some think he is the *ne plus ultra*), while the Jubilees represent the boy,—the tearing, rowdy young fellow, in his first stage of musical growth.

There are musical people of the present age who ask, "What were those Jubilees you talk about?" Some of them may add, "I find in my good mother's library a stack of chorus music marked 'The Jubilee Collection'; and among those pieces are works written by our native composers, together with great oratorios and some trash. What does it all mean? When did the Jubilees occur?"

I will try to answer those questions, premising that there could not have been Jubilees without Patrick Sarsfield Gilmore; and we must know his history to know that of the Jubilees.

It is well understood that all talented men are of Irish parentage, for that naturally includes the present writer (!) as well as Mr. Gilmore,—or rather "P.S." as all his friends called him. As a boy he lived

in Salem, Mass., and quite early in life he was a member of the Salem Band, and afterward its leader. His next step forward made him, in 1852, a member of the somewhat famous "Ordway Minstrels," in Boston, then playing in the little hall of the historical "Province House," where, in colonial times, the governors and nabobs held high court,—or "high jinks," as we may properly call it.

If we here allow a spirit of discursive moralizing to take possession of us, we shall have a fine chance to make mental pictures of the old colonial days, to see in fancy the red-coated king's officers, the bedizened governor and his courtiers, the young bucks and belles of the period, the guards of honor in and about the diminutive but cozy little place of royal revelry, and then to compare it all with an entertainment prepared for our modern republican pleasure-loving people,—so entirely different, even in their pleasures. In old times, "pleasures" meant chiefly eating, drinking, dancing, hunting, and love-making. The latter, in its primitive essentials, remains the same, and doubtless will till the end of time, but in other things our modern system of pleasures is vastly different from that of the colonial days. It is true we eat and drink, and we dance a little, but we have evolved a large class of people to entertain us in various ways, and to do it without any effort on our part. One species of this entertainment is, or was, negro minstrelsy; perhaps we might call it "low jinks." We see a band of these fun-providing people holding their revelry in that same Province House hall, and what a cruel contrast is thus made by the irony of fate! Where English nobles once held court, we now see the Irish boy, Patrick Gilmore, snapping his fingers in derision at nobles or their king,—and yet only in the spirit of professional fun, for he with his good brethren are thus earning their daily bread.

From out the frame of that picture we may now withdraw the aspiring boy, P. S. Gilmore, for he shortly after graduated into one of the military bands in Boston. Step by step he climbed the ladder, and finally we had "Gilmore's Band." "P.S." was an active, restless "hustler," and his band was soon on the top of the wave. When the war broke out, Gilmore showed at once the stuff he was made of. He was an ardent "off-for-the-war" man. Meetings to help along enlistments for the army and navy were being held everywhere. Gilmore and his full band constantly played at these meetings, and I dare say played out of pure patriotism. With his band in gay uniforms and ribbons flying from their hats, as in old days, he even paraded the streets of Boston, drumming up recruits for the Massachusetts 24th Regiment.

The next step was that he and his whole band volunteered as soldiers, regularly enlisted as the band of the 24th, and with that regiment went to the war. It is on record that he and his men were always on hand to cheer up "the boys" with good music when they most needed it, and he even got some of the bright young spirits of that crack regiment to form a minstrel company. In fact, he showed his energy and good fellowship in every situation.

After about a year's service in North Carolina, his band, like most of the regimental bands, was mustered out. General Banks, commanding the Department of New Orleans, urged Mr. Gilmore to go to that city and become the chief director of music in his command. He accepted, and was a very popular man in that capacity. He organized one very large school-children's music festival, and it doubtless gave him a good preliminary experience in managing large numbers of performers.

When the "cruel war was over" Gilmore went back to Boston, and once more had "to hustle for a living." He reorganized his band, brought it up to its best estate, and for several seasons gave Sunday night sacred and popular concerts in Music Hall or Boston Theatre. He was a venturesome manager, paying high for drawing cards, and usually had a big orchestra and chorus in addition to his band. He did all the drilling and directing of the musical forces himself, attended to the financial details, and managed to get valuable assistance from the newspapers; in fact, he manifested an energy which was astounding. His large "pull" on the military element in Boston was a great help to him. In the midst of this activity in public entertainments, he formed a partnership (Gilmore & Wright) for the manufacture of band instruments.

I mention all these points to show that Mr. Gilmore was a very bright, energetic man. And whether he lost or made money, his cheery temper always remained unruffled and unclouded. His popularity was great; and all his earlier ventures and activity were simply an apprenticeship for really large doings a little later.

I cannot say positively whether the embryo idea of a Jubilee emanated from him, or whether it took form from the chance suggestion of some one else; but I believe it to have been a Gilmore idea because of the peculiar make-up of the man. He was an earnest, loyal American. All the Southern States had come back into the fold, and we were once more a glorious Union. Peace and plenty reigned. Gilmore was just the sort of man into whose head would come buzzing the idea that the nation should have a big, rollicking family jubilee to celebrate the happy state of the country. Boston was the place above all places in which to hold it. [*] It should be a musical and social reunion,—a magnificent *jubilate*. Such it was in reality.

Mr. Gilmore had the ability to inspire a very large number of people with a belief in him and his idea, who were willing to become financial guarantors. Accordingly a wooden building of good acoustic properties was promptly erected on the Back Bay lands, near or on the site of the present Art Museum, [**]—a building capable of holding fifty thousand persons, including a big chorus of ten thousand and a great orchestra of one thousand. The audience was to be seated in chairs on a level, oblong floor and in the deep balcony which ran round the sides and the end facing the stage. A great organ was built for the occasion; also a bass drum, the head of which might have been ten or twenty feet in diameter. This drum was a special point of attraction; it seemed as big as a Fourth of July balloon.

The musical part of the Jubilee—all things considered,—was noble and dignified. The great chorus, the great orchestra, the great organ, the great drum, and the great singer, Parepa-Rosa, with her wonderful, never-to-be-forgotten rendering of the *Inflammatus,* may seem, at this distance of time and development of musical taste, as something only "great" to laugh at. Yet, when a whole serious-minded community like that of Boston "took stock" in it, and the spirit of the idea was carried out happily, is it not perhaps rash to mock at it? Have not the results been far-reaching, doing their work in this world of evolution just as the chromo prepares the way for high art? Who can say that a large share of Boston's musical reputation was not earned by the Jubilees?

Returning to details, it will surprise many to know that the orchestra numbered quite a thousand—with the patriotic Ole Bull at the head of the violins, and Carl Rosa playing at the same desk. Gilmore had engaged all the principal sopranos of Boston, constituting a "bouquet of artistic singers." These were placed on a special raised balcony between the orchestra and the chorus, and they sang in unison the *obligato* parts as they occurred in the choral pieces.

Great care had been exercised all through the preceding winter in preparing the choristers, who were scattered all over New England,—every village and town contributing a quota. They were supplied with the Jubilee music, and the leaders and directors of all these people had the *tempi* (Italian plural for "time") given them. During many months it was a busy time for Carl Zerrahn, as general music director, and his aids. They had to travel from town to town to drill the choristers, or to see that the preparations were going on auspiciously.

[*According to his own account, Gilmore took his idea to New York and Washington first before settling on Boston, which was also thoroughly reluctant in the beginning.]

[**That is, the old Museum of Fine Arts in Copley Square.]

When all the singers finally came together the result was pretty good. But a chorus of ten thousand persons would naturally occupy a wide space, and they would inevitably drag the *tempo*. Mr. Zerrahn often had to show good generalship by rushing up the aisle which separated the two divisions of the big choral army in order to get near enough to beat the laggards into time.

Mr. Gilmore was a modest and a wise man, and conducted but little of the music himself; but that little was great,—for did he not direct the "Anvil Chorus"? Will Boston, or at least its Jubilee participators, ever forget the sensation it had when the one hundred firemen—each in his belt, helmet, and red flannel shirt, carrying a long-handled blacksmith's hammer at "right shoulder shift" like a musket— marched into the hall and on to the stage in two files of fifty, and then separated far enough to form a red frame for two sides of the orchestra, which meanwhile was playing the introduction to the "Anvil Chorus"? Reaching their special, *real* anvils, the firemen faced the audience, lifted their hammers to the proper position, and at the right musical moment of time began to pound the anvils,—right, left, right, left,—while the great orchestra and chorus played and sang the melody.

If ever "the welkin rang" it did then!

In addition to the sounds from a hundred anvils there was the great organ, military band, drum corps, all the bells in the city achime, and a cannon accompaniment. This last came from two batteries of well served guns stationed at a short distance from the building, and a gun was fired off by electricity on the first beat of each measure. A small table was placed on the stage, close to the director, with a set of electric buttons, each having a wire leading to a gun. Mr. John Mullaly was the artist who pressed the button; the gun did the rest. These guns were similarly used for all national airs.

At the termination of the "Anvil Chorus" there was enormous applause. The whole mass of people rose to their feet, jumped up and down, and nearly dislocated their arms by waving handkerchiefs, fans, hats, parasols, even babies. I am sure that I was never in any great assembly where such wild, almost frantic cheering and applause was heard. Fifty thousand people in a wooden building can make some noise.

The dear, wonderful old *maestro,* Verdi, did certainly furnish a great opportunity for P. S. Gilmore. It is equally certain that Verdi never dreamed of the possibilities contained in the "slam-bang" popular melody. When the piece was ended, the gentlemen firemen would march out; and, the applause continuing, they would march back again and go through the whole exciting performance once more.

During the festival, some of the composers like J. K. Paine and Dudley Buck directed their own compositions. Mr. Eben Tourjee directed *Nearer, my God, to Thee,* and other hymn tunes.

This first festival was held in June, 1869, and lasted a week. Performances were given afternoons only,—nothing in the evenings, except a large, very successful ball given on Friday evening. People poured in from all parts of the country; distance was no hindrance,—they came from the far West and even from California.

On June 17th, the President of the United States, General Ulysses S. Grant, with Admiral Farragut, Admiral Thatcher, Commodore Winslow, a numerous staff, and the Governor of the State, all in full uniform, were present at the performance.

The financial part of the Jubilee was satisfactory. There was a very large income, $290,000, and a correspondingly large outlay, $283,000. All professional people, except the few who declined to receive pay, were paid. The care of the finance had been taken off Mr. Gilmore's shoulders. After every bill was paid, a respectable balance remained. This balance, together with the proceeds of a benefit concert, $32,000, making together $39,000, was, very properly and very handsomely, handed to Mr. Gilmore.

For musical completeness I give the programme of the first concert, June 15, 1869, which will serve as a type of all.

1. GRAND CHORAL, "A Strong Castle is our Lord,"
   Luther.
2. TANNHAUSER OVERTURE, Select Orchestra of 600, ... *Wagner.*
   Directed by Mr. JULIUS EICHBERG.
3. GLORIA from the Twelfth Mass, .. *Mozart.*
4. AVE MARIA, ... *Bach-Gounod.*
   Sung by Madame PAREPA-ROSA.
The violin obligato played by two hundred violinists.
5. NATIONAL AIR, "The Star Spangled Banner,"
   Key.

   Sung and played by the entire force with
   Bells and Cannon.

Intermission fifteen minutes.

6. AMERICAN HYMN, ... *Keller.*
7. OVERTURE, "William Tell." ...... *Rossini.*
8. INFLAMMATUS from the "Stabat Mater,"
   Rossini.

   Madame PAREPA-ROSA.
9. CORONATION MARCH, from "Le Prophete," 1000 performers, ... *Meyerbeer.*
10. ANVIL CHORUS, from "Il Trovatore," *Verdi.*

All the forces; 100 anvils, performed on by 100 members of the Boston Fire Department; Bells and Cannons.

11. MY COUNTRY, 'T IS OF THEE, words by REV. S. F. SMITH, D.D. All the forces; the audience requested to join in singing the last stanza.

CHAPTER XXIII

The second Jubilee was held in 1872, and, like all repetitions of a similar nature, it was found to be impossible to get up a popular excitement equal to that which attended the first one. It was therefore not a financial success. The new building designed for it, and everything else, was on a larger scale, and not so easily handled. There were some notably fine features, but the whole was less of a strictly home affair.

Gilmore's plans again showed his genius. They were bold, well conceived, but very costly. He went to Europe, and "talked the crowned heads" (that was the popular phrase) "into letting their crack" military bands come over to play in the Jubilee. He obtained the band of the Grenadier Guards from London, about forty-five strong, under Dan Godfrey; a German infantry band, about thirty-five men, under Saro; and that of the Garde Républicaine, from Paris, of about fifty-five men. It was said that this latter was reinforced by fine artists from the opera, and was not therefore a fair sample of French bands. There was also a little insignificant band, the Royal Constabulary, from Ireland.

These bands had an English day and German, French, and Irish days. The English band was good, the German, too brassy, the French, magnificent. The latter opened with Meyerbeer's "Torch-Light Dance" *(Fackeltänze)* and won instant success. They had a double quartette of saxophones, four fagotti, a double fagott, and some very large tubas: and the total result was so round, full, and soft, that all musicians were captivated with the deep diapason volume of sound. Their performance of the *William Tell* overture was superb.

It is to be remembered that, in 1872, the political antagonism between the French and Germans was great. The Franco-Prussian War had left rankling hatred between the two peoples. The sight of a German to a Frenchman was like shaking a red rag in the face of a bull; consequently, on the day the French band of La Garde Républicaine marched down the broad aisle in full uniform, surrounded (in their imagination) by their enemies, the German musicians, it was certainly an anxious moment for the Frenchmen. It seemed to me—perhaps it was the effect of the sympathetic current created by the situation—that they were pale with anxiety. It was to be their battle-field; they were to be judged by prejudiced listeners, and they were on their mettle.

The performance of the band was musically so perfect that all prejudice was annihilated. Metaphorically the Germans embraced the Frenchmen; we were all of one brotherhood—politics and race differences had vanished—the music had disarmed all evil spirits. We were simply musicians, ready to award praise to merit. When the band ended the overture, the players all about them were as wild in their applause as the general public. And I am sure I saw some of the Frenchmen wipe away tears of joy at their well-won victory.

Mr. Gilmore had captured several rare lions and lionesses for his musical menagerie, chief among whom was the royal lion, Johann Strauss,—the famous waltz-composer from Vienna,—and Madame Peschka-Leutner, a coloratura singer of extraordinary ability. This lady captivated her audiences with her clear, telling, high, and powerful soprano voice, her almost matchless execution, style, and other rare vocal gifts. She was a genuine success.

Then there was Madame Rudersdorf, a splendid singer, of broad, classic, oratorio style. She was of great value to the city of Boston, for she settled there and became a teacher of teachers.

Strauss, violin in hand, conducted the orchestra daily, in one of his most popular waltzes, and also in some little knick-knacks, such as the *Pizzicato Polka,* which became at once a great favorite. His manner of conducting was very animating. He led off with the violin bow to give the *tempo,* but when the right swing was obtained and the melody was singing out from the orchestra, he joined in with his fiddle as if he *must* take part in the intoxication of the waltz. While playing or conducting he commonly kept his body in motion, rising and falling on his toes in a really graceful manner.

It was natural that Strauss, the composer of the *Blue Danube,* should be an object of great interest to a large part of mankind and womankind. The man who had furnished the human family so many blissful moments, was bound to be an idol; and he had worship enough during the limited time allotted him to face his new-made Boston admirers. We must not forget that on all public parades he had his valet with him,—in gorgeous livery, a cockade on his hat, a brown and golden belt round his waist, a heavy cloth coat on, and over his arm (with the mercury at 90) a heavy cloak to place round his master, the king of waltz-makers, in case of need. This warmly dressed, though picturesque valet, always stood just at the front edge of the stage with his eyes fastened on his master. Some cynic has said, "No man is a hero to his valet." I take no more stock in that saying, for I think Strauss was a hero to his. We must judge somewhat by appearances in this world, as they often furnish our only ground for judgment.

This second Jubilee had a "coda," or tail, in the shape of a financial deficit, but the noble army of martyr guarantors "faced the music" like men.

Mr. Gilmore reached the apogee of his greatness at the period of these festivals. To conceive and carry out such plans showed much forethought and executive ability. First, to get those large military bands over from Europe—foreseeing that it would set the European world to talking of Gilmore and his band—was a pretty big thing; and then to follow it up (after he moved to New York City) by actually taking his New York band over to Great Britain, France, Germany, and (I think) Italy, was certainly not only bearding the lion in his den, or carrying coals to Newcastle, but it was undertaking a financial venture of the most uncertain kind—and yet Mr. Gilmore, with clear vision of success in his eyes, boldly carried out the project, and returned from Europe with all his colors flying.

I think it can be seen that the brave, loyal bandmaster, Patrick Sarsfield Gilmore, filled a good page in the musical and social history of our country. We hopefully believe he now rests in peace.

XII

Philip Hale
Selections from his columns in the
Boston Home Journal,
1889-91

[Philip Hale (1854-1934) and H. T. Parker (the next and final author in this anthology) were the dominant critics of music and the theater in Boston for over three decades. Hale was born in Vermont, went to Yale, read for the law, and even practiced law in Albany from 1880 to 1882 before embracing music as a profession (a delay brought about in part by the traditional family distrust of music as a way of making a living). After giving up law for his first love, he went to Germany to study organ, piano, and composition, following the accepted path to higher musical knowledge trod by so many Boston musicians, among them Paine, Chadwick, and Horatio Parker. In 1887 Hale returned to America and Albany to the profession of organist and choirmaster; he continued to perform even after he had taken up journalism, but criticism became an important part of his life even in Albany, and in 1889 Hale came to Boston to write for the *Boston Post* and the *Boston Home Journal,* which paper he served until 1903.

From the very beginning he demonstrated a breadth of knowledge and a versatility that transcended narrow critical reportage. His writing gracefully encompassed social and philosophical questions surrounding music and theater, as well as a sound practical consideration of the events he witnessed. He also wrote extensively on nonartistic topics, for the most part in columns devoted to the humorous observation of the foibles of humanity, such as the "Taverner" column in the Journal and, more famously, the *Herald* column, "As the World Wags." When he moved to *The Boston Herald* in 1903, he was a securely established critical power in the city; however, the thirty years at the *Herald* were truly the years of "Philip the Great" (or "the Terrible," depending upon one's point of view). In those decades Boston could boast of two critics, Hale and Parker, with international reputations at least equal to those of the powerful New York critics of the day (Krehbiel, Finck, Henderson, Aldrich), and Hale had an additional accomplishment to his credit: in 1901 he took over the writing of the Boston Symphony program notes from William Foster Apthorp (*q.v.*), and he presided over them until his retirement in 1933. Hale's Symphony notes are highly informative introductions to a wide range of music, and they have been considered by many to be models of their kind. Some of these essays were collected in book form (*Philip Hale's Boston Symphony Program Notes,* edited by John N. Burk, another distinguished BSO program annotater, and published the year after Hale's death).

The selections here come from Hale's early days in Boston, his *Boston Home Journal* period. They are chosen, not only to demonstrate their author's journalistic skill, but to present a general view of Boston musical culture as it approached a new century, particularly as seen through the eyes of a gifted and involved contemporary musician. A comparison of Hale's writing with the 1822 columns of the *Euterpeiad* and then with Dwight's 1840 *Dial* essay yields a revealing pattern of change and growth in Boston's musical culture. The critic's stance has evolved from that of the crusader on the musical frontier to that of observer of a musically rich and sophisticated city. But Hale, too, was a crusader, if not on the order of Dwight; the meaning of the cultural crusade seems, however, to have changed profoundly, along with society's other preoccupations, in the intervening half-century.]

Boston Home Journal

[October 19, 1889: Reflections upon the brilliant and highly individual art of the new conductor of the Boston Symphony Orchestra. The first concert of the season prompts the *Journal's* new critic to compare

Artur Nikisch with his predecessor, Wilhelm Gericke.]

The First Symphony Concert.—In applauding Mr. Nikisch, the patient and abiding work of Mr. Gericke should not be forgotten. He gave the orchestra technique. He taught it precision, he called attention to detail. Without the noble rage of the born conductor, he gave a cold and finished reading of whatever work was on his desk. He seemed to abhor contrasts; he shrank from great effects; he appeared at times to entertain a contempt for brass instruments. Gorgeous and daring coloring was not so dear to him as a pale monochrome. So the orchestra became under his leadership an admirable machine, which one looked at and admired. Not without reason, then, did an irreverent New Yorker dub it, "The Boston Music Box."

The work of Mr. Gericke has made possible the first success of Mr. Nikisch. Rhythm, sudden contrasts, crescendos carrying all before them, depend first upon the technique of the performer. Well might Mr. Nikisch, in modestly acknowledging the praise of the audience, turn and point to the men who had so well carried out his wishes.

What Mr. Gericke lacked, seems to be the distinguishing characteristic of the musical nature of Mr. Nikisch. He is highly endowed with imagination, and this imagination is under control. One may quarrel with his ideas, but his ideas at least are interesting. Take for example the "Coriolanus" overture. Some musicians, men whose opinions are of weight, object to his reading of the second motive, which is said to portray the prayers of women; though for that matter the overture might as well be called "King Lear" or "Hamlet"; for it is simply great music. They say it was almost effeminate, untraditional, not as Beethoven wished it.

Pray, how did Beethoven intend it to be played? Would he, himself, have directed it twice exactly in the same manner? We know by the testimony of his hearers that he played his own compositions for the piano with great freedom and almost capriciously.

Why should not a director be allowed to have his own conception of a work, provided that conception be a beautiful or effective one?

But some one may say Mr. Nikisch did not show due "piety" towards Beethoven. Now there is a false and true piety. Rubini was deservedly hissed when, not content with the great air in "Don Giovanni" as Mozart wrote it, he sang, instead of a sustained note, the phrase given in accompaniment to the violins. A pianist, however, who today plays a piece of Couperin exactly as it is written, overladen with ornaments added by the composer on account of the scanty resources of the instruments of that time, shows doubtful taste and false devotion. Again, the modern German organists in playing the works of

Bach, play as a rule with full organ and say they follow in the footsteps of Bach. Yet according to the testimony of Adam Hiller in his life of Bach, written only thirty years after the death of the latter, "he understood the art of combining the stops in a most cunning manner, and of using each according to its character"; and in Bach's correspondence, we find him asking that the tremulant of his organ should be put in order.

Whether Mr. Nikisch's treatment of the second motive of the overture was traditional or not, it was certainly effective, particularly when towards the close it follows the warning notes of the horns.

The other numbers of the program were the Introduction to "Die Meistersinger," an entr'acte from "Rosamunde" and Schumann's Fourth Symphony.

In the beautiful music of Schubert the work of the flute, oboe and clarinet was excellent both in tone and phrasing. The reading of the Wagner overture was in many respects novel and as a whole impressive; agreeably distinct, with a fine sense of the relative values of the parts in the most intricate contrapuntal passages.

There had been a good deal of comment about the choice of the symphony for the opening concert. It is without doubt true that the peculiar genius of Schumann did not lie in the direction of symphonic writing. He was a man of great ideas, with but little sense of orchestral color and a tendency to vagueness and uninteresting digressions.

The Schumann whom Zola apostrophizes as "despair itself, the ecstasy of woe, the end of all, the last song of mournful purity heard in air over the ruins of the world"—the true Schumann is seen in the Kreisleriana, the piano quintet, the Lieder. And yet what passages of wild grandeur and unearthly beauty does this often despised Fourth Symphony contain.

Its performance was a revelation. Even the first movement lost much of its inherent ugliness, and nothing could be more dramatic than the rest of the Symphony beginning with the Romanze. The sixteen measures leading from the delightful Scherzo to the last movement were declaimed with overwhelming effect. The tones of the trombones, horns and trumpets under the direction of Mr. Nikisch are no longer "pillowy protuberances."

The new conductor led quietly, at times a little stiffly, without the score before him. If a conductor can dispense with the score, so much the better; for so can he exert more powerfully his personal magnetism, just as an orator who uses no notes plays more easily upon the passions of his hearers. To do this successfully a man must of course be favored by nature; and if he is able to memorize only a few bars, it certainly is then the part of wisdom to use a score of fairly coarse print.

The first afternoon audience was cold; it is true there were many present who had paid a high premium for seats which, I believe, Mr. Higginson originally intended for impecunious students and lovers of music. Possibly some of these good people were surprised at the absence of a calcium light; or they perhaps expected that Mr. Nikisch would be lowered from the ceiling to the director's stand by means of an invisible wire. The audience of the following Saturday night gave Mr. Nikisch a hearty welcome and generous applause.

This first concert has shown conclusively that Mr. Nikisch is a conductor of rare endowments. Future concerts will show whether the "individuality" already complained of will prove to be individualism; whether instead of nine parts Beethoven and one part Nikisch we shall be obliged to have our Beethoven still more diluted.

[November 16, 1889: From a review of a Boston Symphony concert in which Nikisch conducted symphonies by Haydn, Mozart and Beethoven.]

"The art of art," says Walt Whitman, "the glory of expression . . . is simplicity. Nothing is better than simplicity, nothing can make up for excess or for the lack of definiteness." . . . Nowhere in music is this simplicity more imperatively demanded than in the works of Mozart. His melodies are so free, so perfectly balanced, his harmonies are so constructed, that they lose instead of gain by any attempt to give to them increased "expression." Now Mr. Nikisch has taken liberties in overtures by Beethoven and Weber for which he has been severely criticized. These were chiefly slight changes in tempo, generally found in connection with second motives and episodes. These liberties have found, on the other hand, warm admirers and earnest defenders; and the reasons for applauding instead of condemning are many. But take the first movement of the G minor symphony as played under Mr. Nikisch, was it as beautiful to the ear that night as it is to the eye upon the printed pages? This wonderful child of inspiration and science is an *allegro molto* beginning with a melody given in octaves to the violins; the accompaniment is played by the other stringed instruments. It is an Italian song of restrained passion, of quiet intensity, such as is found in the first movement of Mozart's G minor quintet; it is direct, going straight to the mark, as terribly in earnest as many of the musical sentences of the old man Verdi. It stands at the very beginning of the symphony. Mr. Nikisch treated it sentimentally; he coquetted with it. It was beautiful, but it had as it were an artificial beauty; it was a woman bedizened and bedecked instead of the naked goddess, rosy and palpitating. Had this been the second motive instead of the first,

there might have been a reasonable excuse; but surely at the beginning of a composition written so frankly and honestly, the rhythm should have been more sharply defined, and the melody given with more directness. I do not speak of any "traditions," I do not speak of the "composer's intentions"; it seems to me looking at the score that in this case Mr. Nikisch failed to find the proper rhythm, and so the melody suffered; its sensuous warmth cooled and it became lukewarm. And the whole movement halted a little, and it seemed as though Mozart had put on airs of affectation.

Yes, if the proper tempo is not found, the melody is ruined. How beautiful, for example, was the trio of the minuet in the same symphony; where if the "time" had been hurried one jot, the exquisite phrases allotted to the wind instruments would have been meaningless and confused. The minuets of Mozart and Haydn are often spoiled through the inability of conductors to discriminate between a scherzo and a minuet.

How should the first five measures of Beethoven's Fifth Symphony be played? Perhaps there is no passage in instrumental music about which conductors so essentially differ. Colonne of Paris who gives a singularly virile "reading" of this first movement, declaims the first phrases with the eighth notes heavily and deliberately detached; while his "holds" are as long sustained as the "holds" of Mr. Nikisch. With Wagner they hear Beethoven's voice crying, "Hold my *fermate* for a long time, so as to inspire awe. I do not write them merely for a joke, or as though I wanted time to ponder on what comes after." (And our orchestra held the long sustained tones without wavering; no easy task.) Mr. Nikisch's performance of the symphony has brought out much adverse criticism; it certainly was remarkable, at times curious and almost perplexing; it was radically different from others which have been heard and applauded. Was it therefore wrong? Were all the others right? Now it is easy to say the conception of Mr. Nikisch was bombastic and "un-Beethovenish." . . . But this fifth symphony abounds in daring violations of rules: there are passages of great difficulty which were once thought impossible and were omitted; there are mysterious and overwhelming things hinted at darkly which are followed suddenly by grotesque ideas. It is a Gothic cathedral where grinning gargoyles squat by the side of the statue of the Virgin.

There were passages which under Mr. Nikisch's direction assumed new and unpleasing forms. Perhaps a second hearing would confirm this opinion; perhaps it would remove it. In hearing a work which has been so often given, a musician must necessarily have preconceived ideas of its proper performance;

if the performance agrees with them he is apt to praise the conductor. But his ideas may be erroneous. Are there any formulas for directing the fifth symphony? Is there any carefully prepared receipt which no conductor should be without?

And there were portions of the work which were grandly worked up by the conductor and superbly played by the men. How full of beauty was the opening of the scherzo! How exciting was the approach to the finale, and how imposing was the declamation of the first pages of that finale!

The great audience, which had given hearty signs of approval after each number of the symphonies, at the end of the concert broke out in wild and long continued applause. And the orchestra deserved this tribute; for although there was at times a noticeable lack of precision and unity, the individual and ensemble as a whole was remarkably good. In this connection it may be proper to remark that the orchestra, while it has gained in fire and swing and all the details necessary for producing great effects, has apparently lost a little of that exquisite and delicate finish which characterized the concerts of Mr. Gericke. This is spoken of the orchestra as a whole, and not of the individual members, for nothing could have excelled the work of the double-basses, bassoons, and in fact all the individual playing heard last Saturday. To combine the qualities of finish and power may appear an impossible task; yet the superb orchestra of M. Lamoureux comes very near to this perfection. Better than unrelieved polish and such careful attention to detail that the effect of the whole is lost, is a performance full of virility, manly beauty and dramatic intensity, even though exaggeration may enter and annoy.

Six programs have thus far been presented to music lovers of this city; and not one of them includes the work of a French composer. Is Mr. Nikisch acquainted with any of the compositions of the French school?

[After four years in Boston the Hungarian-born Nikisch (1855-1922) returned to Europe, eventually to assume the conductorship of both of Germany's greatest orchestras, the Leipzig Gewandhaus orchestra and the Berlin Philharmonic. As far as is known, he was the oldest great conductor to make recordings, and his 1913 HMV recording of Beethoven's Fifth is the first full-scale symphony performance to be captured on records. This recording has been transferred to LP and is currently available as an import. The large features of the interpretation correspond very well to Hale's description of the BSO performance. The Schumann Fourth Symphony performance of the previous review seems to be similar in important respects to the recorded interpretation by Nikisch's successor in both Berlin and Leipzig, Wilhelm Furtwängler.]

[1889-90: Selections from Hale's "Causerie" column. Observations upon the year's end, pianists and pianos, singers and songs, orchestras and audiences, musical nationality, and much else.]

The year does not die amid the crash and roar of pianofortes. D'Albert came to his bedside and played to him, and the feeble old man was stunned by the *fantasie* of Schubert, for it was as the noise of a whip, and the noise of the rattling of the wheels, and of the prancing horses, and of the jumping chariots. The light of youth shone in his eyes when he heard the pieces of Liszt, and his blood turned to wine, and like Faust he dreamed of fair women. But Sunday he listened to the sublime harmonies of the "Messiah," and Friday night men singers and white-robed women sang for him the Mass for the dead.

. . . . .

So there is this week a lull after the musical storm and confusion of the past months. Concert has followed concert; and the hearer has had but little time to breathe or digest. The musician, whether he sing, play or direct, is now the mark at which we all shoot pointed arrows, or throw the bludgeons of our own make. He is ever before the public. Even his private life seems to be a matter of public interest. Take the case of Mr. Nikisch, whom some regard as a Lohengrin, brought by an ocean steamer for the salvation of our city; while others eye him askance and follow the worthy example of Master William Perkins (now with God) who in his sermons "used to pronounce the word Damn with such an Emphasis, as left a doleful Echo in his Auditors' Ears a good while after." And this is in Boston. How changed the sentiment of the people; does it seem possible that John Adams could have said of the promising youth, Peter Chardon, "This fellow's thoughts are not employed on songs and girls, nor his time on flutes, fiddles, concerts and card tables; he will make something"? For now we are either all musicians or we hope to be. We spend our money for concerts and pinch ourselves in other ways. Weak women stand during long programs that they may thus catch the crumbs which fall from the table of the rich man who wished to generously give a public banquet and has been thwarted by wicked speculators. [Note: This is a reference to the widespread ticket scalping that often frustrated BSO founder Henry Lee Higginson's desire to keep the admission prices low.] The columns of the journals are filled with learned disquisitions upon taste and traditions. Surely musicians will soon be a privileged class; they will be exempt from jury duty and will be sure of seats in the horse cars. And yet I have read somewhere that in Sweden in the fifteenth century, if one killed a musician, the crime was, if not absolutely permitted, at least tolerated, as the murdered man was held to be a dangerous criminal solely on account of his profession; and the only penalty the assassin paid was an indemnity to the heir of the dead man, this indemnity consisting of a pair of shoes, a pair of gloves and a three-year-old heifer. Upon an appointed day, the murderer, the heir and a few lookers-on met on the top of a steep hill. The heifer whose tail had possibly been greased was led to the summit. The heir took hold of the animal's tail, the murderer hit the calf; if the heir could stop her before she was at the foot of the hill, he could keep her for his own; if he could not stop her, the calf still belonged to the assassin.

. . . . .

Has the pianoforte of modern build been an unmixed blessing to music as an art? It undeniably has brought nearly all music to the knowledge of any one who has ten trained fingers. It is easy to say with some that it is an instrument of torture which breaks up happy homes, kills neighborly good will and devastates communities. Louis Pagnerre has written a book which bears the title, "The Evil Influence of the Piano on Music as one of the Arts." . . . And Riehl of Munich sees in the piano the great corruptor of music of this century, and he boldly says there will be again no great epoch in the history of music until the day when the voice and violin have vanquished the piano; "but we shall not live to see that day."

. . . . .

The singer and hearer react upon each other; the hearer soon becomes incapable of distinguishing good from evil, and the singer is careless, frivolous, and has for the audience a good-natured, ill-disguised contempt. Singers in the true sense of the word grow rarer each year. How many who apply for even church positions can read at sight or have musical knowledge enough to tell at a glance whether the key of the anthem put before them is E flat or C minor? Nor are they ashamed of their ignorance. How many who rush upon the concert stage have mastered tone production? If they have good voices, many are too lazy or too impatient, or too conceited and ignorant to learn their trade. Yet perhaps their conduct is excusable when they see the applause and money given to German men and women who, to be sure, in the catalogue go for singers—the descendants of the people of whom Frederick the Great said: "I had rather hear my horse whinny and snort in an aria than have a German prima donna in my opera house." . . . But our audiences, even though the voices of these favorites are disagreeable and untrained, endow the singers with "intelligence," and give them credit for "intellectuality," and then fall down and worship the gods of their own hands,

even as the man mentioned by Isaiah the prophet.

. . . . .

It is also a question whether so many orchestral concerts are not an injury to the state of the body musical. Some people of sensitive ears and impressionable spines go to the Saturday concerts as other men go to a dram-shop. They crave sudden and startling effects; they demand gorgeous instrumentation and odd rhythms. Their delight is in the cymbal, and they wait patiently for the triangle. What to them is a string-quartet of Haydn or a motet of Palestrina?

. . . . .

Fortunately choral societies still exist and flourish in this city; the readiness of men and women to quietly attend the necessary rehearsals and go through the inevitable drudgery attending the preparation for a concert is a surer sign of true musical interest than the buying of seats for Symphony concerts at an exorbitant price that it may be known of men. Sunday night the "Messiah" was given by the Handel and Haydn society . . . the choruses, as a whole, were admirably sung, but the soloists were not equal to the severe demands made upon them. The tenor part of the chorus, so often the weak spot in such societies, was surprisingly good. The measures of "Since by man" and "For as in Adam" were certainly more effective as sung by the full chorus than if they had been given to a quartet. There will always be a dispute as to how far improvers and restorers of a work of the last century should go. It is often said that Bach and Handel, had they lived in our own day, would have availed themselves of the resources of a modern orchestra. There are two answers to this statement: First, they did not live in our day, and their works, besides their great intrinsic worth, are interesting from the historical standpoint, and this interest ceases when we hear them arranged according to our modern ideas. Again, they were acquainted with nearly all of the instruments used in the modern orchestra, the clarinet being the most notable exception, and they also had at hand instruments not in use to-day, such as the oboe bassa, oboe d'amore, viola da gamba, viola da spada, viola pomposa (invented by Bach himself), not to mention a variety of violins, trumpets, and bassoons. Why, then, were they not used by Handel; and how did Handel fill up the passages which now to some seem empty? It must not be forgotten, however, that the works of Handel were essentially vocal, for symphonic art did not exist. When Handel wrote an aria he looked upon the accompaniment as background. His was an age of great singers, and he wished the voice to be supreme. . . . But modern ears rebel against simplicity. And it must be remembered that comparisons between the works of musicians of different centuries are useless and impertinent; a composer must be judged by what he did during his life in comparison with the composers of his own day. When we hear a work of Handel, with the additions of Franz, or even Mozart, we do not hear the work of Handel as he conceived it. Such additions, it is true, seem valuable in the absence of all knowledge as to how Handel himself accompanied his works upon the organ or clavier. Franz has shown taste and becoming reverence; an example of outrageous meddling can be seen in Bülow's additions to the Cat's fugue of Domenico Scarlatti.

. . . . .

How stands this question of nationality with us Americans? Is there any composition of long breath written by an American composer which at first or fortieth hearing strikes the listener as free from the marked influence of either the German, French or Italian school; *apart;* distinctively American; a work which could only have been written by an American? We have many composers of American birth who in their works show both talent and skill; but have we any American School of Composers? Or is it possible for such a school to exist? Have we in music any "inborn qualities to be ascribed either to the influence of Nature or of manners or of peculiar instruments originated by rude people?"

We are a new people, an heterogeneous body. From the Indians whom the settlers found here we could derive but few musical ideas. . . . We have to look at the early French and the negroes; later at the Germans and Swedes; for the first settlers at the North believed with Galen as quoted in Roger Ascham's "Schoolmaster" that "Much Music marre Men's Manners." We have, it is true, the banjo, a "peculiar instrument originated by rude people;" and whether this originality came from the Arabs and is the same as the Senegambian "bania," or whether it is allied to the Bandore or Pandora, the fact remains that it is the only instrument peculiar to this country. The Germans have organized their singing clubs and sing in the German language, German part songs; the Swedes, the Welsh have done the same. These elements have staid apart and as yet there has been no fusion for good or for evil. But how about the Creoles and the negroes?

This brings up the subject of negro minstrelsy; the original and the bastard form. To trace its origin, its triumphs, its decadence, its real or fictitious influence, would be a work of service and a valuable document for the future History of North American music. The Negro Minstrels of today are by no means the idols of our youth. Who now imitates the negro dialect? The songs smack neither of the plantation nor the camp meeting. The deadly "topical song" has done its work, and the glory of burnt cork is departing.

Gone too are the real and so-called negro melodies heard so often that they were possibly not appreciated. It is easy to say that many of the melodies were stolen from other nations; that they were too often of a sickly sentimental nature with a superabundance of golden-haired ladies, and graves dug in extremely unhealthy localities; but, with the exception of the Harrigan-Braham tunes, have we now any characteristic airs so simple and of such haunting beauty as "Old Folks at Home," "Carry me back to old Virginia," "My old Kentucky home," "Uncle Ned" and others of the Foster school. The Americans then were sentimental. They sang of log cabins and mocking birds, even though occasionally slaves were flogged or sold. To-day they peddle votes and sing of "boodle."

Gone too is the dancing of that day. Where can be seen the wild frenzy of "Nicodemus Johnson?" Where is the double shuffle, the pigeon wing? To be seen upon the levee or upon the deck of a Mississippi steamer, danced by roustabouts; but they are vanishing from the stage, and in their place we have imitations of Fred Vokes and the unearthly Majiltons, and the dance of the divided skirt.

Gone too are the orators who entered with umbrellas and carpetbags and gave information in regard to the crisis. Gone too are the negro character sketches, such as the delightful and realistic "Watermelon Man" of McAndrews. The banjo has fallen from its high estate, and is now picked at by girls who play upon it transcriptions from Wagner.

Look over the volumes of music which belong to maiden aunts who in their youth were looked upon as women of accomplishments; it is like visiting a neglected graveyard. Side by side with the "Wrecker's Daughter Quickstep" and "Gen. Persifor F. Smith's March" we find the songs sentimental and "comic" once sung and whistled throughout the land by men, women and children. There is the song with the melancholy refrain of "She fell in love with a ham-fat man;" there is the once favorite ditty of

"Sally come up,
Sally come down,
Sally come twist your heels around."

Yes, these words were often silly, often coarse, yet there was in them a flavor of individuality which almost approached nationality.

Did the results of the war kill the stage negro? Was the negro only interesting so long as he was a bone of contention, a rallying cry of political parties? Or did the rise of the Irish in America drive him from the stage? Whatever the cause may be, negro minstrelsy is dead; nor does any modern American composer deign to look at plantation song or dance as possible material for rhythm or color.

It is true that many of the earlier piano pieces of Gottschalk, such as "La Bamboula," "La Savane," "Le Bananier" show the strong Creole-negro influence: unusual accentuation—strange melodies of unaccustomed intervals which might soothe the Snake God,—dances with rhythms now halting, now frenzied, fit to accompany swamp-orgies and human sacrifices. Our composers of today have neglected to work in this field, and Gottschalk who has been both over-praised and under-estimated was not the man to found a school or leave disciples.

To-day the most characteristic tunes we have are the songs and dances introduced in the plays of Harrigan. And yet it is perhaps not fair to say that this music has a national flavor; it is rather local, as are the plays. For such sketches as the Mulligan series cast side-lights upon New York life as it is under the reign of the Irish-American; he is the hero of the scene, though around him revolve negro and German with procession and picnic. The scenes, the jests, the allusions are local, often unintelligible to people of other cities. They are not merely adaptations of foreign comedies changed to suit the place; they have sprung from New York soil. They are full of "the blab of the pave, tires of carts, sluff of bootsoles, talk of the promenaders." The conditions of life, the sudden changes from the tenement to Murray Hill, the negro preacher, the German baker, the ward politician with his heelers, the ever shifting panorama of New York life is in these plays, is in the music of Braham. You cannot imagine one of the Mulligan melodies originating in London or Paris or Berlin; it is the epitome of the recklessness, contempt for authority, and grotesque sentimentalism which are seen in the characters of the plays. These melodies could not have been written in another atmosphere, under another sky. They have a distinct flavor.

Is it likely that we shall ever have a national music or music of strong characteristics? It seems doubtful; we are without a musical past, nor were we a musical nation. We have many composers of talent who study here and abroad and write much that is admirable; but so far as nationality goes, the music might as well be signed with a foreign name. There is a tendency with us to imitate other nations in dress and ideas; and individuality is almost wholly disregarded. Our audiences are too apt to admire and applaud at dictation; and a foreign name or the mysterious fiat of a society leader often awes the crowd. It looks as though for some years to come we should blindly submit ourselves to the Germans. It is here at least the musical language. German is spoken at the rehearsals of orchestras composed of men of various nationalities, and supported by Americans. And

when the chief supporter and patron of the Boston Symphony orchestra wished the other day to express to the orchestra his personal gratification at the work of the past year, it is said that he composed with care a letter in the German language which was read aloud in German by an imported German.

. . . . .

The musical season is over, and the wearied players and singers, and the hearers who have given repeated proofs of great physical endurance can now recruit their strength for the coming year. After all the pianos have been the keenest sufferers, and the unprovoked attacks of such pugilists as D'Albert upon naturally peaceful instruments remind one of a story lately told by Legouvé. Once at a concert in Paris Liszt had cruelly maltreated a beautiful Pleyel pianoforte, and after the inspired Hungarian monk had left his seat, Pleyel drew near and with woeful face examined the strings. "I am looking over the field of battle," he said with tears in his voice, "and I am counting the dead and wounded."

. . . . .

Much ink has been shed since October . . . over the Battle of the Operas . . . the Italian and the German. Instead of enjoying that which was good at Mechanic's Hall and that which was good at the Boston Theater and condemning that which was bad at either place, the musical people were divided into two unreasonable factions who squabbled over the name, Wagner; as if Wagner had anything to do with the production of opera in Boston. Were an Italian opera sung by Germans, excuses, apologies were made for its introduction in the repertoire, on the ground that the "Master" Wagner had approved of it or at least had tolerated its existence. So too this name of the great composer is often used in this city as a measuring rod, a test-tube in all matters musical. There is but little discussion concerning the merits of the work: the question is, what did Wagner say about it? The Waltzes of Johann Strauss are delightful and musical—because Wagner approved of them; they can therefore be enjoyed and applauded. Mendelssohn wrote little music of real value—Wagner said so. Meyerbeer was a dismal failure as a writer of operas—Wagner said so. And so on throughout the catalogue of Wagner's personal likes and dislikes. The fact that music was not born and did not die with Richard Wagner does not seem to occur to these good people; and it would seem as though they believed that his musical judgments, often the expression of malice and disappointment and gigantic conceit but interesting as an exhibition of the workings of a splenetic mind (as when he assured a friend of mine a year before his death that Chopin was merely a chocolate-maker and Schumann a builder of sequences), were delivered from the Bayreuth

Temple as he sat upon the tripod, while nature gave assent with thunder-crack and earthquake shock.

The sight of the people of this city paying the prices demanded and enduring the physical discomforts and poor performances during the "operatic season" was ludicrous and pathetic. They eagerly listened to Italians and Germans and their applause fell upon the just and the unjust,—upon an Albani, and even upon a Kalisch. Some found fault with the Italians because they were guilty of singing; others were rash enough to condemn the Germans because they studiously refrained from singing.

. . . . .

[May 21, 1891: A disquisition upon "A Boston Habit," the tendency of Bostonians to criticize.]

The people of Boston are reported, and no doubt truthfully, to be of a critical spirit concerning everything that pertains to art, and they plume themselves both upon the fact and the report. The columns of the newspapers, the talk at the clubs, the conversations in parlors and street-cars, are proof of a widespread interest in art that finds expression in criticism. If a new painting, or a new play, or a new musical composition is put before us, it is the food of the popular mind for a day or two. If the leader of a "new movement" or the preacher of a new gospel tarries here for a season, the lion is hunted without delay. He is easily caught, indeed, he often courts pursuit; and he is poked with questions until he roars. Then the roar, as well as the mane and the length of the tail, is discussed and criticised. So years ago certain philosophers of the Epicureans and of the Stoics once encountered Paul, saying, "May we know what this new doctrine, whereof thou speakest, is? For thou bringest certain strange things to our ears; we would know therefore what these things mean." For they spent their time in nothing else, but either to tell or to hear some new thing.

Now, any discussion of that species of popular criticism that is simply slavish adoration culminating in a "fad" is foreign to the purpose of this article. Neither is there any inquiry here into the capabilities or functions of recognized, professional critics, a race of long suffering, much-enduring men; for whether their criticism be destructive or complimentary, they themselves are criticised upon all sides, and they are constantly reminded that their opinions are simply those of so many individuals and, therefore, entitled to no special weight. We have here to do simply with the mental unrest into which the apparition of any new work throws so many of the unemployed, an unrest that only finds relief in spoken opinion and in long letters to the newspapers.

In spite of the saying "where everybody criticises, no one produces," this excess of open opinion might be regarded as a gratifying symptom of the healthy condition of the artistic body, were it not for the fact that in nine cases out of ten the opinion expressed may be reduced to "I like it" or "I don't like it." Or the proclaimer of the opinion is mentally controlled by a theory, and the hobby-horse upon which he exercises is of large proportions. Take the case of a play recently produced, a play that has excited much comment—or call it criticism. The theatre-goer that seeks only amusement and does not wish to have certain unpleasant problems of life thrust upon his attention at once condemns the play, root and branch. On the other hand the man that believes that the time is out of joint and that these problems should absorb the attention of mankind not only praises it unduly but he is impatient at the success of plays of a different nature and of actors that do not seek to bring about social regeneration by their performance upon the stage.

Again, it is found in nearly every instance of popular criticism that the quadruple element of subjectivity that must enter into any final estimate is entirely lost sight of. This element has been so clearly expressed by Mr. John Addington Symonds that his words are worthy of quotation. "The mind of one individual, qualified by certain idiosyncratic properties, and further qualified by the conditions of his race and age, is brought to bear upon the product of another human mind, itself qualified by certain idiosyncratic properties and further qualified by the conditions of a certain race and century." . . . Now nearly all the amateur critics that deal in opinions take no account of the "moral, political, religious, aesthetic, sensuous sympathies and antipathies playing an inevitable part." Each one is inclined to measure by the pocket-rule of his own individuality. There is a lack of discrimination, there is, too, often an utter want of comparison. Miss Wilkins is compared to de Maupassant, and greatly to her advantage. The characters of Ibsen are judged as though they lived in a New England town. Realism is hankered after, and when it presents itself there is an outcry. Idealism is sought, and when it is found, it provokes yawns. And before everyone who wishes to create a great work of art, there arises the awful vision of the Young Person, with pallid face, and with hands ready to cover ears or eyes.

XIII

Henry Taylor Parker
Selections from *Eighth Notes:*
Voices and Figures of Music and the Dance
(Boston, 1922)

[H. T. Parker (1867-1934), the other half of Boston's famous pair of rival critics, was, unlike Hale, not a musician—it is said, in fact, that he couldn't read a note—but he brought to music a deep love, a broad knowledge, and a keen intelligence which transcended his technical shortcomings. Like Hale, Parker was a New Englander (he was born and died in Boston), but he was a Harvard rather than a Yale man, and he received his early schooling in England. Upon graduation from Harvard he became New York correspondent for the *Boston Evening Transcript,* then went to London as foreign correspondent for the *Transcript* and the *New York Globe.* After he returned to New York and a local job with the *Globe,* he was asked to put his vast amateur's expertise in music and the theater to use in opera criticism for the *Globe,* and thus began a brilliant career covering the musical and theatrical arts, as well as their respective social worlds.

In 1905 Parker returned to Boston and the *Transcript,* which he then served until his death. "H.T.P." or "Hell-to-pay," as he was variously known, enjoyed power and reputation fully comparable to Hale's. He was often a stern judge, though at the same time balanced and discerning. He could be a master of irony, but he did not sacrifice truth to the turn of phrase, and if his phrases were not as graceful or succinct as those of Hale, they often carried thoughts which ran deeper. The selections here carry us into the first two decades of the twentieth century and focus upon certain great artists who were important to Bostonians. They are part of a group of essays which was, in Parker's words, "originally strewn through the columns of the *Boston Evening Transcript* . . . they have been astutely assembled and ingeniously coördinated by my friend, Neil Martin." The first essay deals with the great conductor Karl Muck, who led the Boston Symphony Orchestra through the stormy period of the First World War—his tenure ended with his imprisonment as an enemy alien, essentially for the crime of being a German.

Parker wrote much and well about opera; he was a strong (though by no means uncritical) champion of the original Boston Opera Company, which was one of the premier companies of the world during its brief but gilded existence (1909-15). When he died, Parker was near the successful end of a long campaign to bring the touring Met back to Boston. These discussions of three great singers, Caruso, Garden, and Fremstad, reveal Parker's acute and appreciative judgment in matters operatic. Both Fremstad and Garden were principals of the Boston Opera Company. Caruso did appear in Boston but not often—he entertained an active dislike for the city.

Parker's *Eighth Notes* was at one time reprinted (1968). Quaintance Eaton's excellent history of *The Boston Opera Company* (1965) contains an entertaining account of both Hale and Parker.]

Eighth Notes

MANY-SIDED MUCK

One sort of conductor, like Mr. Toscanini, invites his hearers to receive his impressions of the music that he chooses, to listen to Mozart or Beethoven, Tschaikowsky or d'Indy, after it has passed through his temperament. He plays upon his men as some pianists play upon their instruments in order that the orchestra may express himself quite as much as the composer whose name stands upon the program. Those of another sort regard themselves as only means to an end—and that end is the clearest and fullest communication of the contents of the music in hand as the composer wrought and felt it. These conductors approach a given piece, be it a simple symphony by Haydn or an intricate tone-poem by Strauss, with an eye single to its peculiar traits. They apprehend its structure, assimilate its substance, penetrate its moods, assort and adjust its details to the underlying or dominating musical and poetic content, discover its accent and eloquence, and then to their utmost seek to communicate all these things to their hearers. They differentiate each piece that they undertake from all the rest. They give to each its individual voice.

Dr. Muck, when he graced the Boston Orchestra, was such a one. He sought only the substance, the spirit, the peculiar life of the music as it came from the composer's hand. His personal distinction was to be impersonal before his music, but not impersonal in the negative sense. Rather, he had as many personalities as there were composers and pieces on his programs. He made himself and his orchestra the eloquent and the characterizing voice of each. No conductor of our time has seemed to have so few limitations of sympathetic understanding and answering emotion.

The secret of this discrimination, this truly interpretative quality, this self-subordination, lies, perhaps, in the qualities of Dr. Muck as man no less than as musician. His work has proved him a man of strong and fine intellect, of alert, nervous and sensitive mind. He was schooled in the liberal studies; he knows other arts than the one that he practices; he has lived in the world of cultivated men and not merely in the world of makers of music; he looks upon life shrewdly and humorously. He has the penetrating, discriminating and orderly mind that springs from mental discipline and mental training. He understands before he feels, and the breadth and the fineness of his understanding he has proved from Bach through the composers of our own particular place and hour. But mental qualities alone make only a dry conductor. He must have emotional understanding and responsiveness as well. On this score, again as his work has proved him, Dr. Muck is no less finely strung. His is the alert, sensitive, nervous spirit that enters into the moods and the emotions of the symphony, the tone-poem, or the concert piece before him, and that seizes and reflects them vividly and vitally. As he has proved time and again, he is sensitive alike to the varied poetry, the varied drama, the whole range of the expressive quality of music. He has kept it an emotional speech. Such a union of mental and emotional qualities does not in itself round a conductor. He must add to them the intrinsically musical qualities—the feeling for beauty and poignancy of tone, for musical design and form and ornament, for the underlying and distinguishing melody, for the songful utterance, for the charm and the power of ordered sound. Dr. Muck knew no less this purely musical sensitiveness. He is the man of

intellect, the man of feeling, who has found the conducting of music the normal and instinctive outlet for these qualities. His mental, emotional and musical traits stood ever in even balance.

By general consent, the Boston Orchestra under Dr. Muck was the incomparable orchestra of the world. His purpose was to make it as perfect an instrument as he could compass. He would not have it merely more eloquent than other orchestras; for that, however high the standard, is relatively a common criterion. He would have it eloquent with the rare and ideal eloquence in which fulfillment matches vision. To that end he shaped his programs and ordered his rehearsals. For that end he lavished all his powers tirelessly and stimulated all the powers of his men. They answered as though they knew and felt the goal. At the close of his long last term in Boston the orchestra stood at the apogee of attainment. It was as perfect an instrument as a human instrument could well be. It was perfect in the range, the balance, the euphony, the elasticity, and the sensibility of the blended tonal mass; perfect in the luminous utterance of music; in the manifold force of voice that it yielded, in diverse richness and coloring, in the variety of its march, in rhythmic suppleness and felicity, in its eloquence of mood and passion, image and suggestion, poetry and drama. The orchestra was a virtuoso orchestra in the highest sense of the word. It was even more than a virtuoso orchestra because it warmed its virtuosity with glowing beauty and winged it with the multifold strength of ordered and sensitive powers. It delighted the ear, it transported the imagination. Its voice was an emotion in itself. They say that the old and dying Vieuxtemps sent for the young Ysaye that he might hear one of his violin concertos played as he had imagined it. So more than one composer, of old or newly dead, might have been fain to summon the Boston Orchestra under Dr. Muck to hear it play his music. The fortunate living came and heard for themselves and departed rejoicing. In their hearts they may have even said: "Did I really write so?"

It is perilous to bear the measuring rule to the orchestral Olympus. But surely it is safe to say that no living conductor has assembled in himself more of the attributes of a great conductor or held them in juster balance than Dr. Muck. *Servans servorum Dei*—the servant of the servants of God—the early Popes used to proudly call themselves. So Dr. Muck might have called himself the servant of the composers whose music he played. He transmitted music to us in the living image of its form and substance, in the voice and in the emotion, as it seemed, in which it was created. Divining, he imparted. Imparting, he enhanced and intensified. For in him is that faculty of divination and that quality of impartment which differentiates the great conductor from the merely able practitioner of his art. The composer writes in emotion, sometimes in an emotion that the music hardly embodies and releases. Divining, penetrating, Dr. Muck enters into this emotion, transmits it, and sometimes releases and heightens it as though he were freeing that, which from sheer intensity of feeling, holds the composer almost tongue-tied. As widely as these composers range, so ranges Dr. Muck's divination. And to do and to be these things is to be a very great conductor.[*]

CARUSO—TO HIS UTMOST

In this queer operatic world of ours there have been no audiences like those which Caruso assembled because, in truth, there have been no singers like Caruso. A large part of his hearers, whatever he sang, seemed to come from those who regarded him as one of the unique personages of the time, as Paderewski was to be seen and heard among pianists or Mme. Bernhardt among players. This company go to see her though they know not a word of French and barely heed the play when she is off the stage. So they hear Paderewski, though the piano and its "literature" are sealed books to them, and so they heard and saw Caruso, careless of the opera in which he was appearing or of the part that it yielded him. Enough for them that they looked upon him and listened to him.

And what manner of Caruso went they forth to see and to hear? Surely not the Caruso who used to stand four-square to the audience and pour forth his flood of song. But rather the singing-actor who learned, with commendable perseverance, to penetrate the skin of a character, to be personage in the musical drama, and not merely an acclaimed tenor singing this part or that. In the last decade of his service at the Metropolitan Opera House he was no longer the tenor of the "golden voice," enrapturing audiences by the opulence of his mellow and glowing song; for the quality of Caruso's tones and his ways with them much changed with the passing years. As time matured his voice so did it ripen his imagination and develop his means until his tones became the voice of his personage, until he himself entered, perforce, into part and drama. Not for nothing may a singer, though he be as eminent as Caruso, work year after year with Toscanini.

If the old, golden magnificence had somewhat gone out of the singer's voice, tones remained that carried and imparted emotions variously and poignantly, that revealed the personage who was singing, that took color and accent from the moment of the drama, that characterized, delineated, projected. If once the only emotion that the voice provoked was of the sensuous delight of beautiful and puissant

sound, it continued, to the very end, to thrill. But with a different thrill. It pleased the exacting as much as it satisfied the lovers of "big" and sensuous tone. The magnificent sonorities, the freedom of utterance, the breadth of phrase, the flood of sustained tone, the large vocal intensities endured. It is indeed true that Caruso kept to the end certain vocal idiosyncrasies that made expert listeners grieve and lay hearers rejoice, that he would make his vocal effect even if for the moment he halted the flow or altered the rhythm of the music. Yet the next moment he could shape a phrase, sustain a melody, shade a measure with an exquisite sense of tonal beauty and an equally subtle skill. Moreover, in the quality of that voice as it flooded the theater was a pleasure and an emotion that stirred the common heart of all that heard. There was that, too, in Caruso which commended the man behind. A more honest, a more earnest singer, more willing to do his utmost for his audience and for the opera has never drawn breath. Simple-minded he also was, and his simplicity and his sincerity saved him in operatic impersonation. Admittedly he was no very plausible actor in romantic parts, but when in his honest continence did he offend or amuse the eye? And in his last and mellowed days he was not far from the "grand style" of John of Leyden in "The Prophet" and Eléazer in "The Jewess." Or give him a homely personage among Italian folk to play and he played him vividly and well. He was, for instance, a believable and amusing comedian in Donizetti's "L'Elisir d'Amore." He characterized the Canio of Leoncavallo's melodrama stirringly and truthfully.

In "Pagliacci" Caruso had a clear notion of his personage that he wrought into a workable and cumulating histrionic design. From year to year, he amplified it with much illuminating and defining detail. Recall, for instance, the exaggerated whimsies of a strolling player with which his matured Canio cozened the crowd at the beginning of the play; the wiping of the powder from his face as of a player resuming relievedly his own person; the intensity, brooding or ominous, that he threw into his declamation in the play while in action he was but doing the part; the fashion in which he went emotionally dead when he had struck down Nedda; how he returned a little to himself, dragged out of his throat "la commedia e finita" and huddled away, distraught, blind, blank again.

[*The Muck-Boston Symphony recordings of Tchaikovsky and Wagner were the first serious orchestral recordings made by the Victor Talking Machine Company (1917). One of these brilliant performances, the *Lohengrin* Act III Prelude, was once reissued on a long-play record by RCA. Muck's famous European recordings have also been reissued.]

Always, too, Caruso's song was the speech of Canio, as elemental in all his moods, as direct and full-voiced in his emotions, as simple or savage as the character really is. He made tellingly but untheatrically the swift change from playful banter over the lightness of women to the amorous and vindictive words about a wife that he already suspects; he did not overdo the celebrated soliloquy as a Canio might utter it; he sang in the final scenes with the accents of the pain and the passion that rend the clown amid the ironies of the make-believe and the reality. The music of Canio suited the best compass and the best quality of his matured voice. Hackneyed, "popular" and all the rest of the damning adjectives of superior righteousness his Canio may have become. But it remained one of the most remarkable operatic impersonations of our time.

FREMSTAD—MIND AND WILL

Mme. Fremstad had not been long in opera houses before she discovered that the field of the mezzo-soprano is relatively small. To perceive was to will the gradual quest of a new range, little by little enlarging the compass of her voice and persuading it to new timbres. Her voice ever bore the marks of the strain the transformation had laid upon it, but the change, with all its pains and penalties, was worth the accomplishing. For had she not achieved it our opera houses would have lacked the most illustrious singing-actress of Wagnerian parts since Lehmann and Ternina. Only Mme. Easton has matched her since in the singing of them; no one hereabouts in the acting of them.

By force of penetrating will, by keen and tireless mental energy, by goading pride of achievement, Mme. Fremstad seemed to devise, compose and project most of her impersonations. She was no "temperamental" singing-actress who seized instinctively upon a few elementary emotions and by easy ardor and readiness of means gave them tonal and histrionic life and being. In all her parts, except possibly Venus in "Tannhäuser" and Sieglinde in "Die Walküre," wherein complete, secure and long-standing impersonation hid every means to the illusion, it was possible to discover traces of her processes. Her alert and tireless mind, her resolute imagination searched out of music and text and inner vision the moods and the impulses, the rages and submissions, the raptures and despairs of her Isolde. In its earlier days, her impersonation no more than laid these emotions side by side in flat tints. The illusion of tones and action was as the illusion of an Isolde in clear outline and vivid color in a window of glass.

Then, as Mme. Fremstad ripened the impersonation and herself, these emotions began to appear in the round, to melt their lines into long and sweeping curves of feeling, to fuse their colors into a manifold glow, to animate the whole being of an Isolde who went the way of tragic fate. The voice became as Isolde's at the given moment and in the given stress of the music-drama; the action seemed the spontaneous and inevitable complement. Mme. Fremstad, as Mme. Fremstad, added to it only the expressive richness of her tones and the tragic sweep of her movements. Her impersonation was no longer frescoed upon the stage. It had its being there in the emotional life of music and play. Her threefold Kundry, from its darksome and impenetrable wildness in the first scenes, through its sensuous splendors and subtle suggestion in the garden, to the tranquil beauty of the final episodes underwent a similar evolution. By fine and indomitable will of imagination, she mantled her characterization in mystery, shadowed in the earlier episodes, agonized when Klingsor evokes her magic in the seductions of the garden—they are half-mental and so the better within Mme. Fremstad's powers—and haloed in the transfiguration of the end. No Kundry of the international stage probably matches hers. Only she and Ternina have made head against a perversely baffling part.

Mme. Fremstad's Isolde and Kundry were intricately composed, as Wagner's music and characterization bade. Each was at once a finely and largely wrought vocal and histrionic design sedulously proportioned, colored and shaded. Beside these her Brünnhilde seemed a simpler impersonation, in which one elemental mood or passion gave place to another and each was translated into heroic ardor and sweep of voice and action. Out of a young world came her Valkyr, elate and high-hearted; out of a world already shadowed and out of a spirit deepened, she called Siegmund to Valhalla. The high heart was racked in the parting with Wotan but it kept its pride. Then the exaltation, the desolation, the transfiguration of the two other "Ring" dramas—tragic passion upon tragic passion—that Mme. Fremstad, upborn by the music and by her will, came finally to sustain to the end. There were moments in her Brünnhilde when her voice and action struck swift, heroic fire; there were as many more when her sustained intensity of passionate utterance and passionate pause flooded eye, ear and imagination; and once and again the still magnificence of her repose seemed to fill the stage.

GARDEN—MIRROR OF THE MODERNS

Pick, if you will, twenty technical flaws in Mary Garden's singing. Discover, as it is easy to discover, that hers was originally a voice that might have served admirably the purposes of song. She has preferred to make it an exalting, emotional, characterizing and delineative speech. To that end she uses all her vocal resources; for it she will risk any vocal sacrifice, attempt any vocal distortion. The technician will rage at her; singing-teachers count her the abomination of desolation—in their trade; while sensitive ears, trained to the older arts of pure song, in and out of the opera houses, do writhe now and then under the quality of some of her tones and the methods by which she gains them. But she attains no less her real end. Her singing is the speech of the part she is playing. In her tones float the traits and the emotions of the character portrayed. She colors them with every change and process of mood, with every subtlety of suggestion. Hers is a truly magnetic art, the art of the singing-actress, however uneven she may be in the exemplification of it, near its fullness. Hers are modern means to modern ends. With her came a new day in operatic acting and singing.

Miss Garden's singing—or oftener declamation —calls to a more vivid life than any other singing-actress now may, the Thaïs of Alexandrian feasts and the desert convent; the Louise of Montmartre the day before yesterday; the little juggler whom the Virgin loved; the piteous Mélisande, or the tempestuous and brooding Carmen. Her range is wide and she differentiates each of the characters she chooses from it. The heavy-lidded, panther-like Oriental girl, who has thought the thoughts of passion and first feels it when the white-shouldered Jokanaan comes from Herod's pit, is far indeed from the Mélisande, wisp in the wind of fate, trembling to the impulses she hardly knows, moving, living as the vision of a dream. Louise of the dressmaker's shop, palpitating to the surge and the heat of Paris, is no less remote from the little white monk, who sits apart and downcast in the common room and wonders how he, too, —poor juggler lad—shall make his works serve Our Lady. To differentiate and to individualize her characters, to call them, each in its kind, to as intense life as is her own is Miss Garden's chief purpose. And the chief means is the exalted speech that music gives her when such imagination, such communicating emotional force and such self-surrender as are hers, may color her tones.

No one quite knows the voice of Mary Garden; but her hearers know the voices of Louise, of Thaïs, of Melisande and of Salome. She is less the actress who happens also to sing (as Whistler said Leighton "also" painted) than the actress who has discovered that music affords a more imparting and thrilling speech. She is as vivid in her appeal to the eye. Consider Thaïs with her train of dancing and singing girls sweeping into Nicias's house in the exuberant joy of careless and sensuous life; Mélisande still and dreaming in the pale sunshine of the terrace by the empty sea, and with eyes that search its emptiness; Louise rapt in the intoxication of the Paris that spreads the elation of living at her feet; Salome crouching over the silent cistern, whither the executioner has descended; when even Strauss's orchestra makes stillness searching and expectant. Of such are the unforgettable images that Miss Garden summons to the eye and the imagination of her audiences that her characters may live before them. They live, most of all, because of the superb and tireless vitality of the singing-actress behind them. Life —the joy of it, the exertion of it, the reward of it, the pleasure daily renewed of all these things—burns too brightly and too eagerly in Mary Garden for her impersonations to be one whit less alive than is she. Even when she exceeds and overemphasizes as with Fiora in "The Love of Three Kings," or distorts as with Monna Vanna in Fèvrier's music-drama after Maeterlinck, she errs with a certain magnificence.

Miss Garden is the guardian, in America, of the living and vivid "tradition" of the ultra modern opera. It is her knowledge that directs, her spirit that informs whatever is accomplished in this country in the renewal, from time to time, of the beauty and the power of the music into which Debussy has wrought Maeterlinck's "Pélléas and Mélisande." Each hearer of the opera listens for himself. Some there are whom the comparative newness of the idiom of the music baffles until they lose themselves in the pursuit of Debussy's harmonies, progressions, modulations, scales and rhythms. They debate of the details of his musical speech as though they were absolute and exact things and not means to a particular end of expression. They inquire whether such speech may serve other composers and other music-dramas—a matter of pure and futile conjecture. They do serve Maeterlinck's play, and beyond that purpose Debussy had no occasion to go. So Miss Garden's means as singing-actress serve the ends of the opera. Within music that so speaks the spirits of the personages of the play; that stirs with the fate that creeps about them, the singing players must seem the figures of Maeterlinck's dream and Debussy's music. So, indeed, does Miss Garden wholly vanish into the being that she would simulate. So she speaks with the very tones of Debussy's music. So she quivers and swims, pales and brightens in its very atmosphere.

99